Nasty Rumors

*Can You Believe What They're Saying About
the Bible?*

Rod Pinder

Rod Pinder

17133 Drawdy Ct.

Orlando, FL 32820

PastorRodPinder@gmail.com

PastorRodPinder.com

Limits of Liability and Disclaimer of Warranty

Warning – Disclaimer

ISBN 978-0-9889584-8-7

Nasty Rumors

© 2019 Rod Pinder

The Buzz:

What People Are Saying.

Reading *Nasty Rumors: Can You Believe What They're Saying about the Bible?* was a truly transformative experience. It is insightful, engaging, and answers so many questions I have had about the history, origin and authenticity of the Bible. I could feel the Holy Spirit moving as I read. This book has re-ignited my desire to dig into the Word and to live my faith out daily. It is scholarly and well researched, while also fun and entertaining to read. I found myself not wanting to put it down. If you have ever wondered how we can know if the Bible is truly inspired by God, or if it has been accurately transcribed and translated through the years, this book answers those questions and more. It is a captivating read in whatever stage you are in Faith, and I highly recommend it.

- Kathryn Matos, MPA, Assistant to the City Manager, Sunny Ilses Beach, FL

What the world needs is the truth, the whole truth and nothing but the truth, so help us God. And that's just what

God has done! God has, by His grace, given us everything we need to know Him. The truth is the Bible is the Word of God. But until the Word of God is restored to its rightful place - and received for what it really is, the very Word of God - everyone will do what is right in his own eyes and all will suffer. What Rod Pinder delivers is an easy to read, joyful, truthful answer to the Nasty Rumors of our day - a treasure worthy of our time.

> - Carmen Fowler LaBerge,
>   Author, Speaker, Radio host and Evangelical leader
>   https://reconnectwithcarmen.com

In today's post-modern, post Christendom world, it is hard to find resources for help in dealing with the skeptics we engage with. Pastor Rod's book *Nasty Rumors*, although targeted for believers, is a great mix of apologetics and church history that would be convincing even to the critic that Scripture can be trusted as a reliable source. Rod has done the work, the research, and put together a wonderful read for not only the people in the pews but the church leaders among us as well. Today's evangelism and missional engagement requires answers to tough questions. The material found here serves as a wonderful aid in our quest to bring the Good News to a hurting world that questions the validity of the Scriptures we hold as our final rule of faith and practice.

> - John A. Terech Jr. Executive Director of Operations
>   ECO: A Covenant Order of Evangelical Presbyterians

My prayer is that the simple truths of *Nasty Rumors* will penetrate the darkness as a shining star that glows even brighter at night.

- Rev. Charles H. Baxter, State Coordinator, Church Ministry,
  Billy Graham Evangelistic Association

Dr. Pinder is a well-trained student of the Bible, both in the original languages and in a multitude of English translations. He is a Presbyterian minister who has preached the gospel for forty or so years. And he has the heart of a pastor. In *Nasty Rumors*, Dr. Pinder ably presents and debunks eight major objections to the text, content, teaching, gospel, and God of the Bible. It would be good for ministers, elders, deacons, and other church members to read this book, individually and in groups or classes. This book will be especially helpful for believers who realize they are swimming against the stream in an increasingly pagan culture. And, if they are brave enough to open themselves to what is being taught here, even unbelievers might learn something good, true, uplifting, challenging, and new to them.

- Dr. James C. Goodloe IV, *Executive Director*
  Foundation for Reformed Theology
  https://foundationrt.org

I was a member of Rod's congregation for over 15 years until I moved out of state for a new job. He has been "writing" this book for many years, as much of it was familiar. Having it all together in one place is a gift that I truly enjoyed reading and reflecting on. I am a little sad we have to defend the Bible – but *Nasty Rumors* does a great job at doing so while also interspersing a nice dose of Rod's evangelism.

As someone who reads the Bible daily, I found it very helpful in reinforcing the big picture.

The book is very readable and includes a lot of sources - which appeals to me as an academic.

Anyone whose faith is shaken because of a concern the Bible of the 21st century is not reliable will be very reassured by reading this book.

> - Donna Bobek Schmitt, PhD, CPA, Associate Professor of Accounting,
> Darla Moore School of Business, University of South Carolina.

Nasty Rumors is a very engaging read that is also one of the best resources I have ever come across to meaningfully respond to various criticisms of the Bible and of faith itself. I intend to read it through once or twice more, and become familiar with the various chapters in order to deal with different myths and misunderstandings I encounter. I found the chapter entitled "Herman Who" to be especially helpful.

> - Kathy Turner, Follower of Jesus

This is a great book for clergy and lay people alike. Rod uses great illustrations, humor, and solid Biblical content as he dispels various myths we have heard about the Bible. His explanations are thorough but very relatable. I plan on using this book as a book study in my congregation.

- Rev. Anne Horton, Cedarville United Presbyterian Church, Ceaerville, OH

Nasty Rumors is a wonderful combination of insightful reasoning, clear arguments, and rich, personal warmth. The book address real questions Christians have about the reliability of the source book of our faith, providing clear, persuasive answers along with wise, practical advice for bringing the truth of the Bible to bear on the life of all who seek to follow Jesus. This is a book that I, as a pastor and teacher of the Bible, will strive to get into the hands of all the members of my flock."

- Rev. Gary Chorpenning, Pastor, Venice Presbyterian Church near Pittsburgh, PA
  Writer at https://gachorpenning.com

Historical Context, critical thinking and faith application all mixed into one. A must read for all and a great tool for the Christian toolbox!

- Charles Coburn, Commissioned Lay Pastor, Macclesfield Presbyterian Church

How do I know that the Bible is true? The Bible tells me so. As do other historical documents. Dr. Pinder lays out the proof that the Bible accurately records the history of Abba, Father, the Lord our God and his only begotten Son, who "came into the world, not to condemn the world, but to save it." Dr. Pinder shows how today's translations of the Bible are deeply rooted in the translations of old and relate back to the earliest manuscripts known, and how and why one can read them today with the full confidence that today's Bibles truly are "the inspired word of God."

   - Michael N. Hutter Esq. Retired

Nasty Rumors is a gem of a volume. Written thoughtfully and with humor and humility, it provides helpful encouragement for those who have written the Faith off because they have believed the *rumors*.

Useful for everyone who wants to be grounded in the Truth of the Scriptures. I commend this to college students about to take Bible classes at either a Christian or secular school, seminary students who are preparing for ministry, to young pastors in their first parishes to reaffirm their grounding in the authority and reliability of the Word, and to more experienced pastors who may need a reminder of the glory and grandeur of the Bible.

Pastors will find *Nasty Rumors* a great resource for new member classes and confirmation classes. I suggest clergy maintain multiple copies of this book on the shelves of the church library for giving away to interested members and inquirers.

Read *Nasty Rumors* and then read it again. Enjoy freshly the Truth of the Christian Faith as revealed in the Holy Scriptures.

   - Steve Strickler, Teaching Elder,
     Evangelical Presbyterian Church

Acknowledgements

I've heard it said that no one writes a book alone. It wasn't until I started getting ready to share *Nasty Rumors* publicly that I understood how true that statement is. It has been my privilege to surround myself with a virtual research team of people who are smarter than I, and they have helped me enormously. Several times I'd be unsure of a fact or missing a reference, so I would post a question on Facebook. Wonderful friends came through time and again with personal perspectives, references, and theological connections, even French and Spanish lessons. Others gave helpful encouragement when they read snippets from the book as I posted them on line. There are too many contributors to name them all, but here are a few: Tom Biery, Sandi Cole, Ali Dugger, Bill Enns, Tina Ferrin, Cindy Pate Gibbs, Greg Hicks, Barb Koob, Brad Long, Alexandra Mariano, and David Summerford. James Goodloe also made very helpful suggestions on both style and content. The contributions of others are mentioned in the following chapters or footnotes. Countless friends, colleagues, mentors, pastors, and teachers through over 50 years of learning to follow Christ and grow in Him also shaped who I am and what I have written.

Steve Strickler and Gary Chorpenning read and edited the entire manuscript, more than once. Not only did their support, friendship and suggestions make *Nasty Rumors* a better book, they helped me become a better writer. I can't thank them enough. The common disclaimer applies: while I was greatly helped by their insights, I didn't take every bit of advice that was offered. So, they can't be blamed for the errors or oversights that are my own.

Joseph Schlosser of Excellent Adventures! Inc. (www.joeschlosser.net) has patiently helped me through the publishing process with wisdom and encouragement. My gratitude is hard to express. Special thanks also to John Litton of Kobalt Media (www.kobaltmedia.com) for his guidance and creativity with my web site, www.PastorRodPinder.com, and other avenues of media outreach. Both of these brothers have contributed to this project (and others) with competence and grace.

The good Christian people at Woodbury Presbyterian Church provided many of the illustrations in these chapters. They also heard much of the book in sermon form, and were graciously supportive.

My immediate family gave great encouragement and shared some important perspectives and information. I'm filled with gratitude for Jessi and Luis, Mike and Sarah, and especially my wife, Pat. She demonstrates the Bible's reliability, especially at Proverbs 18:22. Liliana and Arabella, to whom this book is dedicated, provided inspiration and fervent hope for a growing generation that will be enriched and guided by God's Word. All these people make me a richly blessed man. If God bless you through this book, you have them to thank.

Cover Design by joeschlosser.net & Excellent Adventures Inc.

Two Personal Notes

It is my custom to capitalize pronouns that refer to God. I have continued that personal devotional practice in writing this book, though I know it is out of vogue. When I quote a translation or other source that does not capitalize the divine pronouns, I have left their words unaltered.

Also, when I read a book, I like to check footnotes. I find it very inconvenient to have to flip to endnotes to follow up on a reference that intrigues me, though endnotes seem to have become the common convention. In this book, notes appear at the bottom of pages instead of at the end of chapters or the whole book. I hope that enhances your reading experience.

Dedication

Dedicated to Liliana and Arabella,

my first two grandchildren,

with the prayer that they will grow up

reading, heeding, and loving

the Word of God,

and be a witness to their generation.

Easter 2019

About the Author

Rod Pinder loves being a husband, dad and, most recently, Papa. He enjoys playing, singing, writing, and arranging a wide variety of music. He has been privileged to serve as a short-term missionary in about a dozen countries around the world. Ordained in 1981, Rod served as a pastor and a church planter. He has been a spiritual director with the Walk to Emmaus and is an adjunct faculty member of the Dunamis Institute. From family to pastoring, from music to missionary work, all these activities have provided Rod with joyous opportunities to help people grow in God's love in Jesus Christ.

In 2019 Rod retired from the pastoral ministry to respond to a new calling. He is now learning to apply his gifts and experience to writing books and blogs, making YouTube videos and podcasts, and speaking. Again, all these enterprises are designed to help people grow in God's love in Jesus Christ.

Future books include:

> ➢ *Preaching in the Power of the Holy Spirit: How God's Word Creates Reality*
> ➢ *The Book of Love: Seven Words to Change Your World*
> ➢ *The Joseph Curve: How God Fulfills Vision*

➢ *Kill the Old Man (It's an Inside Job): How to Die to Self and Grow in Christ-likeness*
➢ *Tiptoe through the T.U.L.I.P.: A Moderate Look at Modern Calvinism.*

For updates and more information, visit www.PastorRodPinder.com.

Preface

Suppose there was a bountiful treasure buried in your back yard. Imagine a chest full of gold, silver, priceless gems, more wealth than you could ever spend. It's on your property. The treasure is yours, and you know right where it is. You can see the mound. You walk over it every day and mow over it every week. However, some people, including some so-called experts, tell you the treasure is buried too deep for you to reach. The ground is too hard for you to penetrate. The gold is fake, the silver is phony and the gems are glass. You'll get dirty digging. You'll wear yourself out and look like a fool, excavating your lawn. Besides, even if the treasure is real, once you pay the taxes, you won't have any wealth left for yourself. What would you do? Would you let those allegations discourage you? Would you leave your fortune hidden in the dirt? After all, retrieving buried treasure sounds like a lot of labor. So, would you just give up? Or would you ignore those negative reports, grab a shovel and start digging anyway? Wouldn't you at least try to find out whether the rumors were true or false? I hope you would at least investigate. Incredible riches are at stake.

I wrote this book because there is a priceless treasure at your disposal. It may not be buried in your back yard, but it is nestled between the covers of your Bible. Like many other people, I've discovered this treasure. It never diminishes. In fact, it makes my life richer every day. Here's an amazing fact: The God who made us loves us enough to tell us how to live life to the fullest. He hasn't left us to our own devices, to figure out the best way to live. His love doesn't abandon us to do whatever we think is best. No. He shows us the way. He reveals it to us in the Scriptures. I want you to experience the same joy, the same meaning, the same growth and spiritual abundance that the Bible has brought to my life and the lives of others through the centuries.

Sadly, some people never start digging. They're immobilized by the naysayers. Those negative reports, those nasty rumors become imaginary barriers. They prevent folks from taking possession of the bounty that is so readily available. Many of God's children live as spiritual paupers when they could be rich. Everything they need and more is just a little dig away, but they subsist in scarcity. What a tragedy!

The purpose of this book to help remove those barriers and let people get to the abundant treasures in the Scriptures. My passion, my mission in life is to help people grow spiritually, as lovers, friends and followers of Jesus Christ. I believe the Bible, along with prayer, faithfulness, and Christian fellowship, is one of the best tools around to help people develop a mature, powerful spiritual life. It breaks my heart to see precious people of God languish in spiritual poverty because faulty philosophies keep them from drawing on the resources at their fingertips.

One of the greatest joys of my life has been the privilege of mining the Scriptures and enjoying the abundance I find there. As a Religion major in college, in seminary, and in graduate school, I've learned much about God's Word from an academic perspective. As a follower of Jesus who reads the Bible regularly to enhance my own spiritual growth, the Scriptures have helped me cultivate a sweet, intimate relationship with the Lord. And as a pastor for nearly forty years I've had the privilege of quarrying the Scriptures weekly to share their powerful, world-rocking message with people through preaching, teaching, writing, making videos, music and other vehicles. All these enterprises converge in *Nasty Rumors: Can You Believe What They're Saying about the Bible?* I draw from decades of experience to help you examine the nasty rumors of the naysayers, and see whether they present real barriers or deceptive mirages.

Primarily this book is written for the normal, everyday Christians who may have heard some of the scandalous scuttlebutt going about concerning the Bible. Maybe the nasty rumors we're about to examine have kept you from digging into God's life-transforming Word. I pray that these chapters will obliterate any barriers that keep you from the riches that are rightfully yours.

I hope this book will also be helpful to Bible students in college and the early years of seminary. It can serve as an introduction to many of the issues and theories your studies will lead you to explore. Perhaps it will be a trustworthy roadmap through the labyrinth of scholarly literature ahead of you.

Pastor friends who have read drafts of these pages have expressed excitement about the book's potential as a tool for a Sunday School class, small group study or other forms of adult Christian Education. I would be thrilled for this work to enhance the ministries of my brothers and sisters, and strengthen the churches they serve. Perhaps some of the stories, insights and illustrations will also be helpful in sermons. Feel free to use anything you like. A Scripture index will be available at PastorRodPinder.com to facilitate the use of *Nasty Rumors* as a resource for teaching and preaching.

This book started as a series of sermons in 2004. My friend, Steve, carried home a copy of those sermons soon after they were preached. One Sunday afternoon, he took them into his study and read them, one after the other. He went into his study as an agnostic, an unbeliever with an open mind. He came out as a brother in Christ! Nothing would thrill me more than for Steve's experience to be repeated in many lives. So, this book is also written for fair-minded agnostics, looking for truth.

Finally, this book speaks to friends and colleagues who might not agree with my understanding of the Bible or its importance to living an abundant life. These pages may not convince them of my point of view, but I hope they will help them understand my perspective and my heart. I have tried to articulate that perspective respectfully and clearly.

Whichever of those categories describes you, or even if none of them does, I hope this book is for you. I pray that it will be a tool that empowers you to uncover the amazing treasure trove we know as the Bible. My fondest dream is that God will use this book to nudge many people to discover the riches of Scripture and that as a result, their lives and eventually our culture will be transformed by God's Word. The Scriptures really are a buried treasure. Dig in!

Contents

Chapter One

Nasty Rumors

Nasty Rumors

There are some nasty rumors floating around out there. Strong accusations are afoot that stain a stellar reputation. These ruinous rumors could shipwreck many lives. You've probably heard some of this gossip yourself. You may have wondered if any of it is true. The rumors are about the Bible. From magazines and movies, from tabloids and TV documentaries we hear the scuttlebutt from skeptical scholars and know-it-all neighbors. You know the rumors I mean. We've all heard them, and inquiring minds want answers.

One typical tale is that the Bible was put together by a group of unscrupulous bishops who only chose the writings that would serve their selfish interests. They wanted to build their personal power bases. Time and again we hear about "lost books of the Bible." The innuendo is that certain books *should* have been included in Scripture, but power-hungry prelates suppressed them. They censored the seditious truth because it threatened their dark designs. Is that really how the Bible came together?

A second slice of slander is that the Bible has been copied so many times, with so many mistakes in each copy, that the message has morphed over the millennia. The word on the street is that the Bible has been so drastically distorted we have no idea what it originally said. Which version of the Bible is "right?" Decriers tell us it's hopeless even to try to find out. Can we recover what the Bible really says?

A similar tidbit notices that the Bible has been translated over and over again. And since something is always lost in translation, whatever the Bible originally said is completely obscured. Is the situation really that garbled?

Here's a fourth, juicy allegation. The Bible is just one of many holy books. It has some great stories and wonderful teachings, but so do the *Bhagavad Gita*, the *Koran* and even the *Iliad* and the *Odyssey*. Like the sacred writings of all religions, the Bible is a compilation of human ideas about God, the universe and so on. When Christians refer to the Bible as the "Word of God," we're either exaggerating or bragging. It's as if we're saying, "My book's better than your book!" That idea feels arrogant and narrow-minded. Is there anything special and unique about the Bible?

And here's a good one. Some say the Bible was written so long ago, in cultures so different from ours, it can't possibly convey anything meaningful or helpful to us today. It's an irrelevant relic that should be consigned to the trash heap of history. Is there no ancient wisdom that could enlighten our times?

A similar supposition goes like this. If you interpret and apply the Bible literally, you end up with some ridiculous ideas and practices. For example, almost no one nowadays believes that the earth literally has four corners (Isaiah 41:9, Revelation 7:1, 20:8), or that the sun really runs daily like a champion across the sky (Psalm 19:4-6). And even the most devout Christian never thinks twice about wearing a garment made of two different kinds of material, though Leviticus 19:19 tells us not to do that. On the other hand, if we only interpret the Bible figuratively we can make it say anything we want it to say. In that case, it says nothing at all. Is there a way to interpret the Bible that makes sense? Are there proper ways to understand Scripture so that it will help us and enrich our lives?

Then there's this common charge: The Bible is full of contradictions. If the Bible says one thing here and the opposite there, both can't be true. And if both can't be true, we can never know which statement to believe. Therefore, we can't trust any of it. Further, if the Bible is the Word of God, how can God contradict Himself, like a careless liar or a sleazy politician? Can those discordant notes be harmonized?

Others allege that because the Bible is filled with "mythological" features like angels and demons, healings, resurrections and other miracles, it describes an unreal world. Primitive peoples could believe that stuff, but we know better. Have we outgrown the Bible?

Finally, there are those who say the Scriptures are inscrutable. The Bible is just impossible to understand, so we shouldn't bother with it at all. Is the Bible's message so far beyond our comprehension that we shouldn't waste our time exploring it?

A Crucial Question

What should we make of these nasty rumors? Should we believe what they're saying about the Bible? We sing the children's song, "Jesus loves me, this I know, for the Bible tells me so." Very sweet. But do we really mean it? Oh, most of us believe that Jesus loves us, but is the *reason* we believe that the fact that the Bible tells us so? Can serious minded grown-ups like you and me trust what the Bible says? In other words, is the Bible reliable? That's one of life's most crucial questions. If the Bible is reliable we have God-given guidance for our beliefs and behavior. If we can trust the Bible we have a lamp for our feet and a light for our path. But if these rumors are true then we're ships without rudders, being carried by the currents of moral fad and philosophical fashion. If the rumors are true we are left to grope our way through the dark, grabbing onto anything that feels like it might be solid or stable.

To put it in more practical terms, if the Scriptures are trustworthy then we have a way to teach our children right from wrong and truth from error. If the Bible is reliable we can get to know what God is like. We can find out who we are and what purpose we have in life. We can love God the way God wants to be loved and experience the joy of living according to His will. Countless people, including myself, have found comfort in times of distress, inspiration, purpose, meaning and more in the words and teachings of the Bible. Cultures have flourished and civilizations been built on the basis of this most influential book in history. But if those rumors are true, we've been duped. If those rumors are true, your ideas about God and life and significance are just as good as mine. Or just as bad. So, in the chapters that follow we're going to look into those nasty rumors one by one. Are they fact or fable? Will the charges stick? Are they totally true? Are they malicious lies? Are they some mixture of the two?

Anatomy of a Rumor

Many rumors grow out of a misunderstanding. There's often a grain of truth behind gossip, but it gets grossly distorted and blown way out of proportion. For example, suppose someone said, "I saw Pastor Rod in a darkened restaurant with an attractive, younger lady." Could that really be true? As a matter of fact, it could. However, there's nothing salacious going on. From time to time I take the church staff to lunch to thank them for their dedication and excellent work. The last time I did that our party included the church secretary and pianist, Leticia and Lauren, not just one but two attractive young ladies. It also included Bill, our custodian/sexton. The guys sat on one side of the table, the ladies sat on the other and there was absolutely nothing untoward about the event (unless you count the fried onion petals, which clearly weren't very healthy). Nevertheless, it is true, someone might have seen me in a restaurant with a younger woman. The facts reported would technically be correct, but the rumor, or at least its innuendo, would be completely false. The rumor would be a perversion of the truth.

Now, why would someone start a rumor like that? I can think of two reasons. First, it may be an honest misunderstanding. Perhaps the person was sitting in a position where only one co-worker and I were visible. That's not likely, but possible. Or, maybe the person saw us during the brief moment when two of the staff members had already left but another and I were still at the table. There were about two minutes when a woman and I were at the table alone. If anyone inferred anything unseemly, he or she simply misinterpreted the situation. The second possibility is that the person intentionally distorted the truth. Perhaps someone holds a grudge for something that I did wrong, or a mistake the church made. Maybe the person feels disappointed in God and finds fault with anything related to Christianity. It might be that the person just doesn't like me. That happens. But for whatever reason, that teller of tales finds satisfaction in twisting the truth and deliberately spreading a bad report.

Is that what we will find about these nasty rumors concerning the Bible? Is there a speck of veracity behind these rumors? Are they based on an honest misunderstanding or do they grow from some more malicious motive? It could be some of both. Either way, regardless of the motives, these rumors do damage. Can we uncover the facts that put these rumors to rest?

A Pastor's Perspective

Before we go on, I need to make it plain why I'm writing this book. I write as a pastor. Brilliant scholars have come out with widely varying writings, videos and other presentations on these subjects. I've studied many of them, but I'm not a professional scholar. Years ago, I did earn an advance degree in New Testament and was privileged to study with some of the leading Bible professors in the country at that time, but I am not a professor. I'm a pastor, and I write as a pastor. That means that I have very little interest in winning an academic debate. The debate is fascinating, but I'll leave that to the more competent people who do it for a living. Further, I don't see it as my place to "defend" the Bible. As Charles Spurgeon famously said, defending the Bible is like defending a lion. All we really need to do is let the lion out of its cage, and it will defend itself.[1]

My heart's desire as a pastor is to strengthen the faith of followers of Jesus. Nothing is more precious than your faith (See 1 Peter 1:7). Your faith is the foundation of your vibrant relationship with God through Jesus Christ and the abundant life that is yours in Him. Your faith is the

---

[1] "Spurgeon's 'Let the lion out of the cage' Quote," https://elliotritzema.com/2012/07/31/spurgeons-let-the-lion-

https://elliotritzema.com/2012/07/31/spurgeons-let-the-lion-out-of-the-cage-quote/ Last visited 1.3.19.

instrument of your salvation (Ephesians 2:8, John 3:16). Winning a debate can be a rush. I've done it a time or two. But that's nothing compared with the exhilarating joy of helping you rest secure and grow in your faith.

As the Apostle Paul said good-bye to the elders in Ephesus, he spoke these ominous words, *"I know that after my departure fierce wolves will come in among you, not sparing the flock; and from among your own selves will arise men speaking twisted things, to draw away the disciples after them"* (Acts 20:29-30). Paul prophesied that outsiders and even professing Christians would twist the truth – maybe out of genuine misunderstanding or maybe with a more malicious motive – and would try to mislead God's people. This prophecy has been fulfilled again and again in the history of the Church. Are the circulating rumors about the Bible another fulfillment of that prophecy? Dan Wallace estimates that tens of thousands of Christians have abandoned their faith because of some of these rumors.[2] Precious people have been drawn away by perversions of the truth. Others, I suspect, remain believers but, in part because these rumors have planted poisonous doubts in their minds, they rarely read the Bible and apply it to their lives. How awful! How tragic! Both groups have been robbed of the great comfort, joy, purpose, direction and more that many of us find in Scripture. These rumors are stumbling blocks. They dishearten believers and discourage people from reading, contemplating, and living God's Word. I write this book to help move those dastardly barriers out of the way. If these rumors are false, it is important, no, it's

---

[2] See the film, *Fragments of Truth* 2018 Faithlife Films, about 70 minutes into the film.

urgent that we know. It matters to us now, and to future generations.

The Stakes Are High

When people believe these rumors, they are tempted to neglect the Bible. They might hold onto their faith in Jesus, but they don't see the Bible as a reliable resource for help and guidance. So, they cut themselves off from this flow of essential guidance, truth and wisdom. Many Christians don't know the Bible because they don't read it. They don't read it because they don't really understand what a valuable treasure it is. In other words, they don't believe it will make a difference in their lives. They don't recognize Bible reading to be a profitable investment of their time and energy. Much of our culture's population would rather peruse novels, watch YouTube or play video games than search the Scriptures. We live in a dark age of biblical illiteracy. Bibles sit in our bookcases or on our coffee tables or computers. We even install Bibles on our phones. That's good, but sadly, many Christians rarely instill God's Word in their hearts and minds.

What a tragedy. We live in complicated times. Suicide, abortion, new family structures, and political polarization are among the many issues that perplex us. The complexities of (post) modern life require great and godly wisdom. If we can gain that wisdom from the Bible, it's both stupid and foolish to ignore it. Like a motorist who runs out of fuel even though he drives right past dozens of gas stations, like the person who lives and dies as a pauper because she doesn't know that she has inherited a fortune, like Dorothy who only had to click her ruby slippers together to get home free, we make a colossal mistake and set ourselves up for trouble when we ignore God's Word.

The rumors insinuate that the Bible is not God's Word. The malicious among the rumormongers want us to run out of gas, to be impoverished, never to make it home again. But if the rumors are false, we have an astonishing treasure trove right at our fingertips. In God's Word we have all we will ever need and more. That is more true today than ever. We live in an age when information is as easy to get as fresh air and clean water. Easier. Books, articles, blogs, teaching videos, courses, sermons and scores of other helpful materials are only a mouse click away. Are you reading a passage of Scripture that's confusing or seems obscure? What did Billy Graham or John Piper or some other anointed preacher say about those verses? Maybe there's a good sermon on line. There are probably several! Has anyone written on the subject you're interested in? Or made a video? You don't have to go to the library or bookstore to find out. The answer is literally in the palm of your hand. Much of the research for this book was confirmed and enriched by watching lectures and debates by excellent Bible scholars on line. We live in times of biblical illiteracy, but we have the amazing potential to be the best-informed generation in history. Let that sink in. We have the amazing potential to be the best-informed generation in history. We could and should be the most knowledgeable group of disciples who have ever lived. The opportunity is ours. We ought to seize it.

A New Reformation?

Imagine what would happen if we took advantage of the riches that are available to us! What could transpire if we invested our intellects deeply in our faith? What would be the results if the vast population of Christians alive today really knew and trusted the Bible? If we did all we could to learn it and live it? I have an inkling, I have more than an inkling that if we did those things, not only would we dispel false rumors and foil fake news, we would experience a comprehensive renovation of our society. No, not just a renovation, a Reformation. A restoration of what God intends for His children. Renewal. Revival. Times of refreshing. Call it what you will. Whatever you name it, this transformation is of utmost importance. We can continue to languish in ignorance, which is actually the opposite of bliss, or we can flourish in the light of truth. We can choose: Dark ages or Reformation? If these rumors are true, then it's futile for us to look for help in the Bible. But if we're dealing with idle gossip, those tales are holding us back from exciting enlightenment and rejuvenation. Can we discover the truth? The stakes are high.

A Special Kind of Love

The gravitational center of the Old Testament is Deuteronomy 6:4-5, *Hear, O Israel: The LORD our God, the LORD is one. You shall love the LORD your God with all your heart and with all your soul and with all your might.* That passage is called "the great *shema*" (שמע) from the Hebrew word for "hear." Most Bible students, whether Christian, Jewish or non-believing, recognize the preeminence of that passage. They're in good company. Jesus understood the same thing. When He was asked which commandment is the most important of all, *Jesus answered "The most important is, 'Hear, O Israel: The Lord our God, the Lord is one. And you shall love the Lord your God with all your heart and with all your soul and with all your mind and with all your strength.'"* (Mark 12:29-30)

Did you notice the significant difference between those two passages? In Mark, Jesus tweaks the great *shema*. He throws in some vocabulary we don't find in Deuteronomy. The phrase, "and with all your mind" is added. It turns out that the words for "heart," "soul" and "mind" overlap in meaning, both in Hebrew (the original language of Deuteronomy and most of the Old Testament) and Greek (the original language of Mark and the New Testament). It's hard to define shades of distinction among those words, and someone could argue that the idea of loving God with one's mind is already present in Deuteronomy. The passage in Mark doesn't really add anything. It just makes clear what Deuteronomy really meant. We are to love God with everything we are. In any event, Jesus specifically tells us here (and in Matthew 22:37) that we are to love God with our minds as well as with other aspects of our being. We love Him with our emotions. We love Him with our affections. We love Him with our wills. We love Him with our desires. We love Him with our service. Yes. But the Bible also makes clear that we are to love Him with our full mental capacities. Our minds.

So how do we do that? How do we engage our intellects in the love of God? At the very least, we love Him with our minds as we think godly thoughts. We think about Him. We think about our faith. We think about Scripture. That's called

Theology. Now, don't let that word intimidate you. This book is not an academic treatise. It's written for normal, intelligent followers of Jesus like you. You don't need a Ph.D. or seminary degree to understand what we're talking about. Nevertheless, these pages may give you some things to ponder. Reading this book is a way to help you love God through thinking. I hope it will help you develop a more thoughtful relationship with God's Word. If these nasty rumors about the Bible are false, if we really can trust the Bible, then one of the best ways to love Him with our minds is to read the Bible and read it intelligently. That isn't the only way to love Him, but it is a special kind of love. This book hopes to help you do precisely that.

The Bible's Answer

The Bible itself responds to these nasty rumors. 2 Timothy 3:16 says, *All Scripture is God-breathed and is useful for teaching, for rebuking, for correcting, and for training in righteousness* (NIV). That's a potent promise. But what help is that to the doubter? What the Bible says about the Bible proves nothing to people who aren't sure we can trust it in the first place. I'm reminded of the man who told his friend, "I understand you buried your mother-in-law at sea. I'm so sorry. I didn't even know she was dead." The friend replied, "Well, she insisted she wasn't, but you know how she could lie." I think the dear lady was telling the truth, don't you? I think the Bible is telling the truth, too. And that powerful verse will answer many of our questions. But first we have to learn what the verse means.

What is "all Scripture?" Does it include those "lost books" we talked about? Does it apply to every word in every version? Every translation? What does it mean to say all Scripture is "God-breathed?" How did that happen? What difference does it make? And how does the Bible teach us? Rebuke us? Correct us? Train us? There's a correlation between this verse and the nasty rumors. Keep reading. As we explore this verse, as we come to a better understanding of what these words mean, our picture of the Bible will become clearer and brighter. And as the radiant truth about Scripture comes into focus, we'll begin to expose the ruse of these nasty rumors.

Chapter Two

Banned from the Bible?

"Lost Books of the Bible?"

Have you heard about the lost books of the Bible? The word on the street is that there were scads of sacred writings that could have been included, *should* have been included as part of our Scriptures, but they were hushed up. Excluded. Banned from the Bible. For example, we've found ancient gospels bearing the names of Peter, Thomas, Mary Magdalene and even Judas! We have books with fascinating tales about the childhood of Jesus. Why didn't these make the cut? How come we have Matthew, Mark, Luke and John, these four and no more? Further, we've found The Acts of Peter, The Acts of John, The Acts of Paul and more. Is somebody holding out on us? Why do we have only the sixty-six[3] books in our Bibles? Who were the doorkeepers? Who were the holy bouncers who decided which books got in and which books got the boot? 2 Timothy 3:16 assures us that *All Scripture is God-breathed,* but who determines what is and what isn't part of "all Scripture?" Why John but not Thomas? Why The Acts of the Apostles but not The Acts of Peter or Paul? How did the Bible come together?

A Backroom Deal?

A speculative suggestion that became surprisingly popular was posited in a 2003 thriller by novelist Dan Brown. This particular rumor spread like wildfire. Pundits still parrot it sixteen years later. About halfway through *The Da Vinci Code*[4] we meet Professor Teabing. He says to the female lead character, Sophie (who is far more competent in the novel than the feminine foil in the film adaptation), "The Bible did not arrive by fax from heaven." Well, that much the author got right. But the rest of what he proposes about how the Bible came to be is raw fiction. It doesn't fit the facts. Professor Teabing spins the yarn that the

---

3 There are 66 books in the Protestant Bible. The Roman Catholic Bible incudes a section known as the Apocrypha or Deuterocanonical books. These have usually been received as helpful but not authoritative until the middle of the 16th century when, as a reaction to the Protestant Reformation, the Council of Trent declared them to have the same authority as the rest of the Bible for Roman Catholics. That seems to be the late exception to the process described in this chapter.

4 Dan Brown, *The Da Vinci Code* © 2003 (New York) Doubleday pp. 230 ff.

Emperor Constantine, anxious to shore up the power of the Roman Empire, turned to Christianity as a means of unifying his domain. Though in the professor's version of history Constantine never became a Christian, he elevated Christianity to the status of the official state religion because he thought it would give him more complete control over his subjects. In a shrewd move to solidify his power, he called all the bishops to convene in Nicaea in the year 325. He ordered them to declare that Jesus was the Son of God – allegedly a novel idea at the time. With an official religion whose founder is said to be divine, no one could oppose what that religion said. And if the emperor controlled the church, the emperor's power would be absolute.

Further, Constantine directed the bishops to write a creed, which would establish the divinity of Jesus. This is supposed to be how and why we got the Nicene Creed. Then, to top things off, Teabing says, "Constantine commissioned and financed a new Bible, which omitted those gospels that spoke of Christ's *human* traits and embellished those gospels that made him godlike. The earlier gospels were outlawed, gathered up and burned."[5] Aha! There's the culprit. Our Bible is the propaganda pamphlet of Constantine's corrupt conspiracy.

A Work of Fiction

Now, *The Da Vinci Code* is just a novel. It belongs to the genre of "historical fiction," light on history, heavy on fiction. Soon after I finished a graduate degree in New Testament I had the pleasure to read James Michener's *The Source*[6]. The caliber of Michener's research blew me away and delighted me at the same time. Much of the information I had studied so hard to acquire was reflected in

---

[5] Ibid. p. 234
[6] James Michener, *The Source* © 1965 by Random House Inc.

that entertaining and informative novel. The story lines were made up, but the historical backgrounds were remarkably accurate. That's how historical fiction should be written. I'm afraid much of the public believes that Brown was equally careful in his research. Or if he wasn't careful in his research, he was at least lucky in his guess. Many folks seem to think that Brown's recasting of history closely resembles what actually happened. Thoughtlessly, some accept "the Teabing Theory" as fact when it's mostly fabrication. Even some professional scholars seem to build their opinions on this flimsy foundation. Yes, Constantine did call the Council of Nicaea in 325, and yes, that council did bless the world with a beautiful creed, a concise articulation of what Christians believe. That much is true. The rest of this rumor, however, is fake history.

Think about it for a moment. Why would Constantine adopt Christianity as a tool to enhance his own power? Because he could claim that Jesus was a god? That would have been a seriously stupid strategy. For centuries, since the time of Augustus Caesar, all the emperors of ancient Rome claimed that they themselves were gods. The religious policy of the Empire had always been that Roman subjects could worship any god or gods they wanted, so long as they worshipped Caesar, too. That's why Christians were persecuted. They wouldn't play along. They wouldn't acknowledge the Emperor as divine. So, they were thrown in prison or burned alive or fed to the lions as a form of entertainment. All they had to do was say, "Caesar is Lord." But they knew better. For centuries until the time of Constantine, Christians were martyred because they knew that only Jesus Christ is Lord. They literally staked their lives on it. If Constantine had wanted to increase the power of the state, he would have never done it by declaring that Jesus is Lord. He would have done what all his predecessors had done. He would have enforced the old decree, "Caesar is Lord." Why concede his power to Jesus? Constantine was not so clueless.

But not only does *The Da Vinci Code* present us with a cartoonish caricature of Constantine, we get an equally grotesque impression of the bishops at Nicaea. We picture the bishops as power-hungry politicians out to enhance their own positions. We envision wealthy prelates in rich robes and velvet finery. Perhaps we think of Cardinal Richelieu from *The Three Musketeers*. But these very bishops had suffered severely for their faith. The last emperor before Constantine was Diocletian. This despot despised the Christian Faith and wanted to extinguish it. From the year 303 to 311 Diocletian oversaw the worst persecution the Church had known until that time. Bibles were banished and ordered to be burned. Flames engulfed Christian homes and meeting places. Believers were tortured and killed. This was the brutal culmination of the first "age of the martyrs." Most of the bishops who came to the Council of Nicaea had been victims of this bloody pogrom. They had been tormented, beaten, jailed and abused. Many of them limped to Nicaea, crippled and mangled for their faith. They came with eyes gouged out. They came marred, scarred and maimed. They came mourning close colleagues, their beloved brothers and sisters who had been killed in the persecution. They were the walking wounded. These faithful shepherds had been persecuted precisely because they refused to deny that Jesus is Lord. The Council of Nicaea didn't invent the divinity of Jesus. The bishops who were there had believed that teaching so strongly that they had sacrificed their bodies and their families for that great, saving truth.

More to the point, I know of no record that says the bishops of Nicaea even talked about which books should be in the Bible. And even if they did, it didn't settle the matter. In the year 367, more than forty years after Nicaea, the bishop Athanasius sent a letter to the people under his care, advising them which books are properly considered Scripture. He lists the 66 books we have, then says, "These are the fountains of salvation, that he who thirsts may be satisfied with the living words they contain."[7] Further, about seventy years after Nicaea the councils of Hippo and Carthage presented lists naming the books that were accepted in all the churches. As we will see later, the process was fluid, but there never was a council that dictated which writings were in and which were out.

We can't really blame Dan Brown. *The Da Vinci Code* is fiction. So, he did what fiction writers do: he made things up. But we should know that the idea that an ambitious body of bishops put together a Bible that would suit their purposes is blatantly false. The facts tell us otherwise. It is remarkable how many intelligent people and prominent educators, even if they know better than to buy the exact scenario fantasized by Dan Brown, still insinuate that the formation of the Bible was an oppressive power play. Take, for example, Elaine Pagels. She teaches Religion at Princeton University and is a favorite authority in documentaries that tend to disparage a traditional understanding of the Bible. Pagels suggests that the books that were chosen to be included in the Bible were only the ones that were "good for institution building."[8] Sound familiar?

So, if the Bible wasn't faxed down from heaven, and if Constantine didn't commission corrupt clergy to develop a weapon of mass domination, how did the Bible come to be?

How the Bible Came Together: Old Testament

Let's start by admitting that there really are "lost books," some of which have never been found. The Bible comes clean on this

---

[7] For a fuller text of this letter, see "Athanasius on the Canon" http://www.bible-researcher.com/athanasius.html

[8] Listen to her interview with Terry Gross on NPR's *Fresh Air* at https://www.youtube.com/watch?v=CQEaBUohYzE

several times, mentioning books none of us have ever seen. For example, in Numbers 21:14-15 we read, *Therefore it is said in The Book of the Wars of the Lord, "Waheb in Suphah and the valleys of Arnon, and the slope of the valleys that extends to the seat of Ar, and leans to the border of Moab."* The quote doesn't tell us much, but it makes us wonder, where is *The Book of the Wars of the Lord?* It's nowhere to be found. Similarly, in 1 Kings and 2 Kings we come across many verses like 1 Kings 22:39, *Now the rest of the acts of Ahab and all that he did, and the ivory house that he built and all the cities that he built, are they not written in The Book of the Chronicles of the Kings of Israel?* Or 2 Kings 20:20, *The rest of the deeds of Hezekiah and all his might and how he made the pool and the conduit and brought water into the city, are they not written in the Book of the Chronicles of the Kings of Judah?* We no longer have *The Book of the Chronicles of the Kings of Israel* or *The Book of the Chronicles of the Kings of Judah.* These aren't just other names for our 1 and 2 Chronicles. They're completely different books, and like *The Book of the Wars of the Lord,* they're gone. Too bad. They would probably be fascinating to read. They might even shed light on events recorded in the Bible. But they're lost. The question, however, is *why* are they lost?

In a similar way, we know that there were plenty of prophets around in the days of Jeremiah. Jeremiah 23:16 says, *Thus says the Lord of hosts: "Do not listen to the words of the prophets who prophesy to you, filling you with vain hopes. They speak visions of their own minds, not from the mouth of the Lord."* Did any of these prophets record their sayings as Jeremiah did? We don't know because, if they did, nobody bothered to preserve them. Books like 1 Kings and 2 Kings helped God's people understand how the Lord was working in their situation, so these books were cherished, protected, and shared. Annuls like *The Book of the Wars of the Lord* or *The Book of the Chronicles of the Kings of Israel* or *Judah* may have been interesting, but people didn't hear the Word of God in them. So, they kept one set of books and lost the other. Likewise, the prophecies of Jeremiah proved to be true. They not only "came true," they revealed the truth about God and His plans and His purposes. They described reality, though the people couldn't see it at the time. So, the people clung to the writings of Jeremiah because they recognized them as the Word of God.

Jeremiah's writings were revered as early as the time of the prophet Daniel. In Daniel 9:2 we read, *I, Daniel, learned from reading the word of the LORD as revealed to Jeremiah the prophet, that Jerusalem must lie desolate for seventy years* (NLT). Jeremiah prophesied during the time of Jerusalem's desolation, which began in 586 Before the Christian Era[9]. During his lifetime, Jeremiah was ridiculed and reviled. A mere seven decades later, however, Daniel acknowledged Jeremiah's writings as nothing less than "the word of the LORD."[10]

Ezra the priest regards Jeremiah's words with the same high esteem. In Ezra 1:1 we read, *In the first year of Cyrus king of Persia, that the word of the LORD by the mouth of Jeremiah might be fulfilled, the LORD stirred up the spirit of Cyrus king of Persia, so that he made a proclamation throughout all his kingdom and also put it in writing.* The decree that follows is the good news that the Temple in Jerusalem is to be rebuilt. God is faithful to His promises. What we want to notice here, however, is that again the

---

[9] In this book I will use the newly preferred abbreviations BCE and CE instead of the traditional designations, BC and AD. However, since it is an important aspect of a Christian worldview that history pivots around the coming of Jesus Christ, I use BCE to mean "Before the Christian Era" and CE for "Christian Era." In what follows, if a date is mentioned with no abbreviations, it refers to a year in the Christian Era, a "year of our Lord."

[10] When the word LORD appears in small capital letters in a quote from the Old Testament, that indicates that the Hebrew word being translated is God's holy name, YHWH.

prophecies of Jeremiah are acknowledged to be "the word of the LORD by the mouth of Jeremiah."

We don't know of any councils that endorsed the book of Jeremiah but rejected any writings by his rivals. We find no conciliar or corporate decrees to receive books like Numbers and 1 and 2 Kings but to spurn *The Book of the Wars of the Lord* or *The Book of the Chronicles of the Kings of Israel* and *of Judah*. In fact, the Bible speaks favorably of these lost books. They were probably very fine literature. They simply weren't recognized by the people of God as the Word of God. Therefore, they fell into disuse and disappeared.

So, here we have a rough picture of how the books we call the Old Testament came together. When people heard the voice of God through a writing, they clung to it. They cherished it as Scripture. When a writing was perceived to be simply a human work, no matter how brilliant it might have been, it was ultimately discarded. By the first century, essentially the books we receive as the Old Testament were recognized as Scripture by most people, including Jesus and the apostles. In Luke 24:44, the risen Jesus says to His disciples, *These are my words that I spoke to you while I was still with you, that everything written about me in the law of Moses and the Prophets and the Psalms must be fulfilled.* The Law of Moses would be Genesis through Deuteronomy. In Judaism, Joshua through 2 Kings were called "the Former Prophets," so Jesus would have been talking about these books as well as the books named after prophets. Perhaps the term "Psalms" here is synonymous with "writings," which would include the wisdom literature (Job, Proverbs, Ecclesiastes, Song of Solomon) and the Chronicler's History (1 Chronicles – Nehemiah) and Esther. In any event, by the time of Jesus something very much like our Old Testament was recognized (and frequently quoted in the New Testament) as Scripture. God's people recognized these books as the Word of God.

How the Bible Came Together: New Testament.

We find a parallel process in the New Testament. Some books are admittedly lost. In 1 Corinthians 5:9, Paul says, *I wrote you in my letter not to associate with sexually immoral people.* The point of that passage, of course, underscores how important the blessing of sexual purity should be to God's people, but we're going to focus on a small but significant detail. This detail gives us some insight into how the New Testament came together. We're talking about the phrase, *I wrote you in my letter* ... What letter? We find this quote in the book we call 1 Corinthians. *First* Corinthians. But it clearly isn't the very first letter the apostle ever wrote to that congregation. Where is the earlier letter Paul is referring to? It's lost. We don't know what else it said (though scholars always have very creative theories). What we do know, however, is that Paul wrote a letter to the Corinthians *before* he wrote what we call 1 Corinthians. We could call that letter "former Corinthians." And it's lost.

Hold on. The plot thickens. In 2 Corinthians 7:8 we read, *For even if I made you grieve with my letter, I do not regret it – though I did regret it, for I see that that letter grieved you, though only for a while.* Here we go again. As we read the surrounding verses, we realize that this doesn't seem like a description of 1 Corinthians. It looks like there was another letter between what we call 1 Corinthians and what we call 2 Corinthians. It's referred to as the "tearful letter." And where is that letter? Again, there are some very complex and speculative answers offered for that question, but the simplest and best answer seems to be that the tearful letter is just missing. Lost. No one bothered to save it.

One more. Look at Colossians 4:16. *And when this letter has been read among you, have it also read in the church of the Laodiceans; and see that you also read the letter from Laodicea.* Have you ever read that letter? Probably not. Again, there are theories. A few scholars think there are reasons to believe that the epistle we call Ephesians is really Laodiceans. There is also a little Latin book of 19 verses that claims to be the lost letter[11], but most scholars agree it's a forgery. Paul says he wrote a letter to the Laodiceans, but it's lost. We don't have it anymore.

Why are these letters missing? Apparently because no one bothered to preserve them. They didn't "live" in the church. They didn't thrive in the community of faith. They didn't help people understand what it means to be the people of God. Believers read 1 and 2 Corinthians, they read Colossians and other epistles in our Bible and said, "Wow, this letter is a keeper!" They kept and copied these letters. They shared them with their friends in other churches. "You've got to read this!" Other letters, regardless of who wrote them, were perceived to have only temporary value. In terms of addressing the lasting needs of God's people, you could say those letters were losers. In any event, they were lost. On the other hand, the letters we still have in our Bibles today were widely treasured. In them followers of Christ heard the Word of the Lord.

The letters of Paul were undoubtedly the first New Testament books to be written. They were gathered into collections at an early date and recognized as Scripture during the lifetime of the apostles, before some other parts of the New Testament were even written. We know this because 2 Peter 3:15-16 says, *And count the patience of the Lord as salvation, just as our beloved brother Paul wrote to you according to the wisdom given to him, as he does in all his letters when he speaks in them of these matters. There are some things in them that are hard to understand, which the ignorant and unstable twist to their own destruction, as they do the other Scriptures.* Notice two things from these verses: First, Peter talks about *all* Paul's letters. This may or may not mean that

---

[11] "The Epistle of Paul the Apostle to the Laodicians" http://www.strecorsoc.org/docs/laodiceans.html Last visited 2.27.2019

he already knew later letters like 1 and 2 Timothy and Titus. It probably doesn't include former Corinthians or the tearful letter, but it does show that there was a compilation of Paul's letters at a very early stage. Second, Peter recognizes these letters of Paul to be Scripture, on a par with the Old Testament. Do you see the New Testament starting to come together?

That's what we see with the epistles, but what about the gospels? Were there missing books there, too? Let's see. Read Luke 1:1-4:

> *Inasmuch as many have undertaken to compile a narrative of the things that have been accomplished among us, just as those who from the beginning were eyewitnesses and ministers of the word have delivered to us, it seemed good to me also, having followed all things closely for some time past, to write an orderly account for you, most excellent Theophilus, that you may have certainty concerning the things you have been taught.*

Luke tells us that *many* people had written about the life and teachings of Jesus. But again, most of those writings apparently didn't thrive in the churches. They didn't help people encounter the risen Christ, so they were dropped by the wayside. Matthew, Mark, Luke and John, these were beloved by believers. These books helped people grow in their faith. So, they were saved and shared and circulated. These became the four Gospels of our Bible.

The Bible was never interested in giving us every possible detail about Jesus and His life. John 20:30-31 says, *Now Jesus did many other signs in the presence of the disciples, which are not written in this book; but these are written so that you may believe that Jesus is the Christ, the Son of God, and that by believing you may have life in his name.* John left things out of his Gospel. Some of that material is found in Matthew, Mark and Luke. Other things aren't preserved anywhere. John says, *Now there are also many other things that Jesus did. Were every one of them to be written,*

I suppose that the world itself could not contain the books that would be written (John 21:25). Yes, there are lost books of the Bible. That's no big surprise. But we have what we need. We have those writings that conceive faith and lead to life.

A Familiar Voice

Picking up on a tender image from the Old Testament (see Psalm 23 and Isaiah 40:11), Jesus described Himself as the Good Shepherd and His people as His sheep. Sheep know the voice of their shepherd, Jesus said. They will not listen to the voice of another. (John 10:3-5) He said, *My sheep hear my voice, I know them, and they follow me* (John 10:27).

Not long ago I phoned my wife on our landline. When she answered I told her that I just wanted to call and say that I thought she was the most wonderful, beautiful and delightful woman in the world. She replied, "Why thank you. ... Who is this?" Okay, that didn't really happen. Oh, she's witty enough to have delivered that line, but for the record, she did not. It isn't that all those statements about my wife aren't true. They are, but she knows me. She knows the kinds of things I would say. She recognizes my voice. It's silly to think she wouldn't. Isn't this the phenomenon we see in the earliest stages of the Bible's formation? There was no authoritarian imposition of arbitrary orthodoxy. Some writings reverberated in the hearts of believers, and those writings were recognized as Scripture. Christians kept the books in which they recognized the Shepherd's voice. Professor Dan Wallace of Dallas Theological Seminary suggests that Christians recognized the "intrinsic authority"[12] of certain early writings. It isn't so much

---

[12]"Daniel Wallace: Did the Ancient Church Muzzle the Canon?" https://www.youtube.com/watch?v=wcWbV3QUfIg

that the church determined which books are supposed to be in the Bible, but that they discovered the books in which they heard the Good Shepherd's voice. They preserved the books in which they heard the Word of God.

After the Apostles

After the age of the apostles, the New Testament continued to take shape for two or three centuries. Christians would talk to their friends about books they found inspiring and inspired. As still happens today, church members would ask their pastors or bishops to recommend reading material. And pastors would talk to each other about it, formally and informally. As we said earlier, the process was pretty fluid. Many of the books were universally recognized by Christians everywhere, but others were more "iffy." Books like *The Shepherd of Hermas* and *The Epistle of Barnabas* were very popular and well received, but were finally passed by. Other books, like James, Hebrews, 2 Peter and Revelation were often in question. The former were ultimately excluded, the latter incorporated. Here are a few highlights of the process by which those decisions were made.[13]

Marcion and His Followers

The question of which books should be in the Bible and which books should be out became a hot button issue in the middle of the second century. A man named Marcion of Sinope, who grew up in the church and died about 160 CE, caused the crisis. He had some

---

[13] More detailed accounts of the history of canonization are readily available. I recommend chapter 3 of F.F. Bruce, *The New Testament Documents: Are They Reliable?*, © The Inter-Varsity Fellowship 1943, reprinted 1965

very strong and strange ideas about God and the Bible. Marcion took seriously the Apostle Paul's essential teaching that salvation comes by putting one's trust in Jesus Christ, not by doing good works or observing the Law. The Law, of course, refers to the teaching of what we call the Old Testament. However, Marcion took this insight of Paul so seriously that he rejected the Old Testament in its entirety. He went so far as to assert that the God of the Old Testament, the God of Abraham, Isaac and Jacob, was a different god from the God and Father of Jesus Christ. The former god was evil, the latter God sent Jesus to save us from this dastardly deity.

In addition to rejecting the whole Old Testament, Maricion only acknowledged those parts of our New Testament that agreed with his theology. In fact, he came out with his own Bible. The Marcion Bible included only one Gospel, a highly edited version of Luke, and ten Pauline epistles. Further, even the letters of Paul were subject to heavy redaction and reduction. Passages that seemed to affirm the whole biblical story, like Romans 9-11, were left on the cutting room floor. His Bible did not include 2 Timothy 3:16, so Marcion seems to have missed the fact that all Scripture is inspired by God to correct us (among other things), not the other way around.

Unfortunately, many Christians today are still functional Marcionists. While there is an encouraging and growing awareness in the Church that God is using both the Messianic Jewish and Gentile Christian believers to "tear down the dividing wall" and form the "one new man" promised in Ephesians 2:14-16, there are still Christians who ignore the Old Testament. They see the Old Testament as inferior to the New, instead of recognizing that the New is the culmination and completion of the Old. We've already seen how Jesus said He fulfilled the Old Testament (Luke 24:44. See also Luke 24:27, Matthew 5:17, John 5:39). But too many Christians start their Bible reading with Matthew's Gospel and never look back. In this way they deprive themselves of the richness of their spiritual heritage. They fail to understand countless Old Testament references made by Jesus and the apostles. They never plumb the depths of the grace of the Lord, who used fallible people and a flawed history to accomplish His redemptive purpose. Further, we all share a tendency to snip out the parts of Scripture we don't like. The "whole counsel of God" (Acts 20:27) is vast and hard to grasp. I know I don't understand it all myself. But if, like Marcion, we scratch the parts of Scripture that stretch us, we will settle into a smug, dark ignorance and never grow. How tragic.

An Early List

It was probably in response to the pastoral crisis stirred up by Marcion that church leaders began to provide people with lists of books that were helpful. We have a list of authoritative (or better, self-authenticating) books from around 175 CE. It's called the Muratorian Fragment or the Muratorian Canon. The word "canon" comes from the Greek word κανων which means ruler, as in a measuring device. Not only is the Bible the yardstick by which we measure our lives, Bible scholars use the word to refer to a list of accepted or authoritative writings. The Muratorian Fragment includes the Old Testament and most of the New Testament as we know it. However, it's missing Hebrews, James, 2 Peter and 3 John. The fragment recommends *The Shepherd of Hermas* to be read, but not as Scripture. The very beginning of the Muratorian Fragment is missing. It starts by referring to Luke as the "third Gospel." However, there is ample evidence that that the four Gospels had already been collected and circulated in the order we know, Matthew, Mark, Luke, John.

The Second Great Commission

In 332 CE (seven years after the Council of Nicaea) Constantine asked the bishop Eusebius of Caesarea for 50 copies of the Bible to distribute among churches in the growing new capital, Constantinople. Dan Wallace calls this event "the second great commission."[14] The emperor did not dictate which writings to include, rather the bishop knew the books that were in use and blessing God's people. He had written about the process in his book, *Ecclesiastical History*.[15] Though there is some doubt about James, Jude, 2 Peter, 2 John and 3 John, there is reason to suspect that the Bibles Eusebius produced included the same books we find in the Protestant canon[16]. The consensus that began to emerge even in apostolic times was becoming more and more clear.

An Easter Letter

Before Easter in 367 the bishop Athanasius of Alexandria sent a pastoral letter to the Christians who looked to him for guidance and leadership. Among other issues, such as the date of Easter that year, he discussed which writings were found to be helpful and authoritative for the person who wanted to follow Jesus Christ. We have already heard his tender description of these works. "These are the fountains of salvation, that he who thirsts may be satisfied

---

[14] See "Dr. Daniel Wallace – The Second Great Commission: Constantine and the Making of the New Testament." https://www.youtube.com/watch?v=KtWbqsmdZGw&t=521s Last visited 1.16.19.
[15] F.F. Bruce, *The Canon of Scripture* ©1998 F.F. Bruce, pp. 197-203, InterVarsity Press, Downers Grove, Illinois
[16] Ibid. pp. 74, 198-199 and 204

with the living words they contain."[17] The heart of a loving pastor, concerned for the spiritual well being of his people, shines through that sentence.

By the fourth century many books, like those we mentioned earlier in this chapter, had been written. As people tried to express their own understandings of who Jesus really is, and as authors mixed the Gospel with their own favorite philosophies and theories, a confusing diversity of writings threatened to divert people from those early books in which believers heard the Shepherd's voice. Like pretenders to a royal throne, some of these books were put forward as equal to the books recognized as God's Word. To dispel any confusion, the bishop shared with his people what he knew to be most helpful. Taking his cue from the Gospel of Luke, he wrote, "... it seemed good to me also, having been urged thereto by true brethren, and having learned from the beginning, to set before you the books included in the Canon, and handed down, and accredited as divine."[18] If there was ambiguity about the books Eusebius included in the Bibles he published, there was no question for Athanasius. Exactly the books we call the Bible were listed by the Bishop of Alexandria.

Councils and Canon

Athanasius, however, did not settle the matter completely. He did not have the authority to do so.[19] However, two African Councils,

---

[17] For a fuller text of this letter, see "Athanasius on the Canon," http://www.bible-researcher.com/athanasius.html ¶6 Last visited 2.27.2019

[18] Ibid. ¶3

[19] Dr. Pagels' accusation that Athanasius issued this list to solidify his own power ignores the facts, smacks of Dan Brown conspiratorial mentality and approaches character assassination. "Interview on the Gospel of Thomas – Elaine Pagels NPR Fresh

one in Hippo in 393 CE and the other in Carthage in 397 CE affirmed precisely the books Athanasius endorsed.[20] While the process remained somewhat fluid, the biblical canon as we know it had pretty much emerged in full by the end of the fourth century.

God's Canon

We should emphasize the fact that, in this process, the Church did not so much *determine* which books were to be in the Bible as they *discovered* which books were to be in the Bible. The question was not, "Which books do *we* want in the Bible?" The real question was, "Which are the inspired books which *God* has given to us?" The canon is not so much an authoritative list of books but a list of authoritative books.[21] The process was more discernment than decision. As F.F. Bruce says, "One thing must be emphatically stated. The New Testament books did not become authoritative for the Church because they were formally included in a canonical list; on the contrary, the Church included them in her canon because she already regarded them as divinely inspired, recognizing their innate worth and general apostolic authority, direct or indirect."[22]

Echoing a biblical truth taught in places like Hebrews 8:5 and 9:23, which indicate that the earthly worship of ancient Israel was a copy of heavenly reality, James White talks about $canon_1$ and $canon_2$. $Canon_1$ is the Bible, as it exists in God's mind, the Bible as

Air https://www.youtube.com/watch?v=CQEaBUohYzE&t=962s 12:50 Last visited 2.27.2019

[20] F.F. Bruce *Canon* pp.232-233

[21] See "Daniel Wallace: Did the Ancient Church Muzzle the Canon?" https://www.youtube.com/watch?v=wcWbV3QUfIg&t=195s Last visited 2.27.2019

[22] Bruce, FF *The New Testament Documents: Are They Reliable?* © The Inter-Varsity Fellowship 1943, reprinted 1965 p.27

God inspired it. The task of the church was to sort through the many things that were written and discern which writings were of God. "The canon exists," White explains, "because God has inspired some writings, not all writings."[23] The works that were recognized as God-breathed were included in canon$_2$, the Bibles we have on earth.

The canon did not come about as part of a plot or ploy by powerful church leaders to impose their will on the people. That rumor is simply false. Rather, as we saw earlier, God's people resonated with God's Word. The Lord's people knew His voice. "In other words, the Spirit's work was 'bottom up,' not 'top down'; it was God's people gathered in worship and service to Christ, who passively received, from the hand of God by His Spirit, a functioning, sufficient knowledge of the canon. This led then to the outward, official recognition by the ecclesiastical structures of later church history."[24]

And here's the exciting thing. God's people still hear His voice as He speaks to us through His Word. "Despite the nit-picking of skeptics and even the encroachment of unbelieving naturalism that pervades many theological seminaries, God's people hear the voice of their Lord in the writings that make up the Old and New Testaments."[25]

Needless to say, not everyone hears the Shepherd's voice in Scripture, only His sheep. Not everyone recognizes God's Word in the Bible. John Calvin explains:

---

[23] James White, *Scripture Alone* ©2004 James R. White loc 1577 of 3917, an online eBook

[24] Ibid loc. 1692 of 3917

[25] Ibid. loc. 1939 of 3917

"For as God alone is a fit witness of himself in his Word, so also the Word will not find acceptance in men's hearts before it is sealed by the inward testimony of the Spirit. The same Spirit, therefore, who has spoken through the mouths of the prophets, must penetrate into our hearts to persuade us that they faithfully proclaimed what has been divinely commanded. ... Let this point therefore stand: that those whom the Holy Spirit has inwardly taught truly rest upon Scripture, and that Scripture indeed is self-authenticated; hence, it is not right to subject it to proof and reasoning. And the certainty it deserves with us, it attains by the testimony of the Spirit. For even if it win reverence for itself by its own majesty, it seriously only affects us when it is sealed upon our hearts through the Spirit. Therefore, illumined by his power, we believe neither by our own nor by anyone else's judgment that Scripture is from God."[26]

1 Corinthians 2:14 says, *The natural person does not accept the things of the Spirit of God, for they are folly to him, and he is not able to understand them because they are spiritually discerned.* Without the work of the Holy Spirit in their lives, skeptics cannot understand the process outlined above. To them it sounds like folly. Foolishness. Those who don't know the Shepherd can't recognize His voice. So, they have to make up theories that appeal to their limited understanding. They hypothesize about how the Bible came to be and why so many people believe it. They invent rumors like "the Teabing Theory" and spread them. Perhaps we can't blame them. We should certainly love and pray for them. But we must not buy what they're selling. What shall we say about this

---

[26] John Calvin, *Institutes of the Christian Religion, Volume 1,* Edited by John T. McNeil, Translated by Ford Lewis Battles, (Philadelphia) Westminster Press © MCMLX by W.L. Jenkins 1.7.4, 5

nasty rumor that the Bible was put together as part of an evil conspiracy to dominate the masses? It doesn't fit the facts. Dismiss it.

A Look at "Lost Books."

Before we go on to the next nasty rumor, let's take a quick glance at a few of the "lost books" and see if they confirm our explanation. Let's peek at some of the books the devotees of Professor Teabing suggest we should include in our Bible. What do we find in these "lost books of the Bible?" Was the Church right in giving these books the ax? Are they on a par with the books we recognize as Scripture? Let's look at three samples.

The Gospel of Mary Magdalene

One of the books we hear much about is The Gospel According to Mary Magdalene. We only have parts of this book, namely chapters 4, 5, 8 and 9. In 4:5-7 we read, "Peter said to Mary, Sister we know that the Savior loved you more than the rest of woman. Tell us the words of the Savior, which you remember which you know, but we do not, nor have we heard them. Mary answered and said, What is hidden from you I will proclaim to you."[27] We've already heard from John 20:32 that the fourth Gospel was written *so that you may believe that Jesus is the Christ, the Son of God, and that by believing you may have life in his name.* But Mary promises to share truth that was unknown even to the apostles themselves! Do you buy that?

---

[27] "Gnostic Scriptures and Fragments: The Gospel According to Mary Magdalene" http://www.gnosis.org/library/marygosp.htm Last visited 2.27.2019

The Gospel of Peter

The Gospel of Peter starts with Jesus' trial and contains only 60 verses. It diverges from the canonical account in a number of ways, but the strangest idiosyncrasy is the account of two gigantic males – presumably angels – escorting a gargantuan Jesus from the tomb, followed by a talking cross.[28] Does that fit with what we hear in God's Word?

The Gospel of Thomas

We find 114 verses in the Gospel of Thomas. Verse 105 says, "Jesus said, 'Whoever knows the father and the mother will be called the child of a whore.'"[29] In the last verse we read the following:

> "Simon Peter said to them: 'Let Mary leave us, for females don't deserve life.'
>
> "Jesus said: 'Look, I will guide her to make her male, so that she too may become a living spirit, resembling you males. For every female who makes herself male will enter the domain of Heaven.'"[30]

---

[28] "The Gospel of Peter, Tr. Raymond Brown"
http://www.earlychristianwritings.com/text/gospelpeter-brown.html Last visited 2.27.2019

[29] "The Text of the Gospel of Thomas"
http://www.holybooks.com/wp-content/uploads/Gospel-of-Thomas-Scholars-Version.pdf Last visited 2.27.2019
[30]Ibid.   (Some defenders of the Gospel of Thomas want to claim that this last verse is a later addition to the work. It's easy to see why this verse could be embarrassing, but we only have three

Do you hear the voice of the Good Shepherd in that verse? I don't.

Try It Yourself

So, what do you think? Are these writings on a par with Matthew, Mark, Luke and John? Do they belong in the same Bible with books like Acts, Romans and all the rest? In other words, do you suppose God's people heard His Word, recognized His voice in these works? Did you?

Of course, I've given you selected samples. On the first reading they feel ludicrous, ridiculous, hilariously absurd. But maybe I didn't represent these books fairly. So, check me out. You can easily find these works in their entirety on line. In the footnotes you already have links for the gospels of Mary, Peter, and Thomas. The other books, mentioned earlier in this chapter, are just as easy to find. I invite you to read them for yourself. If you really believe that these books – often mere fragments of books – might be serious contenders for canonical status, take the time to check them out. Be sure to read the New Testament, too. See if you think they are on the same level.

When we look at these so-called "lost books" touted by the rumor mill, we can see why they became, well, canon fodder. They were expendable. They were lost because God's people didn't bother to keep them. The books in which they heard the inspired Word of God, these are the ones God's people kept.

---

manuscripts of Thomas, and two of them are fragments from the middle of the work. No existing manuscript ends at verse 113.)

Chapter Three

A Copy of a Copy of a Copy ...?

A Parlor Game

Have you ever played the game "telephone?" You know, the one where someone writes down a fairly complex sentence then whispers it to someone who whispers it to someone else who whispers it to the next person until everyone in the room has a chance to hear and repeat the message. When the last person shares what she heard everyone is amazed and amused at how much the message has changed. It can be a fun game, and it underlines one of the important reasons we should never listen to or spread rumors. Our church elders played this game at a recent meeting. I copied a sentence from the first draft of this book, "A second slice of slander is that the Bible has been copied so many times that it has changed dramatically over the centuries." By the time that sentence went through the eight of us who were present, what we got was "The second sentence of the Bible is too long." That's quite a difference!

Some people say this process of distortion happened with the Bible. It was written so very long ago and copied over and over again. We don't have the actual scroll Isaiah wrote. We don't have King David's sheet music. We don't have the first edition of Matthew, Mark, Luke, or John, nor any of Paul's letters on his personal stationary. All we have are copies. Hand copies at that, since neither the photocopier nor the printing press had been invented when the Bible was written. How, then, can we be sure the message of the Bible hasn't been distorted like the messages in the parlor game?

Well, for one thing, the rules of the game "telephone" are designed to breed mistakes. If you're playing that game, you only get to hear the message once. You can't ask the previous person to repeat or clarify any details. If you didn't catch part of what was said, you have to guess what it might have been, then pass that on to the next player. You see, if the message doesn't change, the game isn't any fun.

The scribes who copied the Bible, on the other hand, made every effort to see to it that the message *didn't* change. Sometimes, of course, they had the document they were copying in front of them. So, they didn't have to worry about not hearing clearly what was whispered in the ear. They could just compare what they copied with what was written, and avoid mistakes. Other times groups of scribes would work together in a "scriptorium." That was a quicker method for making multiple copies. One person would read out loud the book to be copied and all the scribes would take dictation. Here, of course, you do have a greater opportunity for errors, don't you? So, the scribes devised rules that helped them keep mistakes to a minimum. They came up with checks and balances. For example, they would agree always to have a certain number of words or a certain number of letters on each line. They would also agree to have a certain number of lines on each page. At the end of the day they could go back and count the letters or words per line and the lines per page. If they found too many or two few they would know a mistake had been made and could go back and fix it. Often, in fact, defective copies were destroyed.

They were serious about getting this right. Devout scribes were copying sacred books, and they wanted to preserve the message. Occasionally in the early years, professional scribes, who might or might not have been believers, were employed. But they, too, were careful because their reputations were on the line. Mistakes were made, but not as many as you might think.

The Story of the Scrolls

Let me tell you a story. It starts in 1947, 13 miles from Jerusalem. A Bedouin shepherd boy was searching for one of his goats in the Judean dessert. In the process he threw a rock into a cave, hoping to scare his goat out of hiding. Instead, he heard a crackling noise, like the shattering of glass. When he went in to check it out, he found a big clay jar with some scrolls in it. He reported what he found and, over the next 9 years, archeologists discovered about 850 scrolls in eleven nearby caves. These are the famous "Dead Sea Scrolls."

You've probably heard about the Dead Sea Scrolls, but may have wondered why they're important. One reason is that among those scrolls they found copies of every book of the Hebrew Bible except for Esther. Further, when they determined the dates of these scrolls by coins that were found near them and other means, they discovered that the scrolls were written or copied between 200 years BCE and the second fall of Jerusalem in the year 70 CE. Until the Dead Sea Scrolls were discovered, the earliest copy we had of the Hebrew Scriptures was a version called the Masoretic Text, from roughly the year 900 CE. That's a huge gap between the time the books of Moses and Malachi were written and the time our best copies were made. We're talking about a period of more than 1,300 years after Malachi, maybe twice that for the books of Moses. But when the Dead Sea Scrolls were discovered, we had an opportunity to compare our very late copies with some fairly early copies. We could see what corruptions had crept in over a millennium or two of copying and recopying. How badly had the Bible's message been mangled in transmission? Skeptics were rubbing their palms and licking their chops, certain the distortions would be many. Some people were sure the Bible we had was very different from the Bible that was written.

The first scroll to be evaluated was a copy of Isaiah. Some folks confidently expected that the Masoretic version of Isaiah we had followed for years would be completely discredited. But guess what they discovered. Most good detective stories have a surprise ending, and this one is no exception. Instead of showing how much the Old Testament had changed, the Dead Sea Scrolls proved how little it had changed. The scribes had been very careful. Oh, there were some fascinating and enlightening details that we can't go into here, and not every scroll was as close to the Masoretic Text as Isaiah. Still, by and large what we found in the Dead Sea Scrolls was very close to the copies we had from more than 1,000 years later. Instead of proving that our text of the Bible can't be trusted, as some detractors had hoped, the Dead Sea Scrolls emphasize how reliable the Bible is.

An Elaborate Science

Nevertheless, copying errors did slip in, with both the Old and New Testaments. We can't deny that. But scholars have developed a very sophisticated science called "textual criticism" or "lower criticism" that helps us recognize mistakes – scholars call them "variants" – and choose which variant is probably the best. This science isn't limited to

Biblical studies. All kinds of literary critics[31] use these tools. After all, the plays of Shakespeare were hand-copied, too. The philosophy of Aristotle was hand-copied, too. The *Koran* was hand-copied, too.[32] So variants found their ways into all of these works. In fact, compared with most other literature, it's amazing how few variants are in the Biblical text.

Textual critics are the super-sleuths, sort of the CSI of literary scholars. They know how variants are likely to happen, and that helps them distinguish which readings are better than others. For example, a scribe is more likely to add a couple of words to explain an idea than to leave words out on purpose. So, the shorter reading is usually to be preferred. It's probably original. Again, a scribe is more likely to try to clarify a passage than try to make it more confusing. That means if one version of a verse is harder to understand than another, the more difficult reading is usually to be preferred. The easier reading is probably an attempt to fix the original. If we can see how a scribe's eye might have slipped and he accidently copied a word from a previous line, we can be fairly confident that's a mistake.

Many of the mistakes are easy to catch: misspelled words

---

[31] In this context words like "critic," "critical," "criticism" do not imply fault finding, but very close study.
[32] While Muslim tradition denies that there are any variants in the Koran (or Quran) Mateen Elass makes a convincing case to the contrary in his blog "Quranic Scribe Rejects Islam!," February 22, 2018 https://mateenelass.wordpress.com/2018/02/22/quranic-scribe-rejects-islam/ Last visited 2.27.2019

(the vast majority of variants are differences in spelling),[33] transposed words, a word or phrase copied twice, a word or phrase copied twice. As I said, it's an elaborate and impressive science, exercised with great artistry. And if there are enough documents to compare, textual critics can come up with a pretty reliable version of what an original text said.

A Gold Mine

With the New Testament we have more than 5,800[34] documents to compare! In 2004, when I wrote the sermons on which this book is based, we knew of 5,600 documents. See how the number has grown in just fifteen years. Further, leading textual scholar Dan Wallace, who teaches at Dallas Theological Seminary and is the founder of the Center for the Study of New Testament Manuscripts,[35] estimates that there are about 1,000 manuscripts yet to be found, mostly in former Soviet countries. As Wallace says, we have "an embarrassment of riches"[36] when it comes to New Testament

---

[33] Skeptical critical scholar Bart Ehrman likes to quip that the scribes couldn't spell any better than his students at UNC Chapel Hill!

[34] "Dan Wallace – Recent Discoveries of NT Manuscripts" https://www.youtube.com/watch?v=SqLSSZ-nRPU&t=6s

[35] The Center for the Study of New Testament Manuscripts http://www.csntm.org. CSNTM travels around the world taking photographs of ancient copies of the Greek New Testament. In the process they frequently discover valuable, forgotten manuscripts. Last visited 2.27.2019

[36] "Daniel Wallace: Is What We Have Now What They Wrote Then? Part 1 – Biola Chapel"

manuscripts. By contrast, the piece of ancient literature of which we have the second most copies is the *Iliad* by Homer. We have about 650 copies of that. See the difference?

In addition to the 5,800 manuscripts we have from the Greek New Testament, we have thousands of ancient translations of the Bible. When we read an ancient translation in, say Latin or Syriac, we can have a pretty good idea of the Greek text the translator was using. We may not be able to determine every Greek word that was translated, but we can certainly tell the extent and the basic sense of the text. That is, we can tell which sentences and phrases were in the Greek manuscript that was being translated. And, of course, the manuscript being translated would be older than the translation.

What's more, we have innumerable writings where early Christian authors and preachers quote the New Testament. As a matter of fact, Bruce Metzger, who is sort of the Sherlock Holmes of textual scholars, says that we could reconstruct the entire New Testament on the basis of those quotations alone!

Further, these 5,800 manuscripts come from all over the ancient world. So, we can compare copies that came from Egypt with copies that came from Syria with copies that came from Greece or Palestine or Rome. Thus, we can see if some local prejudice might have changed a text in a particular area. We can also see how widespread a variant

---

https://www.youtube.com/watch?v=uOv6JItV5-w Last visited 2.27.2019

may have been. It's hard to imagine how the exact same mistake could have been made on three different continents.

Finally, our earliest copies of the *Iliad* are from about 900 years after Homer. By contrast we have copies of the Gospels from the second and third centuries. We even have a fragment of John's Gospel, about the size of a driver's license that may be from about 125 CE, or even a quarter century before that.[37] It is called Papyrus 52 or p52.

So, for textual critics, the New Testament documents are a gold mine. We have thousands of them. They come from all over and we have some very old copies. And what happens when we compare all these documents? We find that it is much easier to be sure about the original text of the Bible than it is of any ancient writings, or even most later writings. In other words, though we only have copies of the Bible, not the original manuscripts, we can be confident that the versions of the Bible we have are a very good reflection of the Bible as it was written. We do not suffer from a lack of evidence. We never have to "fill in the blanks." As James White says, it is as if we have 1,010 puzzle pieces for a jigsaw puzzle with only 1,000 parts. The challenge is to determine what to leave out.[38]

---

[37] "The Earliest Handwritten Copy of a Gospel," goodnewsevidence published May 30, 2013
https://www.youtube.com/watch?v=NOwlhcLcJGM&t=34s Last visited 2.27.2019
[38] "The Reliability of the New Testament Text (Dr. James White)"
https://www.youtube.com/watch?v=LuiayuxWwuI&t=99s 1:14:50
Last visited 2.27.2019

Did errors slip in? Well sure. But given the vast number of manuscripts we have, the number of variants is proportionally far lower than what we find in other ancient writings. As Frank Sinatra famously sang, "Mistakes, there've been a few, but then again too few to mention."[39] We have enough material to see what the mistakes are and correct them, usually with confidence.

Meaningful and Viable

At this point we need to recognize that textual variants vary in importance. Many variants don't matter. They don't change the meaning of a passage at all. You could say that some differences make no difference.

The vast majority of variants are simply discrepancies in spelling. The most common of these relates to what is called the "movable nu." In some streams of Greek grammar, one adds their letter for "n" (ν, nu) at the end of a word if the next word starts with a vowel. It's kind of like our difference between the indefinite articles "a" and "an." We talk about *an* honest man but *a* heavenly being. But should we say "an humble person" or "a humble person?" Either way, the "n" doesn't change the meaning.

There are also outright spelling errors. In Matthew 22:42 some manuscripts talk about Jesus as the "Son of Dabid," but we know that the ancestor being referenced is David. The overwhelming majority of those discrepancies, and others like them make no difference to the meaning of a passage,

---

[39] "My Way" lyrics by Paul Anka 1969

especially since standardized spelling is a fairly modern invention. We call such variants "meaningless."

Other variants exist, but they are obvious mistakes. We can tell just by looking that a mistake was made. One medieval scribe, for example, seems to have copied the genealogy of Jesus in Luke 3 from a two-column document as if it was a one-column document. He just read straight across the column gap, hopelessly gnarling the Lord's family tree. In this manuscript (Codex 109) Pares, not Adam, is the father of the whole human race, and Aram is the father of God![40] This reading would be very meaningful if it were valid, but common sense tells us this scribe was uncommonly sloppy. This reading occurs in only one manuscript and it's fairly easy to explain. That reading just isn't viable. Dan Wallace likes to use the example of someone who tries to quote the preamble to the US Constitution, but mistakenly writes, "We, the people of the United States, in order to form a more perfect onion …" No one would conclude that our forebears were interested in improving a spicy vegetable. We would know the author meant "union." The mistake would be meaningful, but not viable.[41]

In 2 Chronicles 22:2 we're told that King Ahaziah pulled off an amazing stunt. He was forty-two years old when he succeeded his father as king. What's so astonishing about that? His father, Jehoram, died at the age of forty (2

---

[40] See *The Text of the New Testament; Its Transmission, Corruption and Restoration* Second Edition by Bruce Metzger © Oxford University Press 1968 p.194-195
[41] "Bart Ehrman & Daniel Wallace Debate Original NT Lost?" https://www.youtube.com/watch?time_continue=4134&v=wyAB BZe5o68 at 1:08:56. Last visited 2.27.2019

Chronicles 21:20)! For the chronology of that text of Chronicles to work, Ahaziah would have had to have been born two years before his father. While all the Hebrew manuscripts of 2 Chronicles have Ahaziah's ascendency in his middle age, other manuscripts agree with 2 Kings 8:26 in saying that Ahaziah became king at the age of twenty-two. That makes more sense. Forty-two shows up in a handful of English translations (KJV, NKJV, RSV, NRSV). Those translations certainly honor the rule that the more difficult reading is to be preferred, but that wording is as impossible as Codex 109's assertion that Aram is the father of God. It simply isn't viable. More than 99% of the variants are either not meaningful or not viable.[42] We can ignore all of those. Some variants, however, are both meaningful and viable. Let's turn our attention to a few of these.

Four Important Variants:

Among the less than 1% of differences that make a difference, let's check out four of the biggest ones. When presented with two or more possible readings, what happens if we select the wrong variant? How much is at stake? What do we lose if we choose poorly? Will that choice significantly impact the content of our faith?

---

[42] "Daniel Wallace: Is What We Have Now What They Wrote Then? Part 2 – Biola Chapel" https://www.youtube.com/watch?v=unlMULCNDUU Last visited 2.27.2019

(1) The Kingdom, the Power, the Glory

One important example comes from "The Lord's Prayer" in Matthew 6:9-13. No, it isn't the controversy about debts and debtors. All the manuscripts say "debts" and "debtors." The problem is the last part of the last verse of the prayer. *For yours is the kingdom and the power and the glory forever. Amen.* What wonderful words of praise! But you may have been shocked and dismayed to notice in reading a 20th or 21st century edition of the Bible that the prayer stops short before it gets to those majestic words of exaltation. As it turns out, that beautiful and beloved doxology isn't found in many of the earliest documents. They may not have been in the Gospel as Matthew wrote it, or even in the prayer as Jesus taught it.

However, read 1 Chronicles 29:11. When the people of God gave willingly and generously for the building of God's temple, King David blessed God and said, "... *Yours, O LORD, is the greatness and the power and the glory and the victory and the majesty, for all that is in the heavens and on the earth is yours. Yours is the kingdom, O LORD, and you are exalted as head above all.*"[43] That sounds remarkably like the missing words from the Lord's Prayer. In fact, one might suppose that similar words were written in the margin of Matthew 6 as an act of praise by a devout copyist. When the

---

[43] Compare the doxology of every creature in heaven and earth from Revelation 5:13. *To him who sits on the throne and unto the Lamb be praise and honor and glory and power, forever and ever* (NIV)*!* Throne implies kingdom. A different Greek word is used for "power."

next scribe came along, perhaps he thought that doxology was supposed to be part of the text, so he added it in. And it certainly does fit beautifully.

My point is this. No matter how those wonderful words ended up at the conclusion of the Lord's Prayer, they are still scriptural. That is, they still express biblical truth. 1 Chronicles 29:11 tells us so. Regardless of whether those words were originally in the book Matthew wrote, they are eminently biblical, and they are true. The kingdom does belong to God alone. The power and the glory are also His. And we are right to praise Him for that. We are right to declare those words continually, "for the kingdom and the power and the glory are Yours. Amen!" The teaching of Scripture is not changed.

(2) Blessed Trinity

A second example. 1 John 5:7 says, *For there are three that bear witness in heaven; the Father, the Word and the Holy Spirit; and these three are one.* At least that's what it says in the New King James Version. However, this clearest articulation of the doctrine of the Trinity in the whole Bible isn't found in a number of old manuscripts, or in the majority of new translations. For example, in the ESV we read, *For there are three that testify: the Spirit, the water and the blood; and these three agree* (1 John 5:7-8).

So, what happened to *the Father, the Word and the Holy Spirit; and these three are one*? It's hard to conceive why any orthodox[44] Christian scribe would intentionally drop those words from his copy. In fact, however, they are absent from many copies. How can we account for that? The solution seems simpler if we turn the problem upside down. Instead of asking how those words got dropped, we might inquire how they could have been added. It's fairly easy to suppose that a God-loving scribe read what we find in the ESV and older copies, and wrote a devotional note in the margin. That note said, "in heaven, the Father, the Word and the Holy Spirit, and these three are one." Again, a later copyist who used that manuscript saw the note in the margin, interpreted it as a correction and inserted it into the text. We can't prove that's what happened, but it makes more sense than any attempt to explain why a variety of scribes would omit such a powerful statement.

Does that mean that the Bible doesn't tell us about the Trinity? It doesn't mean that at all. Clearly the Bible tells us that the Father is God. The Apostle Paul frequently says things like "the God and Father of our Lord Jesus Christ" (Romans 15:6. 2 Corinthians 1:3, 11:31, Ephesians 1:3, 17, 5:20, Colossians 1:3 etc.).

The Bible also teaches that Jesus Christ is God incarnate. Calling Him "the Word," John 1:1 says *In the beginning was the Word, and the Word was with God, and the Word was God.* Then in verse 14 we find, *And the Word became flesh and dwelt among us, and we have seen his glory, glory as of the only Son from the Father, full of grace and truth.* Jesus

---

[44] There could have been scribes who adhered to Arianism or some other ancient heresy. It is possible that they deleted this phrase because of theological bias.

Himself said, *"I and the Father are one"*(John 10:30) and *"Whoever has seen me has seen the Father"* (John 14:9). Philippians 2:6 speaks of Jesus, *who, though he was in the form of God, did not count equality with God a thing to be grasped* (RSV). And after the apostle Thomas dropped his doubts, he called Jesus, *"My Lord and my God"* (John 20:28)*!* Without a doubt the New Testament teaches that Jesus is God. He is God the Son.

And what about the Holy Spirit? He is called the Spirit of God and the Spirit of the Lord too many times to count. He is also called the Spirit of Jesus (Acts 16:7). Further, 2 Corinthians 3:18 talks about "the Lord, who is the Spirit" (ESV, NIV, RSV and others). So, God's Word says that the Holy Spirit is God.

The Father is God. The Son is God. The Spirit is God. But there are not three Gods, for perhaps the most important verse in the Old Testament says, *Hear, O Israel: the LORD our God, the LORD is one* (Deuteronomy 6:4).

How is God three and yet one? The reality of the Trinity is impossible to grasp with our finite minds. Ultimately, it's a great mystery of our faith. Nevertheless, it is what the Bible teaches. At the Baptism of Jesus, the Father audibly called Jesus His Son, and the Spirit descended on Jesus (Matthew 3:16-17, Mark 1:10-11, Luke 3:21-22). We also see the Father, Son and Spirit in heaven's throne room in Revelation 4 and 5. Finally, the risen Jesus commissioned us to make disciples and baptize them in the name of the Father, Son and Holy Spirit (Matthew 28:19). So, even when we take the shorter reading of 1 John 5:7-8, the Bible still tells us about the

Father, the Word and the Holy Spirit, and these three are one.

(3) A Sinful Woman

The story is told that one day as Jesus was teaching at the temple, His opponents confronted Him with a woman whom they had dragged out of bed with her lover. The accusers said to Jesus, "Teacher, this woman was caught in the act of adultery. Now in the Law, Moses commanded us to stone such women. So what do you say?" After stooping down and writing in the dirt with His finger, Jesus told them, "Let him who is without sin among you be the first to throw a stone at her." Suddenly a huge bolder came flying from the back of the crowd, conked the woman on the head and killed her. Jesus made his way through the crowd to the perpetrator, put His hands on His hips and said, "You know, Mom, sometimes you really burn me up."

Okay, there are a few problems with that version of the story. First, it's an old joke. Second, it never happened. Third, we Protestants can't find where the Bible says that Mary was without sin. She was certainly a woman of great faith and worthy of our honor, respect, and emulation, but her first Son was her Savior as much as He is ours. Most importantly, that version of the story isn't in the Bible. It's a riff on a treasured passage we often find in John 7:53-8:11. The real passage tells one of my favorite stories about the life of Jesus. Unfortunately, like the two passages we just examined, that beloved vignette isn't found in many Bibles either. Let's review the familiar passage.

They went each to his own house, but Jesus went to the Mount of Olives. Early in the morning he came again to the temple. All the people came to him, and he sat down and taught them. The scribes and the Pharisees brought a woman who had been caught in adultery, and placing her in the midst they said to him, "Teacher, this woman has been caught in the act of adultery. Now in the Law, Moses commanded us to stone such women. So what do you say?" This they said to test him, that they might have some charge to bring against him. Jesus bent down and wrote with his finger on the ground. And as they continued to ask him, he stood up and said to them, "Let him who is without sin among you be the first to throw a stone at her." And once more he bent down and wrote on the ground. But when they heard it, they went away one by one, beginning with the older ones, and Jesus was left alone with the woman standing before him. Jesus stood up and said to her, "Woman, where are they? Has no one condemned you?" She said, "No one, Lord." And Jesus said, "Neither do I condemn you; go, and from now on sin no more.

The story is very old. It sounds like things Jesus would say and do. He forgives the sinful and confronts the self-righteous, calling both to a better way of life. I have no reason to doubt that the story is true. But the story isn't found in some good copies of the Gospel of John. If we remove that passage, the narrative from John 7:52 to 8:12 flows just fine. So, most current editions of the Bible set this passage apart with brackets or by some other means.

However, even without that passage, the Bible still tells us how Jesus deals with people like that woman, and me and you, people who have failed in our righteousness. I think of Romans 8:1 *There is therefore no condemnation for those who are in Christ Jesus.* Jesus still says those life-changing words to us, *"I do not condemn you."* The Bible also tells us that Jesus calls us to leave our sinfulness behind. Mark sums up the preaching of Jesus with these words. *"The time is fulfilled, and the kingdom of God is at hand; repent and believe in the gospel"* (Mark 1:15). To repent implies, among other things, that we go and sin no more.

Further, the Bible still shows us how Jesus responds to sanctimonious people, like those who could not cast the first stone. Think of the story of the tax collector and the Pharisee in Luke 18:9-14. As they prayed in the temple, the religious man bragged to God about his own holiness and goodness. The tax collector humbly pleaded, *"God, be merciful to me, a sinner."* Jesus summed up the situation by saying, *"I tell you this man, rather than the other, went home justified before God. For all those who exalt themselves will be humbled, and those who humble themselves will be exalted"* (Luke 18:14 NIV).

The story we're used to finding in John 7:53-8:11 may not have been there in the first release of John's Gospel. We find it in a few different places. Strangely enough, in fact, some manuscripts include this priceless story in Luke's Gospel! My hunch is that whether the story was written by John or someone else, it circulated in the early church. Believers recognized it as God's Word and tried to find a home for it in our Bible. Perhaps it wasn't written by John. Maybe we don't know who wrote it. We don't really know who wrote the letter to the Hebrews, either, but we recognize it as inspired by God. Perhaps the story of the adulterous woman doesn't belong after John 7:52, but it seems to belong somewhere other than the trash bin. Further, what that story vividly illustrates agrees with the rest of Scripture. So, even if we have to relinquish this relished episode, everything it teaches is still in the Bible.

(4) The Longer Ending of Mark

We find the same kind of thing with the only other lengthy variant, Mark 16:9-20. It doesn't appear in a number of reliable manuscripts and is bracketed or otherwise separated in most modern editions of the Bible. And like the other variants we've explored in this chapter, almost all that it teaches is found elsewhere in the New Testament – perhaps even a bit more explicitly.

To comment on everything taught in these twelve verses would require an entire chapter of its own. Instead, I'll simply present the passage below, but in parentheses I'll put references to other places where the Bible teaches what we find in this section of Mark. Then I'll comment on a couple highlights.

> *Now when he rose early on that first day of the week, he appeared first to Mary Magdalene* (Matthew 28:1-10, John 20:11-18), *from whom he had cast out seven demons* (Luke 8:2). *She went and told those who had been with him, as they mourned and wept. But when*

they heard that he was alive and had been seen by her, they would not believe it (Luke 24:10-11).

After these things he appeared in another form to two of them, as they were walking into the country (Luke 24:13-35). *And they went back and told the rest, but they did not believe them* (Matthew 28:17).

Afterward he appeared to the eleven themselves as they were reclining at table, and he rebuked them for their unbelief and hardness of heart, because they had not believed those who saw him after he had risen (Luke 24:36-49, John 20:19-20, 24-29). *And he said to them, "Go into all the world and proclaim the gospel to the whole creation* (Matthew 28:18-20, Acts 1:8, John 20:20-23). *Whoever believes and is baptized will be saved, but whoever does not believe will be condemned* (Acts 2:38, Acts 16:29-33, John 3:16-18). *And these signs will accompany those who believe* (Acts 2:43, 4:30, 5:12, 6:8, 8:6, 14:3): *in my name they will cast out demons* (Acts 16:18, Acts 19:11-16); *they will speak in new tongues* (Acts 2:4, 10:46, 19:6, 1 Corinthians 12-14); *they will pick up serpents with their hands (Acts 28:3-6?); and if they drink any deadly poison, it will not hurt them; they will lay their hands on the sick, and they will recover* (Acts 3:1-10, 5:15-16, 19:11-16, James 5:14-15).

So the Lord Jesus, after he had spoken to them, was taken up into heaven (Luke 24:51, Acts 1:9) *and sat down at the right hand of God* (Psalm 110:1, Acts 7:56, Matthew 26:64). *And they went out and preached everywhere, while the Lord worked with them and confirmed the message by accompanying signs.* (See especially the references about "signs" above.)

I encourage you to check those references. Essentially everything that is taught in this text is repeated, and even expanded elsewhere in the Bible – especially in the book of Acts. Admittedly I find no other reference to believers drinking poison. Paul survives snakebite in Acts 28, though he doesn't pick up the viper intentionally. Everything else is there. So, even if we lose the text, we still keep the teaching.

Now, I personally am not sure that Mark 16:9-20 should be deleted. On the one hand, many good manuscripts omit it, and Eusebius and Jerome said, in the 4th Century CE, that they did not find it in most Greek copies.[45] However, many Greek copies *do* contain it and by 185 CE Bishop Irenaeus quotes verse 19 and says that it's from Mark.[46] [47]

---

[45] "How Badly Has the Bible Been Corrupted? – Daniel Wallace" https://www.youtube.com/watch?v=Os31IEVTDJo (Video no longer available. However, see Robert H. Stein "The Ending of Mark" footnote 23 https://www.ibr-bbr.org/files/bbr/bbr18a04_stein.pdf Last visited 2.27.2019)
[46] Irenaeus: Against Heresies http://www.prudencetrue.com/images/Irenaeus_Against_Heresies_Book_III.pdf Last visited 2.27.2019
[47] For a comedic, satirical treatment of this controversy, see "In Defence of the Last 12 Verses of St. Mark Gospel James White, Wallace & Erhman" https://www.youtube.com/watch?v=ekIyxjyoonU&t=655s Last visited 2.27.2019

What I am sure of, however, is this. Whether we retain the *text* of Mark 16:9-20 or not, we must cling tenaciously to its *teaching*, at least so far as that teaching is corroborated in other Bible passages. It is an indictment if followers of Jesus refrain from preaching the Gospel to all creation. How else will people hear? It is malpractice if we could lay our hands on the sick and they will recover, but we keep our hands to ourselves. And it is foolish when the sick fail to ask for prayer.

The week I wrote this chapter I shared with the elders of our church how I received prayer for healing at the *Growing the Church in the Power of the Holy Spirit* conference of PRMI[48] in May of 2018. God took away back pain from scoliosis and my back has felt better every day since. I also shared how He healed me in a number of other ways. After we adjourned the meeting, one of our elders asked if we would pray for her. She had been suffering from scoliosis and back pain at least as bad as mine. None of the elders left. We all gathered around her, prayed for her and anointed her with oil, just as James 5:14-15 told us to do. And just as James (and Mark 16:18?) promised, she was healed. She left pain free. At this time of writing that was only five days ago but she continues to enjoy feeling great. I believe she is being healed and the pain is gone for good. But what if I'm wrong? The worst possible scenario from here is that she had five pain free days! What a precious gift. And how derelict we would have been had we not prayed for her. In my experience, not everyone who receives prayer for healing experiences the

---

[48] Presbyterian Reformed Ministries International offers the best teaching I've encounterd on the person and work of the Holy Spirit. https://www.prmi.org Last visited 2.27.2019

healing that is requested. Still, I love John Wimber's wise insight, "… if one hundred people receive prayer and only one is healed, it is better than if none receive prayer and no one is healed."[49]

Most textual critics say we should omit the longer ending of Mark from our Bibles. Be that as it may, I fear too many Western Christians have dropped the great truths that passage teaches from the way they practice their faith. In many churches, believers have lost their passion to preach the Good News to all creation so that others may believe, as if those who do not believe are not really condemned (John 3:18). Preachers prepare our sermons with careful exegesis, thought, and even prayer, but how many people expect the Lord to confirm the message with accompanying signs, as He did again and again in the book of Acts and as He does many places today? Many believers edify themselves by praying in tongues (1 Corinthians 14:4), yet some forbid speaking in tongues (1 Corinthians 14:39) as if it were some kind of strange fire.[50] How sad.

Mark 6:5-6 tells us that when Jesus visited his home synagogue, *he could do no mighty work there, except that he laid his hands on a few sick people and healed them. And he marveled because of their unbelief.* Perhaps that's an apt description of Western Christianity today. It bears some resemblance to the congregation I serve. We see a few signs

---

[49] John Wimber and Kevin Springer, *Power Healing* © 1987, HarperCollins Publishers, p. xviii

[50] I do not believe that all Christians, or even "special" Christians should speak in tongues (1 Corinthians 12:30), but that we should all be radically open to whatever the Holy Spirit wants to do in our lives (1 Thessalonians 5:19).

and wonders now and then. We see Jesus heal this person or that person, and we rejoice. But I wonder if we're missing out. I wonder if there could be more. I wonder if our expectations are too low. I wonder if the Lord marvels at our little faith. Even if we should abandon the text of Mark 16:9-20, let's pray that we will enthusiastically recover its teaching.

Did God Really Say ...?

"Did God really say ...?" can be a diabolical question. It was asked by that sneaky snake in Eden and led to the demise of paradise. Yet that is precisely the question textual critics must ask. Did God really say, "For every female who makes herself male will enter the domain of Heaven"[51] and the other things we find in the Gospel of Thomas? If not, then we are right to leave that book out of the canon. Did the Lord really say, *"for yours is the kingdom and the power and the glory forever"* at the end of the Lord's Prayer? If so, we dare not take it away. Proverbs 30:5-6 says, *Every word of God proves true; he is a shield to those who take refuge in him. Do not add to his words, lest he rebuke you and you be found a liar.* Deuteronomy 4:2 says, *You shall not add to the word that I command you, nor take from it, that you may keep the commandments of the LORD your God that I command you.* Deuteronomy 12:32 says, *Everything that I command you, you shall be careful to do. You shall not add to it nor take from it.* Revelation 22:18-19 says, *I warn*

---

[51] "The Text of the Gospel of Thomas" v.114
http://www.holybooks.com/wp-content/uploads/Gospel-of-Thomas-Scholars-Version.pdf Last visited 2.27.2019

everyone who hears the words of the prophecy of this book: if anyone adds to them, God will add to him the plagues described in this book, and if anyone takes away from the words of the book of this prophecy, God will take away his share in the tree of life and in the holy city, which are described in this book." Properly, of course, the quotations from Deuteronomy and Revelation only apply directly to those two books, but the principle about adding to or taking away from God's Word can rightly be applied to all Scripture.

It is the unenviable task of textual critics to evaluate and discern whether something has been added to this manuscript or omitted from that one. Pray for them, that they will do their work with caution, reverence and faithful diligence. Likewise, it is the responsibility and privilege of every Christian to try to live out what God's Word teaches. Unfortunately, sometimes in our behavior and attitudes, we add alien ideas to God's Word or we take away from it by ignoring teachings we'd rather not follow. Isn't that an even greater danger than selecting the wrong textual variant? Let's strive and pray for the same caution, reverence and diligence in our own lives and discipleship, so that we can enjoy the fullness of life God intends for us and shows us in His Word.

A Classic Example

Finally, the vast majority of variants, even the meaningful and viable ones, aren't nearly as large or significant as the ones we just examined. For example, did Jesus teach that some kinds of demons only come out by prayer *and fasting*? "And fasting" is left out of many manuscripts at Mark 9:29, and Matthew 17:21, which expresses the same idea, is missing from some manuscripts altogether. When dealing with the demonic, fasting can be a good idea. But was this phrase another marginal note by a scribe who had discovered how fasting can turbo-boost prayer, and that note got added into the main passage? Perhaps. That also seems to be what happened with the explanation of the angel who troubled the waters in the Pool of Bethesda in John 5:4.

One of my favorite examples, however, involves a single word, maybe a single letter. Look at 1 Timothy 3:16. In the ESV it says:

Great indeed, we confess, is the mystery of godliness:

He was manifested in the flesh,

vindicated by the Spirit,

seen by angels,

proclaimed among the nations,

believed on in the world,

taken up in glory.

The important variant here is on the word "He." The New King James Version says, *God was manifested in the flesh.* As you might have guessed, there are ancient manuscripts that support both readings, "He" and "God." How did this variant come about? The Greek word for "He" is ΟΣ (*hos*). That is what most manuscripts have. However, some manuscripts have the word ΘΕΟΣ (*theos*), meaning "God." Which one is right? What does the original text say? "He was manifested in the flesh" or "God was manifested in the flesh?"

Some very clever scholars have pointed out that a common abbreviation of ΘΕΟΣ (*theos*) is ΘΣ, the first and last letters of the word. When we put the abbreviation for *theos* or God, ΘΣ, next to the word *hos* or he, ΟΣ, we see just how similar the two are. ΘΣ and ΟΣ. Just one little dash distinguishes them. It's very easy to picture a scribe accidently adding the dash or leaving it out. So again, which is right?

Now I should tell you that, as clever as that proposal is, we don't actually have any manuscripts that use the abbreviation ΘΣ in this verse. But here's the important question. If the correct reading is "He," if the verse really says, "He was manifested in the flesh," to Whom does the word "He" refer? Why, to God, of course! You and I have flesh, but it would be grotesquely grandiose to say we are "manifested in the flesh." We're just flesh and blood people. The verse only makes sense, it only means anything at all if it means that Jesus, the One Who is manifested in the flesh, vindicated by the Spirit and all the rest, was and is God. Who appeared in a body? Who became incarnate? Who was manifested in the flesh? God was manifested in the flesh. So regardless of the variant you chose you get the same verity, the same great truth. In Jesus Christ, God became a human being.

Most of the variants that are both meaningful and viable are like 1 Timothy 3:16. They're interesting. I even think they're fun. But in the final analysis it doesn't matter much which variant you choose. The great truths of the Bible are still intact. As Dan Wallace says, "Almost anyone who has spent time with the textual apparatus is amazed at how little the vast majority of variants affect the meaning of the text." [52]

It seems we've spent a lot of time simply saying that, one way or another, the variants in New Testament manuscripts don't matter much. So why expend so much energy if the differences don't make any difference? The reason is that when people hear these rumors about how the copies of the Bible have been changed, they sometimes jump to the false and fatal conclusion that we can't trust the Bible. We can dismiss its message because, even if it was a true book once upon a time, we don't have *that* book any longer. We only have corrupted copies. So why read the Bible? Why study the Bible? Why believe the Bible? Why live our lives according to the teaching of the Bible? That fatal conclusion is based on a faulty premise. The truth is that we *do* know what the Bible originally said in the overwhelming number of passages. And the passages that may not be clear don't deprive us of anything essential. We can be boldly confident that we have the true and original teachings of God's Word.

Yes, the Bible was copied again and again because it has been so powerful and so treasured in the lives of so many people. And no, we don't have the original manuscripts or "autographs." And yes, it is true that there are places where a

---

[52] Daniel B. Wallace in a blog review of *Can We Still Believe the Bible* by Craig L. Bloomberg
https://danielbwallace.com/2014/03/24/can-we-still-believe-the-bible/ Last visited 2.27.2019

word or sentence or even a passage has been changed. But let me tell you something that hasn't changed.

Great indeed, we confess, is the mystery of godliness:

He was manifested in the flesh. In Jesus Christ God became a human being, with a body of flesh and blood just like yours and mine. And because of His amazing love, He offered His body as a sacrifice to take away our sins. That's why He died on the cross. But that's only the beginning of the story.

He was also *vindicated by the Spirit.* Three days after Jesus was crucified, God raised Him from the dead. Thus, God declared once and for all that His Son is Savior and Lord.

Even the heavenly beings know this, because *He was seen by the angels.*

He was *proclaimed among the nations.* He is still being proclaimed. Even as you read these words, He is being proclaimed.

He has been *believed on in the world,* and everyone who believes on Him receives the forgiveness of sins. Everyone who believes on Him becomes a beloved child of God. Everyone who believes on Him shall not perish but have eternal life.

For He *was taken up in glory.* He is at God's right hand, interceding for us. From there He has poured out the Holy Spirit, who brings us to Christ, and transforms us into His image, and empowers us to be His witnesses, and pours God's love into our hearts. And someday Christ will come for us, and we will be with Him forever.

That's what the Bible teaches, and that message has never been changed.

Chapter Four

Lost in Translation

Lost in Translation

One day a lady who had been visiting the US from another country gave a farewell speech to the group that had hosted her. During her stay she had learned a good bit of English, and she desired to express her deep gratitude for the kindness and hospitality she had experienced. She rose to the occasion, stepped up to the microphone and said, "I want to thank you all from the heart of my bottom." I'm pretty sure that's not what she intended to convey, aren't you? Sometimes the meaning of a statement gets lost in translation.

I've had several opportunities to preach and teach, with the help of a translator, in Mexico. On one occasion I was asked to speak on Stewardship. Naturally I incorporated one of my favorite jokes on that topic. It's a little obtuse, but most English speakers who know anything about heaven get the joke pretty quickly. Here's the story: A wealthy man wanted to take his riches with him to heaven when he died, so he had all of his assets converted to gold bullion. He instructed his assistants to stuff the bullion in canvas bags and place it in his casket before he was buried. When the time came, the man died and arrived at the pearly gates, dragging two heavy sacks behind him. St. Peter greeted him with surprise. "No one has ever been able to carry anything with them from earth before. What did you bring?" Proudly the man reached into a bag and pulled out a shiny gold brick. In utter amazement Peter asked, "You brought pavement?"

I shared my plan with my translator before I spoke. He assured me the joke was funny in Spanish, but when I delivered the punchline, only the crickets seemed to get it. I didn't hear a sound from anyone in the audience. Not even a muffled chuckle. Maybe the joke would have gone over a little better if I had said "Peter motioned to the streets of gold and asked, 'You brought pavement?'" In any event, the joke didn't work. I think it just didn't translate well from English to Spanish. (That's my story and I'm sticking to it.) And while the rest of our mission team had a great time teasing me about the flop for the rest of the trip (and even until today), the message I tried to send was not the message our friends in Mexico received. Sometimes meanings get lost in translation.

Most of us know that the Bible was not written in English, but in Hebrew, Aramaic and Greek. So, we have to wonder whether much of the Bible's meaning was distorted as it passed from one language to another. A third rumor we hear is that, since the Bible has been translated so many times, and since each translation is different, we no longer know the meaning of the Bible. It's been lost in a train of translations. What can we say about that rumor?

Should the Bible Be Translated?

Did you know that most Muslims say the *Koran* can't be translated? They say even if you've read the entire *Koran* in English (or German or Spanish etc.) you still haven't read the *Koran*. According to them, Arabic is the holy language. So, if you really want to be a good Muslim, you have to learn Arabic and read the *Koran* as it was written.

Should we say the same thing about the Bible? Should we insist that if you really want to read the Bible you must learn Hebrew, Aramaic and Greek? Emphatically not! In fact, the practice of translating the Bible goes back to the Bible itself. You remember that most of the Old Testament was written in Hebrew while the New Testament was written entirely in Greek. But when the New Testament quotes the Old Testament, which it does hundreds of times, it doesn't quote it in Hebrew. With the exception of a very few words, the New Testament writers either translated Old Testament passages into Greek, or they quoted from the Septuagint (see below) or some other existing translation. The Bible was meant to be translated.

Further, most of the Old Testament and virtually all of the New Testament were not written in the formal language of the court or the academies. They were written in the everyday language of ordinary people. In fact, the style of Greek used in the New Testament is not the classical Greek of Homer, Sophocles and Plato. It's called *koine* or "common" Greek. The Bible was written for folks like you and me. It is right that we hear, read and heed the Bible in our own language.

Every Tribe, Language, People and Nation

The account of heavenly worship that we find in chapters 4-5 of Revelation shows us every creature in heaven and on earth singing to the exalted Christ, *"Worthy are you ... for you were slain, and by your blood you ransomed people for God from every tribe and language and people and nation"* (Revelation 5:9). The Gospel is for all people. God's Word is for every nation. Even in heaven, He is praised in every language. And so, it is natural and right that the Scriptures should be translated into as many languages as possible.

Today the Bible has been translated into a vast number of languages. Dedicated groups like Wycliffe Bible Translators work diligently to translate the Bible into every dialect, so that all people groups can hear and read God's Word in "the language of the heart." Yet there are still more than 1,600 people groups who don't have the Scriptures in their native tongues.[53] It is good to support Bible translators with our gifts and prayers.

---

[53] "The History of Wycliffe" https://www.wycliffe.org/about Last visited 1.18.19

At the other end of the spectrum, we who speak English have so many translations it's almost impossible to keep track of them. There's the CEV (Contemporary English Version), the NCV (New Century Version,) the NLT (New Living Translation), the ASV, (American Standard Version), the RSV (Revised Standard Version), the NRSV (New Revised Standard Version), the ESV (English Standard Version), the KJV (King James Version), the NKJV (New King James Version) and many more. At www.biblegateway.com you can find at least 59 translations of the Scriptures into English, not to mention many other languages. You might say we have more Bibles than we know what to do with.

Good Old King James

Sometimes I could almost wish for simpler times of my childhood, when most English readers read the King James Version. In those days we were all literally on the same page. When you memorized a verse of Scripture and I memorized the same verse, we memorized the same words in the same order. There was a kind of unity. It gave us something in common. And of course, the King James is a beautiful and stately translation. It has a certain loftiness and dignity that is virtually unmatched in the English language.

But I don't want to sound like the religious reactionary who said, "If the King James Version was good enough for Jesus, it's good enough for me." I understand there are drawbacks to the KJV. For one thing, we've discovered a lot of manuscripts since the King James was published in 1611.

Many of those variants that we talked about in chapter three aren't reflected in the good ol' King James.

Further, our language has changed over the last 500 years. We no longer use words like "thee'" and "ye." Thou speakest in such a manner no longer, nor understandest thou it readily. Verily, nor do I. When, as a young teen, I first committed my life to following Jesus, I began reading the Bible. The King James was all that was available to me, or at least it was the preferred translation at the church I attended. I remember how puzzled I was when I got to Matthew 7:2, *For with what judgment ye judge, ye shall be judged: and with what measure ye mete, it shall be measured to you again.* As a seventh grader, I had no idea what "mete" meant. I'd never seen the word before. I had to wait until Sunday to ask my pastor. He was happy to help me, but if I had known to consult the hot-off-the-presses Good News for Modern Man[54] (now known as the Good News Translation or GNT), I'd have read, *because God will judge you in the same way you judge others, and he will apply to you the same rules you apply to others.* That would have made more sense.

Even today, we still have to explain to our children what "hallowed" means when we teach them the traditional version of Lord's prayer. Some modern translations say it in vocabulary we can understand immediately. The NCV says, *May your name always be kept holy.* The NLT says, *May your name be honored.* That may not be as lofty or beautiful as *hallowed be thy name,* but it's the way you and I talk.

---

[54] *Good News for Modern Man: The New Testament in Today's English Version* © American Bible Society 1966

So nowadays we have a slew of English translations of the Bible. There are about a dozen I regularly consult, but there are many good translations I don't take time to consider. The plethora of translations available to us raises the questions, which translation(s) should we use? Which version(s) can be trusted? Have these different translations watered down the Bible's message? Before we can dig into those questions, there are a few things we need to know.

Translations are Translations

First, we have to understand that virtually all of the new translations really are translations. That is to say, they all go back to the original Hebrew, Aramaic and Greek texts. I get the impression that some uninformed skeptics think the newer versions are just updates and paraphrases of the older ones. They seem to think someone read the King James or another older version and tried to put it in the language of his or her day. Then someone else came along and paraphrased the paraphrase. People suspect some meaning is lost each time a new version comes out. But that isn't the way Bible translation happens.

It is true that some versions try to update earlier translations. The New King James is obviously an update of the King James. The same is true of the New Revised Standard Version and the Revised Standard Version. Similarly, even though there was no change in title, the New International Version (NIV) was significantly updated in 2011. The earlier, 1984 edition is (sadly) no longer available. But even these revisions didn't just take the previous English translations and try to bring them up to date. Skillful scholars worked hard, comparing translations with the Hebrew, Aramaic and Greek and making sure that the new versions are faithful to the biblical languages. None of these versions is simply a new edition of an old translation. They are fresh translations of the original languages. We could say each translation descends directly from the Hebrew, Aramaic and Greek. Thus, there was no degeneration of meaning from translation to translation. There are no generations, no layers in between. So, the rumor that we lose biblical meaning in every generation of translation is based on a misunderstanding and is false. Nevertheless, meaning can be lost in a single layer of translation. So how good are the translations we have?

Two Types of Translation

That question leads to a second thing we need to understand. There are essentially two types of translations, representing two different philosophies. There are literal translations and dynamic translations.

Literally Speaking

A literal translation tries to present a word-for-word rendering of the Bible (or any text) from the original language to the target language. If there are idioms or expressions that make sense in the original language but not in the target language, the translator usually trusts the reader to figure out the meaning. A literal translation tries to make as few interpretive decisions as possible. It allows the text to speak for itself. For this reason, literal translations tend to be a bit more difficult to read than dynamic translations.

Some good literal translations are King James Version (KJV), English Standard Version (ESV), NET Bible (NET), New American Standard Bible (NASB), Revised Standard Version (RSV), New King James Version (NKJV).

Suppose you were trying to translate Isaiah 1:18 which says, in the ESV, *"Come now, let us reason together," says the Lord: "though your sins are like scarlet, they shall be as white as snow; though they are red like crimson, they shall become like wool."* Now suppose you were translating for a primitive people group in a tropical region where no one had any idea what snow is. Should you translate the Hebrew word *shaleg* (שֶׁלֶג) as "snow" and explain what the word means in a footnote or an annotation in the margin? Or might you pick a word that provides the same contrast but is familiar to the people, like "coconut meat?" "Snow" is the right word. It would be a literal translation. "Coconut meat" is a dynamic translation. It tries to communicate the right concept or thought.

Or consider Matthew 5:18. In the KJV Jesus says, *"For verily I say unto you, Till heaven and earth pass, one jot or one tittle shall in no wise pass from the law, till all be fulfilled."* But what's a jot? What's a tittle? The Greek word translated "jot" is *iota* (ἰῶτα). It's the name of the smallest letter of the Greek alphabet and looks like this: ι. Most likely, however, "iota" is itself a translation. Jesus would have been referring to the Old Testament Law in Hebrew, not Greek. The smallest letter of the Hebrew alphabet is called "yod." It looks like this: ׳. Chances are Jesus talked about "yod" and, writing in Greek, Matthew translated it to "iota." A pretty close translation, since "yod" is the Hebrew letter that corresponds to our "j," "y" or "i" and "iota" represents those same letters in Greek.

But what about a tittle? The Greek word Matthew used is *keraia* (κεραία). Literally it means a little horn. What? Are there "little horns" in God's Law? Well yes, in a manner of speaking. There are hundreds of them. The Hebrew letter for "b" is ב. The Hebrew letter for "k" is כ. The difference between ב and כ is the "little horn" in the lower right-hand corner of the letter. Similarly, the Hebrew letter for "d" is ד. The Hebrew letter for "r" is ר. See the difference between ד and ר? Again, it's the "little horn," this time in the upper right-hand corner of the letter. Like me, you may find that very interesting, but how do you translate it into a different language?

Clearly Jesus means that every detail of God's Law will be fulfilled. But how do you express *iota* and *keraia* in English? The ESV and RSV translate the phrase, *not an iota, not a dot*. NASB has, *not the smallest letter or stroke*. The NET Bible perhaps comes closest with, *not the smallest letter or stroke of a letter*. The CEV is less literal but more relatable when it says, *not even a period or comma*, and the NLT just says, *not even the smallest detail*. They all convey essentially the right idea, but some are more literal than others.

What's the Big Idea?

A dynamic translation, by contrast, is one that tries to convey correctly the ideas from an original language to a target language. It's the thought that counts, not the exact words. Advocates of dynamic translation say that literal renderings can be too wooden and sound artificial. If different words convey the *meaning* better, then those are the words they say we should use. Suppose I said that if I bought another guitar my wife would hit the ceiling. You would know what I meant. But how would you express that in a different language? If you translated it literally, would the person you were addressing picture my spouse climbing a stepladder and tapping or punching the upper surface in our living room? A literal translation of "would hit the ceiling" into Spanish would be: "tocaría el techo." That would neither make sense nor express what I was trying to say. A better translation, I'm told, would be, "Si me compro otra guitarra, mi esposa se molestaría mucho."[55] "Se molestaría mucho" means something like, "it would bother her a lot." It isn't literally what I said, but it conveys the idea.

Dynamic translations tend to be easier to read than literal translations, but they make more interpretive decisions for the reader. Some good dynamic translations are GNT, CEV, and NLT. *The Message* (MSG) is very popular and highly interpretive.

Of course, no translation can be entirely literal, and no translation is entirely dynamic. In my opinion the NIV did

---

[55] Thanks to Luis Padron of https://padronentertainment.com for his help with Spanish translation.

the best job of striking a balance between the two in all the editions up to and including the one in 1984. The 2011 edition, however sometimes wanders pretty far from a word-for-word rendering and I now consider it a dynamic translation. The same is true of the NRSV.

Why don't we look at some particular verses in different versions of the Bible? That way we'll get a better idea of the differences between these two types of translation.

Led into Temptation

At the end of 2017 Pope Francis I made the headlines when he said that a phrase from the Lord's Prayer should be corrected. According to the bishop of Rome, it is inconsistent with the character of God that He should lead us into temptation. So, he says, we should change the phrase in Matthew 6:13 from *lead us not into temptation* to something like "do not let us fall into temptation." Actually, however, the pontiff isn't the first to suggest this. At Matthew 6:13 the NLT says, *And don't let us yield to temptation but deliver us from the evil one.* The CEV similarly says, *Keep us from being tempted and protect us from evil.* Which is right, these dynamic translations or the literal one on which most of us were raised? The contrast gives us cause to think. It presents us with a rich opportunity to love God with our minds, as Jesus taught us to do. On the one hand, James 1:13 says, *Let no one say when he is tempted, 'I am being tempted by God,' for God cannot be tempted with evil, and he himself tempts no one.* So maybe we should go with the pope and the dynamic translations. On the other hand, Matthew 4:1 tells us that, after the Lord's Baptism, ... *Jesus was led up by the Spirit into the wilderness to be tempted by the devil.* That seems to mean that God might lead us into temptation, as He did with Jesus, even though He Himself does not tempt us.

Only Sleeping

In 1 Kings 2:10 the ESV says, *Then David slept with his fathers and was buried in the city of David.* That's a good literal translation of the Hebrew, and most people would figure out that "slept with his fathers" is a poetic expression – a euphemism. It means he died. And so, the RSV, NASB, KJV and other literal translations have the same word here. David "slept."

However, the expression "David slept with his fathers" might be misunderstood. A young child, who crawled into bed with his parents last night because he was afraid might think that when David did the same thing, they buried the poor guy! So, a dynamic translation would try to clear up any confusion. The NCV says, *Then David died and was buried with his ancestors in Jerusalem.* You see, it doesn't translate the verse word-for-word but thought-for-thought.

We find exactly the same issue in the New Testament. In 1 Thessalonians 4:13, the RSV says, *But we would not have you ignorant, brethren, concerning those who are asleep, that you may not grieve as others do who have no hope.* Again here, "asleep" is a poetic expression for "dead." The literal translations all use some form of "asleep" in this verse. By contrast, the meaning-based translations talk about those who have "died." NLT, NCV, CEV, NRSV all translate it "died."

Which one do you think is better? On the one hand the verse isn't talking about people who are taking a nap. They aren't going through the various stages of the sleep cycle. They aren't snoring. They aren't dreaming. Aye, there's the rub. They're dead. The Greek word Paul used literally means "asleep," but the idea is that they've breathed their last. So maybe it's more accurate to translate the idea and not the word. They're dead.

However, the point of the passage is that Christ, who has already risen from the dead, will one day come back. When He does, believers who have died will be raised again with Him and will live with Him forever. In other words, the point of the passage is that death is only temporary – like sleep. Someday the dead in Christ will wake up! This is the perspective of the Bible as a whole. So perhaps we should stick with "asleep." Maybe a literal translation is better.

A Gut Feeling

Here's another example. There's a great word in the Greek New Testament: *splangchna* [σπλάγχνα pronounced "splankna"]. Literally it means "intestines, bowels, guts." It's the word that's used in Acts 1:18 where we're told that, when Judas Iscariot fell down after he betrayed Jesus, *he burst open in the middle and all his intestines gushed out* (NASB). Usually, however, the word is used in a poetic sense to express deep felt emotion. A gut-wrenching compassion.

Splangchna. It almost sounds like what it means. "I have *splangchna* for you."

You can see how, when we try to translate that word literally, we can run into problems. For example, in the KJV of Philippians 1:8, Paul is telling the Christians in Philippi how deeply he cares for them. He says, *For God is my record, how greatly I long after you all in the bowels of Jesus Christ.* Hmm. Maybe that's a little too literal. (And too graphic!) The NLT renders it well when it says, *God knows how much I love you and long for you with the tender compassion of Jesus Christ.* That isn't as literal, but it makes a lot more sense to modern readers.

We find the same word in 1 John 3:17. The NIV (2011) says, *If anyone has material possessions and sees a brother or sister in need but has no pity on them, how can the love of God be in that person?* The word translated "pity" here is *splanchna.* A very literal translation would be, "If anyone should have the means of life of this world, and should see his brother having need, yet shuts off his bowels from him, how does the love of God remain in him?" That's too literal even for the King James! The KJV says, *But whoso hath this world's good, and seeth his brother have need, and shutteth up his bowels* of compassion *from him, how dwelleth the love of God in him?* The King James added two words, "of compassion," to make the meaning clear. The ESV conveys the right idea when it says, *But if anyone has the world's goods and sees his brother in need, yet closes his heart against him, how does God's love abide in him?* Anatomically speaking, there's a significant difference between the bowels and the heart, yet NKJV, the NASB, the

RSV, the NRSV and others are literally closer to the original when they translate *splangchna* as "heart." Of course, whichever translation you choose the point is clear. If we close our hearts to those in need, if we don't have a gut-wrenching compassion for them, then how can we say God's love is living in us? Lord, please give us Your deep, churning love for people.

Brothers and Sisters

By the way, did you notice that in some of the translations cited above we talked about a "brother" in need while in others we talked about a "brother or sister" in need? That raises an important issue in the new English translations. Not too long ago it was the custom in English to use a masculine word to refer either to males or to males and females. "He" could sometimes mean "he or she." "Man" could sometimes mean "human" or "man and woman." So, when 1 Timothy 2:4 says that God "desires all men to be saved and to come to a knowledge of the truth" (NASB), we know that it means "men and women." That's why the ESV and the NCV say that God wants "all people to be saved." That's why the NLT, the CEV, the MSG and the NRSV say that God wants "everyone to be saved." We all know what the text means. The Greek word is literally the word for "men," but we all understand that it means "men and women." Ancient Greek and Hebrew use masculine words sometimes to refer only to men and other times to refer to all people, just like English did until recently.

Now, however, English has changed. If you mean "he or she," you need to say, "he or she." "He" doesn't mean both nowadays. (Newly proposed words like "zhe" and "zhim" have not been standardized at this time of writing – and may never be.) If you mean "men and women," you need to say, "men and women" or "human beings" or something like that. "Men" doesn't cover it all anymore. You may think it's a good change or a bad change, but you can't deny it. It's how our language is evolving.

This development may raise some of the biggest problems with English translations of the Bible. Sometimes the problems are easy to solve, as we just saw with 1 Timothy 2:4. But sometimes it gets a little awkward. Consider Matthew 16:24. The ESV represents most of the literal translations (including the 1984 NIV) when it says, *Then Jesus told his disciples, "If anyone would come after me, let him deny himself and take up his cross and follow me."* Clearly Jesus isn't talking only about males here. He means anyone. The Greek words are various forms for the word "he," but of course we know it means "he or she." Yet it would be very clumsy to translate it like this, "If anyone would come after me, he or she must deny himself or herself and take up his or her cross and follow me." That sounds silly.

Dynamic translations take a different direction, but it results in a change in the meaning. For example, the NCV says, *"If people want to follow me, they must give up the things they want ..."* Notice that, though misleading gender specificity is avoided, the singular becomes plural. "He" becomes "they." The sense of individual decision is clouded. The idea is basically the same, but not exactly. When the CEV says, *"If any of you want to be my followers, you must forget about yourself ..."* we have a similar problem. The singular is retained, but now "he" becomes "you." That's more specific than what Matthew tells us Jesus said. Jesus wasn't talking about "any of you," He was talking about anyone at all.

Do these distinctions seem too subtle? Maybe I'm being too picky, too precise. Sometimes, however, precision is important. Nevertheless, all the translations say basically the same thing, even if they differ on the details. The point is that the same Jesus who laid down His life for us calls you and me, anyone and everyone to take up our respective crosses and follow Him, no matter what the cost. That reality comes through in all the translations.

So again, which translation(s) should we use? Is there a "best" translation? Each translation has its own strengths and weaknesses. We need to keep three things in mind. No translation is perfect. All the translations are very good. Many translations *is* best. (That last sentence does not contain a grammatical error.) Let me explain what I mean.

No Translation Is Perfect

There are some who believe that the King James Version is the ultimate Bible, better even than the version of the Greek text from which it was translated. Samuel Gipp, sounding a bit like a Muslim talking about the Arabic *Koran*, says that if you cannot read the Bible in King James English, you can only read an inferior Bible.[56] But as venerable as the KJV is, there are challenges that have to be overcome.

Sani C. and the Unicorns

Not long ago a young lady, who goes by Sani C, asked me if unicorns were mentioned in the Bible. My first inclination was to explain to her that unicorns are mythical creatures and the Bible is true. So, no, of course there are no unicorns mentioned in the Bible. Before I followed that impulse, however, I realized this was the kind of teachable moment a pastor lives for. It was time for this delightful pre-teen to learn how to use a concordance and look up passages for herself. It turns out she had a search engine for the KJV on her cell phone. Did you know that unicorns are mentioned in the KJV nine times? (See Numbers 23:22 and 24:8, Deuteronomy 33:17, Job 39:9,10, Psalms 22:21, 29:6 and 92:10 and in Isaiah 34:7.) If I had known they were mentioned even once, I had forgotten! What's the story behind the unicorns?

There is a Hebrew word that occurs only in these verses. We don't know exactly what it means. The word is *re'em* (רְאֵם). About 250 BCE a book called the *Septuagint* was created. This was a very popular and influential translation of the Old Testament into Greek. The *Septuagint* translates *re'em* with *monokeros* (μονόκερως). That word literally means "one

---

[56] KJV 1 https://www.youtube.com/watch?v=MzGrBcCDajE

horn." It could refer to any one-horned creature, not just the horse-like animal we think of today.

Around the year 400 CE St. Jerome translated the Scriptures into Latin. This Latin Bible is called the *Vulgate,* and was the main Bible used in the Roman Catholic Church until fairly recently. Most of the time Jerome used a form of the word *unicornis* where the *Septuagint* had *monokeros. Unicornis* also means, "one horned," without necessarily referring to a unique steed. A few times, however, Jerome translated *re'em* with a form of the word *rinoceros,* meaning "nose-horned." Of course, this is where we get our word "rhinoceros." As I envision the creature described in the passages above, a rhino seems to fit the bill. Read them and see what you think. Most modern translations, however, use a word like "wild ox" or "wild bull."

Some people have used the fact that the word "unicorn" appears in the KJV as a reason to ridicule and dismiss the Bible and the people who believe it.[57] We can understand and explain how the King James translators chose "unicorn." Since they didn't know what *re'em* meant, they depended on the *Septuagint's* and the *Vulgate's* translation. I don't know that we can fault them for that, but it certainly has caused some confusion. No translation is perfect.

---

[57] "What Are the 'Unicorns' in the Bible?" https://www.youtube.com/watch?time_continue=1&v=A9bbRK Wwy20 visited 3.1.2019

A Command or a Promise?

Early in my ministry I preached a sermon on Galatians 5:16. In those days my go-to translation was the RSV. That very good and highly respected translation is still one of my favorites. But no translation is perfect. In Galatians 5:16 the RSV says, *But I say, walk by the Spirit and do not gratify the desires of the flesh.* However, that was different from other translations. The NASB, (another personal favorite) for example, said, *But I say, walk by the Spirit, and you will not carry out the desire of the flesh.*

Wait a minute. That's a pretty important difference. The RSV presents us with a command. The NASB gives us a conditional promise. One says, "Do this, don't do that." The other says, "If you do this, that won't happen." The command pushes us to focus on eradiating the sinful nature at least as much as we focus on living in step with the Holy Spirit. The promise, on the other hand, is that if we walk by the Spirit, the sinful nature will be incapacitated. Just as when we fill a glass with water, air is naturally pushed out, so the Holy Spirit displaces our inclination to sin. These are two significantly different strategies. Which is right?

I looked the verse up in several other translations, and they all agreed with NASB. How could that be? The RSV really is an excellent translation. What did those translators know that others missed? So, I pulled out my Greek New Testament to see what the original language said. A word for word translation would be, "... by the Spirit walk and desire of flesh no not you should fulfill." Sounds like Yoda, I know. But is it a command or a promise? And what does "no not" mean?

I love the story of the linguistics lecture when the professor explained, "In some languages, like English, a double negative equals a positive. In other languages a double negative means an emphatic negative. But in no language does a double positive equal a negative." At that comment, a student on the fifth row muttered, "Yeah, right."

But what about this double negative in Galatians 5:16? What does it mean? I broke out my Greek grammar textbook and discovered that there's a Greek idiom at work here. It turns out that when Greek uses a particular double negative with a "would" or "should" verb (οὐ μή followed by a subjunctive verb, for my fellow Greek geeks), that means something like "it will be impossible." Wow! That means this verse gives us a mind-blowing promise! We don't have to focus on the negative, on not gratifying the desires of the sinful nature. Galatians 5:16 literally says, *If you walk by the Spirit it will be impossible for you to fulfill the desires of the flesh*. Don't focus on the flesh at all. Focus on the Spirit. I was excited and am grateful to have come to understand that profound truth, and I'm still striving to apply it to my life. Nevertheless, I wondered why the RSV said something so different.

A few years after I made that discovery, the NRSV was published. I was eager to see what the new version said in that verse. As soon as I ripped the crinkling cellophane off my brand-new copy I flipped to Galatians and discovered this. *Live by the Spirit, I say, and do not gratify the desires of the flesh*. There it was again, a command instead of a promise. I was puzzled. Why did the RSV and NRSV translators disagree so strongly with every other translation I could find? It bugged me. Decades later I had the privilege to meet Dr. Bruce Metzger. You may remember I mentioned him as the Sherlock Holmes of New Testament manuscript studies. One of the leading Bible scholars of the 20th Century and a personal hero of mine, Metzger had been the editor of the New Testament for the RSV and the over-all editor of NRSV. Here was my opportunity to get my question answered. I carried my trusty Greek New Testament with me to where he was speaking. Finally, my chance came to meet this giant. I couldn't wait to hear the explanation he would give. I showed him the text, explained my puzzlement and said that all the other versions translated it as a promise. Why did RSV and NRSV render it as a command? He looked at the Bible, looked at me and said with some chagrin, "It was a mistake."

A mistake? I was expecting an insightful exegesis of some obscure point of Greek grammar, or maybe the revelation of some manuscript evidence I had overlooked or didn't know. I admire Dr. Metzger all the more for his candid confession. It helps us to know that no translation is perfect. So, when we are seriously studying a passage of Scripture it's a very good idea to look at different translations. All the translations I've studied really are excellent, but none of them is perfect.

Like Father, Like Son

Of course, it isn't only in English that translators encounter challenges. I have great gratitude and respect for the Wycliffe Bible Translators. Well-educated men and women give up comfortable, modern lifestyles to live in often primitive conditions, learn the languages of indigenous people groups around the world and provide them with God's Word in their native tongues. They have an amazing calling and they do it very well. I admire them.

Early in the 21st Century, however, Wycliffe ran into some trouble as they were translating the Bible into Arabic. Of course, the *Koran* has had a great influence on Arabic culture just as the Bible has had on Western culture. There are several places in the *Koran*, like Sura 4:171,[58] which state that it is beneath God's dignity to conceive a son and that Allah is one, therefore there can be no Trinity. These ideas have become endemic to Arabic culture. So, in order to avoid a cultural stumbling block and a misunderstanding for Arabic readers, the Wycliffe translators chose alternate words for "Father" and "Son" when referring to God and Jesus. Thus Matthew 28:19 from the Great Commission would read something like, "cleanse them by water in the name of Allah, his Messiah and his Holy Spirit" instead of *"baptizing them in the name of the Father and of the Son and of the Holy Spirit."*[59] I believe the intentions were noble but the result was disastrous. If someone puts his or her trust in a Jesus who is not the incarnate Son of God, does that person really have saving faith in Jesus Christ? Responsibly, Wycliffe has changed their policy on this issue.[60] The

---

[58] http://corpus.quran.com/translation.jsp?chapter=4&verse=171 visited 6.20.18

[59] "Wycliffe Defends Changing Titles for God" http://www.wnd.com/2012/02/wycliffe-defends-changing-titles-for-god/ visited6.20.18

[60] "WEA Divine Familial Terms Oversight Group Provides Feedback to Wycliffe and SIL on Bible Translation Guidelines"

controversy demonstrated that translation can be touchy in any language and that no translation is perfect.

Most Translations Are Good

We've explored some of the problem areas and missteps in translation in order to help us see some of the issues that are at stake when we read a translation of the Bible. However, I would not want you to get the wrong idea. Please don't falsely conclude that the translations can't be trusted. By and large such problems are few and far between. In my nearly 40 years of preaching I've spent a good deal of time comparing translations and checking them against the original Hebrew and especially Greek. As far as I can tell most of the English translations do an excellent job of rendering God's Word into our language. Yes, there are a few problem passages in different versions. Nevertheless, while I may have my preferences, I would not hesitate to recommend any of the translations cited in this chapter to my fellow disciples who want to grow in their relationship with Jesus.

Many Translations Is Best

That being said, we may still want to ask which translation is best. You might have already guessed my answer. Many translations is best. That's no grammatical goof. We are blessed with incredible wealth in English translations.

https://www.wycliffe.ca/wycliffe/newsroom/release.jsp?uuid=6f8 92d78b7 visited 6.20.18

Bright, faithful, God-loving scholars have prayed and toiled over the original language Scriptures. They have done their best to share the fruit of their labors with us. How foolish we would be to limit ourselves to a single version! Read many translations. Compare them. Think and pray deeply about the differences, and learn from each one. No translation is perfect. Most translations are good. But many translations is best.

The Big Picture

It is true that different translations are better for different purposes. As I indicated above, dynamic translations tend to be easier to read than the literal ones. So, if you're reading large chunks of the Bible at a time, why not use a translation you find comfortable? One that speaks your language? Too many Christians have never read the entire Bible. I hate to sound judgmental (for I know that with what measure I mete it shall be measured to me again!), but that really is an intolerable situation. (See Chapters Nine and Ten.) How can someone try to be a follower of Jesus Christ, how can one seek God with all his or her heart, soul, mind, and strength, but not read the very Word in which He has revealed Himself?

It's desirable and reasonable for mature believers to have a good grasp of the scope of the whole Bible and what it teaches. Who were Eli, Elijah and Elisha? What can we learn from them and where can we read about them? What are some particular characteristics of the prophecies of Isaiah? Jeremiah? Ezekiel? Hosea? What are the themes of Romans,

1 Corinthians, Galatians? We can't apply the transformative messages of these books to our walk with Christ if we don't know what they say. And the best way to know them is to spend time reading the Scriptures. I wrote this book to help dispel misleading rumors, to remove stumbling blocks that might hinder God's people from reading God's Word. I did it because knowledge of God's Word is crucial to living the abundant life that comes from abiding in Christ. That's how badly I want you to read the Bible.

"But I can't understand the Bible" is the excuse I often hear. I get it. Understanding the Bible sometimes takes effort. There are still things that are beyond my grasp. But let me assure you, the more you read it the more sense it makes. The more sense it makes, the more it guides and enriches your life. So why not make it as easy as possible? Why not read the Bible, at least the first time through, in a translation that's easy for you? No translation is any good if it isn't read. So, experiment. Sample several versions, literal and dynamic, and find one that fits your style. Then read it. Read it cover to cover. You can start with the New Testament then go back to the Old if you like, but read it. Then read it again, maybe in a different translation this time. Getting the big story is crucial to understanding all the smaller parts. (See Chapter Nine.)

A Closer Look

Sometimes, however, we want to dig into particular passages. When we want to study a verse or paragraph or chapter closely, a word-for-word translation is indispensable. Yet even then it's wise to compare translations. If you are preparing to preach or teach on a particular section of Scripture, or if you just want to dig deep in your devotional life, studying a specific passage in multiple translations is an invaluable tool and a priceless privilege.

A Wealth of Resources

In Chapter One we mentioned that Christians in our culture have so many resources at our disposal we should be the best informed and most influential generation of disciples in history. Two on-line resources I recommend are Bible Gateway[61] and Bible Hub.[62] Not only can you find a cornucopia of translations and other resources at these websites, they will also let you look at many translations of a single verse or passage on the same screen.

God's Word is richer and deeper and higher than we, with our finite minds, will ever comprehend. As the Lord says in Isaiah 55:9, *For as the heavens are higher than the earth, so are my ways higher than your ways and my thoughts than your thoughts.* Even if we were fluent in the biblical languages and submersed ourselves in the Hebrew, Aramaic and Greek Scriptures, we would not understand everything about God. Any translation will only give us a slice of God's Word. So why not go back for seconds? Thirds? More? Each translation can help us grasp a different detail or see things from a different angle. Using many translations allows us to

---

[61] https://www.biblegateway.com
[62] http://biblehub.com

breathe in more deeply the inspired Word of God.

Try it for yourself. Pick a few of your favorite passages. Read each passage in several translations. What are the similarities? What are the differences? What do the differences mean? Does one translation clarify the meaning of another? Does one translation seem radically different from the others? Meditate on the passage. Chew on specific words and phrases. Think and pray deeply. I bet you will find yourself drawing closer to God as you dive deeply into His Word.

Feast or Famine?

Some people say that the Bible has been translated so many times we can't possibly know what it originally said. In fact, the opposite is true. The cornucopia of translations at our disposal makes it possible for all of us to savor the Scriptures in ways that were available only to a few linguistic scholars just a generation or two ago. Today we can partake of a smorgasbord of Scripture. We face a feast, not a famine of God's Word.

Has the meaning of the Bible been lost in translation? Only in the sense that no translation is perfect. Minor linguistic issues pop up from time to time. But the overall message is there in virtually every translation, clear as can be. Any translation contains more than we can fully understand. And when we explore the Scriptures in the many translations that are available to us, we pick up rich nuances and subtleties that deepen our knowledge of God. Rather than worrying about what might have been lost in translation, we can take advantage of all that has been gained in the wealth of translations at our fingertips.

Chapter Five

Just Another Book?

Just Another Book?

"The Bible was written by mere mortals in ordinary human words, so ultimately it's just another book. It contains good teachings, but no better than the *Koran*, the *Book of Mormon*, the *Upanishads* and the sacred writings of other religions." This is another allegation many people believe about the Bible. Is it true, or is it just another nasty rumor?

Inspired by God

The classic Christian answer, of course is that the Bible is different from all other writings because the Bible is inspired by God. 2 Timothy 3:16 says, *All scripture is inspired by God and is profitable for teaching, for reproof, for correction, and for training in righteousness* (RSV). That's a really good answer, so long as the Bible is inspired in a way that no other writings are. So, we have to ask what we mean by "inspired?"

Many writers and artists claim that they were inspired to create their works. Does that put those creations on the same level as the Bible? Singer-songwriter James Taylor once said, "I don't really write the songs, I'm just the first to hear them." Likewise, Michael Jackson advised young composers, "Don't work so hard to write the music. Let the music write itself."[63] Michelangelo famously claimed that he didn't create his sculptures, he simply released them from blocks of stone. It's as if these and other works of art already existed in some mystical realm, and the writers/artists simply discovered them. That's a type of inspiration. Is that what we mean when we say the Bible was inspired? Did Moses somehow "discover" the Passover story? Was David just the first to hear the 23rd Psalm?

Sometimes we say a composition is inspired by an object or event. The words to "The Star-Spangled Banner" are a reflection on the Battle of Fort McHenry during the War of 1812. In 1962 music producer Bob Crewe was half-way dozing through a late-night movie. When actor John Payne's

---

[63] I heard both of these quotes in television interviews of which I have not been able to find recordings.

character slapped Rhonda Fleming's character in the face, Crewe woke up to hear the leading lady respond, "Big girls don't cry." The next day Crewe and Bob Guadio massaged that line into the second hit song for The Four Seasons.[64] Similarly the Beatles' "Penny Lane" was inspired by a street in Liverpool, where the Fab Four grew up. "Shame on you, your mama said. Shame on you, you cried in bed" is a good line. So are, "Suzanne, the plans they made put an end to you" and "There is a barber showing photographs of every head he's had the pleasure to have known." But does anyone think they are on a par with *And as you wish that others would do to you, do so to them* (Luke 6:31)? Does the word "inspired" mean the same thing when it's applied to all these quotations across the board?

People often tell me after worship, "You must have been peeking through my windows this week" or "That sermon was just for me." Fellow preachers tell me they hear similar comments on Sunday mornings. To be sure, there have been times when I felt like the Holy Spirit prompted me to say or write something for reasons I didn't understand, then later discovered that God used those words to touch someone who was listening. I'm confident that was the nudging of the Holy Spirit, but I'm reminded of the girl who was watching her pastor/father work on a sermon. "Dad," she said, "How do you know what to write?" "Well, honey," the father replied, "God tells me." The daughter furrowed her brow, scrunched up her face and asked, "Then why do you keep scratching stuff out?" I believe God's Spirit does guide us when we

---

64 "Big Girls Don't Cry"
https://en.wikipedia.org/wiki/Big_Girls_Don%27t_Cry_(The_Four_Seasons_song) visited 3.1.2019

preach and write books and serve Him in other ways, but this is on a very different order from what we mean when we talk about the Bible as inspired.

Muslims believe that the *Koran* is an exact replication of *The Book of Books,* which rests eternally by the side of Allah. The *Koran,* Muslims say, was dictated to Mohamed by the angel Gabriel over a period of twenty years. Mohamed, unable to read or write, later recited what he heard to scribes. The Latter-Day Saints make a similar claim about *The Book of Mormon.* They say that in 1822 the angel Maroni told Joseph Smith where to find the *Book of Mormon,* which was written in a form of hieroglyphics on tablets of gold. Later Joseph Smith sat behind a curtain and translated the tablets to a series of secretaries. Do you know anyone who thinks the Bible was inspired in such a manner?

Breathing Out or Breathing In?

In the last chapter we discussed times when consulting different translations can enrich our understanding of a Bible passage. This is one of those times. In the NIV, 2 Timothy 3:16 says, *All Scripture is God-breathed and is useful for teaching, rebuking, correcting and training in righteousness.* (Cf. ESV, NASB and others.) *Inspired by God,* which we read in the RSV, has been replaced by *God-breathed.* This is a very literal translation of the Greek word *Theopneustos* (θεόπνευστος). The Apostle Paul seems to have coined this unique word by combining the word for "God" (*theos,* θεός) and the word for "breathe out" or "blow" (*pneo,* πνέω). The idea is not that God breathed *into* the words that humans had written, making those writings come to life. Nor does it mean that God breathed into the writers as they wrote. No, the Scriptures themselves were somehow breathed out by God. (So "exhaled" or "expired" might be a better translation than "inspired," but what we usually mean by "expired" is very different from what the apostle wants to say about Scripture!) The claim that the Scriptures were breathed out by God sets them apart from every other writing, even works that we might otherwise call "inspired." As far as we can tell, Paul invented the word *theopneustos* to describe a divine quality that cannot be ascribed to any other composition of any kind. The Declaration of Independence, Bach's "Mass in B Minor," DaVinci's "The Last Supper," people might describe these and other opuses as inspired, but none of them is God-breathed. That term describes the Scriptures alone. That is what the word was minted to mean, and we would be wrong to apply it to any other composition.

Carried Along

Sometimes you'll hear preachers and others refer to the people who penned Scripture as "the inspired writers." It's a catchy phrase. I think I've slipped and used it myself. But the Bible doesn't talk about the writers as "inspired." A different word is used to describe them. Look at 2 Peter 1:20b-21, ... *no prophecy of Scripture comes from someone's own interpretation. For no prophecy was ever produced by the will of man, but men[65] spoke from God as they were carried*

---

[65] There is no doubt that parts of the Bible were composed by women. One thinks of the Song of Miriam in Exodus 15, or the

along by the Holy Spirit. The Scriptures are inspired or God-breathed, but the speakers and writers were carried along.

So what does it mean to be carried along? Twice in the Book of Acts the word translated "carried along" here (*phero*, φέρω) is used to describe a ship being driven by the wind or currents (Acts 27:15, 17). It's also the word that is translated "rushing" in Acts 2:2, when the Holy Spirit was poured out on the disciples, *And suddenly there came from heaven a sound like a mighty rushing wind, and it filled the entire house where they were sitting.* Those are rich and evocative images to apply to this understanding of the Bible writers being carried as they spoke and wrote, but *phero* is a very common word that means "carry, bring, bear." The Holy Spirit provided the impetus and momentum for the Bible writers. The Holy Spirit brought them, bore them, carried them from the starting point to the point of completion.

Further, Peter says we need to notice *first of all, that no prophecy of Scripture comes from someone's own interpretation. For no prophecy was ever produced by the will of man* (2 Peter 1:20b-21a). The Bible is fully aware that there are people who claim to speak for God, but only articulate words of their own imaginative invention. Remember the false prophets in the time of Jeremiah. In Jeremiah 23:16 we read, *Thus says the LORD of hosts: "Do not listen to the words of the prophets who prophesy to you, filling you with vain hopes. They speak visions of their own minds, not from the mouth of the LORD."* Then and now

---

Song of Deborah in Judges 5. In 2 Peter 1:21 the apostle is using "men" in the generic sense that we discussed in Chapter Four.

there are religious writings and pronouncements that claim to be from God or pretend to offer supreme guidance for our lives. The Bible insists that such writings are qualitatively different from the Scriptures themselves.

The Bible was *not* just written by mere mortals in ordinary human words. The human writers did not merely speak or jot down their own brilliant insights and ideas. Instead, *men spoke from God as they were carried along by the Holy Spirit* (2 Peter 1:21b). This is the first-person testimony of actual Bible writers. Who should know better than they? The Bible is not "just another book." It is God-breathed, and penned by authors who were carried by the Holy Spirit.

A Promise Fulfilled

By the way, this fits precisely with what Jesus told his disciples on the night before His crucifixion. In John 16:12-15 we read, *"I have much more to say to you, more than you can now bear. But when he, the Spirit of truth, comes, he will guide you into all the truth. He will not speak on his own; he will speak only what he hears, and he will tell you what is yet to come. He will glorify me because it is from me that he will receive what he will make known to you. All that belongs to the Father is mine. That is why I said the Spirit will receive from me what he will make known to you"* (NIV). Explicitly with the Gospel writers, and I think with all of Scripture, the Spirit of truth guided them into all truth as they wrote.

When I was in seminary, "source criticism" was considered an important field of study. I still find it helpful for comparison when we can discern the prior writings and oral traditions that were behind the words of Scripture. Often the supposed sources are nebulous, and their reconstructions tend toward the fanciful, but when they're accurate we can gain great insight by seeing how the Bible writers edited and improved those sources. What many people forget, however, is that the Gospel writers did not depend primarily on written sources, oral tradition or fallible human memories, as critics like to allege. Rather, the Spirit of truth guided the Bible writers into all truth. The Spirit made known to the writers what He received from Christ and the Father. He carried those writers along. The Spirit was the immediate and ultimate source behind the writings. So, what we have in Scripture is more important than other earthly sources, whatever they may be.

It is really no stretch to say that what was explicitly true of the Gospel writers was also true of the other authors of Scripture. They were guided and carried by the Holy Spirit as they recorded the message God breathed. As the Nicene Creed reminds us, the Holy Spirit "spoke by the prophets."

Methods of Inspiration

But can we zero in a little more on what it means to say that Scripture is God-breathed and that the writers were carried along and guided by the Holy Spirit? How did that happen? What did it look like?

Dictation

Some Christians seem to think that saying the Bible is God-breathed means that the Lord dictated the Scriptures word-for-word to the prophets and apostles. The Spirit must have whispered to Moses, *In the beginning God created the heavens and earth ...* (Genesis 1:1) and Moses transcribed the very syllables he heard. The same was true for David, Nehemiah, John, Luke, Paul and all the other Bible writers. Other Christians think that theory is too wooden and simplistic. They insist that the Bible was not dictated at all. I think we'll find, however, that the truth is not as simple as either extreme. The inspiration of Scripture is a multi-faceted gem.

We know that certain parts of the Bible were dictated because those passages tell us so. For example, in the second and third chapters of Revelation we find seven letters that the glorified Christ wanted sent to each of seven churches. In Revelation 2:1 John writes, *To the angel of the church in Ephesus write: "The words of him who holds the seven stars in his right hand, who walks among the seven golden lampstands."* What follows is a small series of affirmations and challenges that the risen Jesus wants expressed to that church. We find similar little letters starting at Revelation 2:8, 12, 18, 3:1, 7 and 14. Clearly the idea is that the Lord told John what to write and the apostle took it down, word-for-word.

We often find a very similar phenomenon in the Old Testament. Isaiah, Jeremiah, Amos or some other prophet will introduce a message with words like, *Thus says the LORD*. Almost as frequently we find, *The word of the LORD came to me.* Other times they'll interject a phrase like, *declares the Lord.* We find a perfect example in Isaiah 55:8-9, *"For my thoughts are not your thoughts, neither are your ways my ways," declares the* LORD. *"As the heavens are higher than the earth, so are my ways higher than your ways and my thoughts than your thoughts."* The point is clear. Sometimes, at least, the Lord told prophets precisely what to say. In other words, these prophecies and pronouncements were dictated by God. But is it necessarily true that every part of the Bible was inspired in the same way? Might there be other methods of inspiration? RC Sproul claims the church has always stopped short of saying that biblical inspiration is the same as dictation.[66] Could it be that some passages are dictated, but not all?

Inspired Research

Sometimes it does not seem that the Holy Spirit is dictating the message, but that He is working through other mechanisms. Consider the preface Luke wrote to his two-volume work, Luke and Acts. Luke 1:1-4 says:

> *Inasmuch as many have undertaken to compile a narrative of the things that have been accomplished among us, just as those who from the beginning were eyewitnesses and ministers of the word have delivered them to us, it seemed good to me also, having followed all things closely for some time past,*

---

[66] "Inspiration, Infallibility, Inerrancy" https://www.youtube.com/watch?v=e-ogEfklzCo Last visited 1.21.19

*to write an orderly account for you, most excellent
Theophilus, that you may have certainty concerning
the things you have been taught.*

Luke read what others had written. He talked to eye
witnesses. He did careful research. Why should he go to all
that trouble if the Lord was just going to dictate to him the
words we read in Luke and Acts? Did all of Luke's diligent
historical research count for nothing? Of course not. Luke
used it as he wrote. He recorded what he had learned.

Further, Luke's opening paragraph is designed to make this
point: "You can trust what I've written because I've studied
the matter very carefully." This assertion lends credibility to
his work. If the words had been dictated to him, wouldn't it
have been more effective for the beloved physician to have
simply said, "You can trust these books because God told me
exactly what to write?"

If Luke and Acts were not dictated, does that mean that these
works are not God-breathed, or that Luke was not carried
along by the Spirit as he wrote? Are these writings somehow
less inspired than Revelation and the prophets? If that's the
case, then it just isn't true that *all* Scripture is God-breathed,
for these are all recognized as Scripture. Or does it mean that
inspiration doesn't have to happen the same way every time?
The Lord can do anything. He can even inspire historical
research! Luke was carried along by the Spirit just like John
and Jeremiah. If you doubt it, just read what he wrote.
Dictation is one way the Scriptures were God-breathed, but
not the only way.

Copy That

There are many places where the Bible repeats itself, almost word-for-word. We call these "parallel passages." Compare Psalm 14 with Psalm 53. The first three verses are identical except that where Psalm 14 says *The LORD,* Psalm 53 says *God,* and where Psalm 14 says *turned aside* Psalm 53 says *fallen away.* There are significant divergences in the next verse or two, but the last verse of either psalm is exactly the same. One seems almost to be a copy, or better yet, an edition of the other. There are passages in the books of Kings and the books of Chronicles that tell the same stories in very nearly the same words. For example, the stories about King Hezekiah are fascinating. When we compare 2 Kings 18-20 with Isaiah 36-39, we find many places where one account seems to have been cut and pasted from the other. When we read 2 Chronicles 29-32 we get a different slant on the same story.

Likewise, when we examine Matthew, Mark and Luke we find both remarkable similarities and revealing differences in content and wording. In fact, one excellent way to study these Gospels and to get a taste of the unique flavor of each is to explore the similarities and differences in parallel passages.[67] For example, read Matthew 9:9-13 alongside Mark 2:13-17 and Luke 5:27-32, where Jesus calls a tax

---

[67] One can find online parallel passages from the Gospels printed side-by-side for easy comparison at http://biblehub.com/parallelgospels/ (last visited 3.1.2019) In my experience the most helpful English tool for this practice is still Aland, Kurt ed., *Synopsis of the Four Gospels: English Edition* © United Bible Societies. 1982

collector to follow Him. Check out these passages for yourself and you'll get a glimpse of what I mean.

When the Bible echoes in one place what it said somewhere else, are the echoes in any way less God-breathed? No. Even if the author of 2 Kings copied and edited passages from Isaiah, even if Luke took his cue from Mark (which seems to be one of the many narratives mentioned in Luke 1:1) and other early sources, these authors still wrote as they were carried along by the Holy Spirit. After all, those passages were worth repeating. Why should the Spirit refrain from telling Micah to quote Isaiah, or vice versa? Or having both quote a common source? (Isaiah 2:1-4 and Micah 4:1-5)[68] Perhaps each received the same words separately, but even if one repeated the other, he did so under the special guidance and inspiration of the Holy Spirit. Either way, God gave us His Word in the words of Scripture.

When we take the Bible at face value (and we'll talk about that in the next chapter), we see that, while not all of it was dictated, all of it was God-breathed. The methods may be different, but the result is the same.

God's Word or God's Words?

This reality has led many modern students of God's Word to suggest that, since inspiration doesn't always mean dictation, perhaps God didn't always breathe the exact words. Maybe

---

[68] My teacher, James Luther Mays, argues that this passage was added to both books decades after these prophets lived. James Luther Mays, *Micah: A Commentary*. Westminster, Philadelphia. 1976. pp.95-96

sometimes He inspired the ideas and left the wordsmithing to the human authors. Is the Bible an exact compilation of the very words of God, or just the "Word of God" in some vague, general sense? These are two distinct paradigms of inspiration. The first paradigm is known as "the plenary verbal inspiration" of Scripture. It means that every word, at least in the original manuscripts, was chosen by God. A very widely acclaimed expression of that view is found in the *Chicago Statement on Biblical Inerrancy*[69]

The second paradigm, that God inspired the ideas but not the vocabulary of Scripture, seems to be growing in popularity nowadays. I think it would have been the common conviction among the faculty when I was in seminary. For that reason, it always struck me as a bit strange that they trained us so vigorously in doing word studies. They rightly wanted us future preachers and teachers to pay painstaking attention to the exact words of Scripture, even if they didn't believe the words themselves to be inspired.

But what does the Bible itself say on this particular question? There is, of course, no question that the Scriptures were written down by humans. Consider John 1:45, *Philip found Nathanael and said to him, "We have found him of whom Moses in the Law and also the prophets wrote, Jesus of Nazareth, the son of Joseph."* The Law and prophets were recognized as Scripture and therefore as God's Word, but Philip tells us that Moses and the prophets did the actual writing. That leaves us to ask, whose words did they write;

---

[69] The Chicago Statement on Biblical Inerrancy with Exposition. http://www.bible-researcher.com/chicago1.html Last visited 3.1.2019

their own, or God's? In Exodus 24:4a we read, *And Moses wrote down all the* words *of the* LORD (emphasis added). In Jeremiah 30:1-2 we find something similar. *The word that came to Jeremiah from the* LORD: *"Thus says the* LORD, *the God of Israel: Write in a book all the* words *that I have spoken to you"* (emphasis added). According to these verses, the authors were human, but the very words are God's. What we have in Scripture is not only the Word of God in a general sense, but also the actual words of God in human vocabulary.

Sir Duke

How is it possible for the Holy Spirit to have guided the Bible writers to the right words yet still preserve their individual personalities? Let me suggest an analogy. I happen to be an amateur musician, and my hobbies include arranging music. If I write a part for a trumpet, I know it will sound very different if it's played on a saxophone or sung by a human voice. Same notes, different sound, different feel. So, I try to write parts that feature the uniqueness of each instrument or voice. That's simply part of arranging music. More precisely, however, I have even written parts not just for this or that instrument, but for particular musicians. I've composed parts not just for the flute but for Mindi, the marvelous flautist at the church I serve. I wrote one whole arrangement around a line I wanted to hear sung not just by a tenor but by Ray's misty tenor voice. Their individual artistry helped create the timbre I wanted to hear. Jazz aficionados will recognize that Duke Ellington was the absolute master of this art

If a genius like the Duke and even a wannabe like me can assign different musical lines to various voices to achieve the effect we want, how much more capable is the Holy Spirit of orchestrating the Scriptures so that they come out as a magnificent symphony?

I imagine that if you had met the author of Mark and asked him, "How was your day?" he would have replied, "First I woke up, then immediately I got out of bed. After that I immediately washed my face and said my prayers. Then immediately, I ate breakfast. When breakfast was completed, immediately ..." If you've ever read through Mark's Gospel you recognize that "immediately" is one of his favorite words. Mark's story of Jesus advances at breathtaking speed. So, when the Holy Spirit wanted a fast-paced Gospel that oozed urgency, He breathed it to Mark. When the writer's personality came through the writing, it was just what the Spirit wanted.

Likewise, if you had asked the apostle Paul about his day, he might have answered in a sentence that was three miles long, travelling through a maze of syntax and complex grammar. So, he was the perfect candidate to write a letter like Romans. Of course, Paul sounds like Paul and Mark sounds like Mark and John sounds like John. Of course, all the Bible writers sound like themselves. Why shouldn't they? They played and sang in their own voices, just as the Spirit orchestrated. The individuality of each author doesn't detract from our understanding of biblical inspiration, it enriches it, for those who know the score.

Ten Testimonies

The Bible is different from every other work or writing because it is God-breathed and its authors were carried along by the Holy Spirit. That's what the Bible says about itself, and for those who believe the Bible, that is all the evidence we need. Still, it might be helpful if there were some corroborating witnesses. A skeptic might say that the Bible's claim to be the Word of God is like a politician's insistence that she is honest. Is there any outside evidence that what the Bible says about itself is true? Apart from its own assertions, how can we know the Bible is the Word of God?

We are not the first ones to have raised that question. In the 1600s a group of devout and faithful students of God's Word gathered in London, England to wrestle with important questions of faith and share their answers with the greater Church. The result was three famous foundational documents, *The Westminster Confession of Faith*, *The Larger Catechism* (a doctrinal guide for preachers) and *The Shorter Catechism* (to be memorized by children). *The Larger Catechism* asks this question: "How doth it appear that the Scriptures are of the Word of God?" In other words, how can we know the Bible is God's Word? The answer it gives is beautiful and brilliant. "The Scriptures manifest themselves to be the Word of God, by their majesty and purity; by the consent of all the parts, and the scope of the whole, which is to give all glory to God; by their light and power to convince and convert sinners, to comfort and build up believers unto salvation: but the Spirit of God bearing witness by and with the Scriptures in the heart of man, is alone able fully to persuade it that they are the very word of

God."[70] This profound paragraph points to seven separate testimonies to the divine nature of Scripture. There a few more. For the next several pages, let's examine a total of ten witnesses to the Bible's character as God's Word.

(1) Majesty

The Bible has a singular majesty that is worthy of God's Word. Psalm 29:4 says, *The voice of the LORD is powerful; the voice of the LORD is full of majesty.* What's true of God's voice is also true of His Word. Explore it for yourself and see if that isn't true. Read Psalm 23 or 90 or 103 or any of the psalms. You won't find such lofty language or profound truth in Shakespeare, Pope or Poe. It's magnificent. It stirs the soul. Read 1 Corinthians 13, the great love chapter. Read the Sermon on the Mount. Read Romans 8, which starts with, *There is therefore now no condemnation for those who are in Christ Jesus* (v.1) then passes through *And we know that for those who love God all things work together for good, for those who are called according to his purpose,* (v. 28) only to climax with, *For I am sure that neither death nor life, nor angels nor rulers, nor things present nor things to come, nor powers, nor height nor depth, nor anything else in all creation, will be able to separate us from the love of God in Christ Jesus our Lord* (vv.38-39). I challenge you to find a passage equally profound in Plato, Aristotle or Kant. You can't. Read *The*

---

[70] The Larger Catechism, Q 4 *Confessional Standards of ECO: A Covenant Order of Evangelical Presbyterians,* Westminster Shorter Catechism Q 4 https://www.eco-pres.org/static/media/uploads/eco_confessional_standards_digit al_12.11.18.pdf p. 103 Last visited 3.1.2019

Koran, The Upanishads, The Bhagavad Gita and see if they compare. None can hold a candle, or even a match to the majesty of Scripture.

(2) Harmony

Second, we hear a lush harmony in the many voices of Scripture. This is what *The Larger Catechism* calls "the consent of all the parts." We already saw how the various voices of the Bible writers create the rich resonance of Scripture, but there is also delightful harmony among the notes.

Some critics like to point out what they see as contradictions in the Bible. For example, in Matthew 16:20 we read, *Then [Jesus] strictly charged the disciples to tell no one that he was the Christ.* Unfortunately, that seems to be a favorite verse of many modern American Christians and the unofficial mission statement of some churches. In Matthew 28:19-20, however, Jesus says, *"Go therefore and make disciples of all nations, baptizing them in the name of the Father and of the Son and of the Holy Spirit, teaching them to observe all that I have commanded you. And behold, I am with you always, to the end of the age."* In one place the Lord charges the disciples to tell no one about Him and in the other He commands them to tell everyone. Which is it, Jesus?

This seeming contradiction is easily resolved when we look at each passage in its context. Early in Matthew's telling of the story, in chapter 16, the disciples have only recently realized that Jesus is the Christ. They cannot yet fully grasp what that means. They don't understand the fact that He came to sacrifice His life to take upon Himself the punishment for our sin. They don't understand that he will rise from the dead and win eternal life for all who put their faith in Him. But when we get to chapter 28, all of that has been accomplished. Now they have the complete message and it is time for them to tell the world this life-changing good news. There is no contradiction at all. In fact, the tension between those two verses makes the story more powerful.

Allow me to use another illustration from music. If you were to go to a piano and play a middle "c" (the white key to the left of the two black keys) it would sound fine, provided your piano is in tune. If you were to add to that a "b" (the seventh white key to the right, just after the three black keys) and play them together, it would sound horrible! The two notes would clash in a jaw jarring dissonance. However, if you add an "e" and a "g" (playing every other white key starting with middle "c") you'll hear a C major 7th, one of the most beautiful chords in music and a perennial favorite for writers of love songs. The dissonance between the "c" and the "b" is still there, but in the context of the full chord that clash adds to the beauty of the whole. We'll spend all of Chapter Seven looking at alleged contradictions in the Bible, but we will find that many of them are resolved in resounding consonance.

(3) One Story

Third, the Bible tells one story. It has a central theme and one principal character. The whole Bible is a narrative of God's relationship with human beings, culminating in the person of Jesus Christ. In John 5:39 Jesus says, "*You search the Scriptures because you think that in them you have eternal life; and it is they that bear witness about me."* It is obvious that the New Testament bears witness to Jesus Christ, but Jesus was talking about the Old Testament. The New Testament had not been written yet. The same truth applies to Luke 24:27, where the Risen Jesus is talking to two of His disciples, *And beginning with Moses and all the Prophets, he interpreted to them in all the Scriptures the things concerning himself.* The whole Bible, including the Old Testament, is one story. It's the story of Jesus Christ.

Of course, that doesn't mean the Bible reads like a novel from cover to cover. It tells part of the story pretty much continually from Genesis through 2 Kings. After that, 1 Chronicles goes back to Adam and carries the narration a little farther as you read on through Nehemiah. Then we zoom in with the poetry books (Job, Psalms, Proverbs Ecclesiastes, Song of Solomon) and the prophets to bring out more details. The story climaxes as the Gospels relate all the events surrounding the earthly life of Jesus. Acts tells us about the early church. The New Testament letters fill in more details and reflect on the meaning of the whole. Finally, Revelation points us to the end of the story.

To be sure, there are numerous stories within this one story. There are sub-plots and sub-sub-plots. We find spellbinding sagas about Moses, Joseph, David, Elijah and others. Intriguing vignettes unfold within each of those stories: Moses meets God in the burning bush. Joseph is accused of rape. David smacks down Goliath and so on. Yet when they are all sewn together, these stories form one grand narrative. They point to the One who accomplishes God's plan and fulfills all God's promises. The Messiah. The Son of God. Jesus. The Christ.

In Chapter Nine we'll unpack a seven-word summary of the full scope of Scripture. When we understand the implications of one meaning-packed verse, we clearly see the point of the whole Bible. I John 4:19 says, *We love because he first loved us.* That's it. You could say that's the moral of the story. And where do we see God's love more perfectly than in Jesus Christ? Nowhere. A few pages ago we looked at Question 4 of *The Larger Catechism.* Now let's look at Question 5. It asks, "What do the Scriptures principally teach?" And the answer is, "The Scriptures principally teach, what man is to believe concerning God, and what duty God requires of man[71]." What, then, should we believe about God? Above all, that He is love and He first loved us. And what duty does God require of us? Love. Love God. Love others. Love is the Great Commandment and the New Commandment. We love because He first loved us.[72]

The Bible was written over a period of about 1,500 years by roughly forty authors. This was before the word processor, before the printing press, before the advent of professional editors, yet all these writers contributed to one great and unified story. From *In the beginning God created the heaven and the earth* (Genesis 1:1) to *The grace of the Lord Jesus be with all. Amen* (Revelation 22:21), it all points to God's unfathomable love for us in Jesus Christ. How can this be?

---

[71] Ibid.

[72] A presentation of the Gospel message based on 1 John 4:19 can be found in Rod Pinder, *The Little Book of Love,* www.PastorRodPinder.com/LittleBook

Simple. Though the Scriptures were written by many hands in several different centuries, they were breathed out by one eternal God.

(4) Accurate History

Fourth, the Bible gives us accurate history. For reasons that escape me, some historians tend to downplay the veracity of the Bible when compared to other ancient documents and records. In fact, supposed historical inaccuracies are used to perpetuate another allegation that the Bible isn't to be believed. But there's plenty of corroborating evidence that the Bible tells us what really happened. We'll look at four examples.

In my student days a theory that was commonly accepted among historical-critical scholars was that the first five books of the Bible were not written by Moses. Instead, they consisted of passages snipped from four more or less distinct sources and glued together into a single mosaic. Scholars seemed to believe that the Law of the Lord resembled a ransom note clipped from magazines and pasted onto a sheet of paper. This notion was known as the Documentary Hypothesis. The latest of these four sources was the "Priestly Document." It was supposed to have been written after the Babylonian exile, sometime after 538 BCE. One key excerpt ascribed to the "Priestly Document" is the Aaronic Benediction found in Numbers 6:22-26:

> The LORD spoke to Moses, saying, "Speak to Aaron
> and his sons, saying, Thus you shall bless the people
> of Israel: you shall say to them, The LORD bless you

and keep you; the LORD *make his face to shine upon you and be gracious to you; the* LORD *lift up his countenance upon you and give you peace."*

If historians were right, however, this beautiful blessing was not given through Moses. It wasn't composed until nearly a millennium after Moses' death.

In 1979 archeologists made an explosive discovery. At a dig at Ketef Hinnom, near Jerusalem, they found two tiny amulets each containing a small silver scroll. It took years to carefully unroll the scrolls. Guess what they read? That's right, a quote from the Aaronic Benediction. What's so unusual about that, you may ask. The scrolls are dated from the 7th Century BCE, roughly 100 years before the "Priestly Document" is supposed to have been written.[73] The silver scrolls do not prove, of course, that the benediction really dates all the way back to Moses, but they do undermine certain presuppositions of skeptical historians. This shouldn't surprise us. The Bible gives us accurate history.

Consider a second example. Some historians, predisposed to believe the kinds of rumors we're exploring in this book, supposed that King David never really existed. Like King Arthur of England, David was suspected to be a mythical figure. The stuff of legend. But in 1993 archeologists uncovered revealing fragments of the Tel Dan Stele.[74] In this

---

[73] "The Blessing of the Silver Scrolls"
http://www.biblearchaeology.org/post/2010/01/06/The-Blessing-of-the-Silver-Scrolls.aspx#Article Last visited 3.1.2019
[74] See "Tel Dan Stele" https://www.bible-history.com/archaeology/israel/tel-dan-stele.html Last visited 3.1.2019

stone monument a king (probably Hazalel of Syria) proudly claims credit for the deaths of King Joram of Israel and King Ahaziah of Judah, "of the house of David." Dating all the way back to the 9th Century BCE, this stele is foolproof evidence from outside the Bible that David and his dynasty in Judah were real historical entities. Another embarrassing blow for skepticism. Further, the story corroborates the events recorded in 2 Kings 9, how Joram and Ahaziah died in battle on the same day. Stealing the king of Syria's boastful thunder, however, the Bible tells us that Jehu the Israelite, not Hazalel the Syrian, was responsible for the double regicide.[75] Since ancient kings liked to exaggerate their accomplishments, I'm sure the Bible gives us accurate history on this point as well as the others.

Our third example comes from the reign of Hezekiah of Judah. In 701 BCE, Sennacharib of the Assyrian Empire came to capture Jerusalem by laying siege to it. Rather than allowing the Assyrians to cut off the water supply for the city, which flowed from the Gihon Spring outside the city walls, 2 Chronicles 32:30 tells us, *This same Hezekiah closed the upper outlet of the waters of Gihon and directed them down to the west side of the city of David. And Hezekiah prospered in all his works.* Hezekiah hurriedly dug a tunnel from the spring to the city. One crew started at the spring and the other inside the city wall. Remarkably, they met somewhere in the middle. Hezekiah's tunnel was uncovered more than a hundred years ago. One can visit it today. More

---

[75] See also 1 Kings 19:17 where God tells Elijah, "And the one who escapes from the sword of Hazael shall Jehu put to death, and the one who escapes from the sword of Jehu shall Elisha put to death."

recently, in 2004, the end of the tunnel was discovered at the Pool of Siloam.[76] This is the site where Jesus healed a man who was blind from birth (John 9). The pool is mentioned in 2 Kings 20:20, *The rest of the deeds of Hezekiah and all his might and how he made the pool and the conduit and brought water into the city, are they not written in the Book of the Chronicles of the Kings of Judah?* Archeologists continue to find artifacts, which fit with the facts of the Bible. The Bible gives us accurate history.

Let's look at one more find, maybe the most famous of all: Jericho. The ruins of Jericho were discovered around the beginning of the 20th century. The evidence is clear: those "walls came tumblin' down." In fact, they found an inner wall and an outer wall, with space for apartments between them. This correlates with Joshua 2:15, which tells us that Rahab the prostitute lived in a house that was built into the city wall. John Garstang and William Albright were certain that the findings at this site line up with the Joshua story. Admittedly, Kathleen Kenyon's theory and methodology led her to the dubious conclusion that Jericho was destroyed long before Joshua, though in a manner strikingly similar to what the Bible describes.[77] So you'll have to choose whom you believe. As for me and my house, the finds at Jericho corroborate the Bible's accurate history.

---

[76] "The Siloam Pool: Where Jesus Healed the Blind Man" https://www.biblicalarchaeology.org/daily/biblical-sites-places/biblical-archaeology-sites/the-siloam-pool-where-jesus-healed-the-blind-man/ Last visited 3.1.2019
[77] "Jericho: Does the Evidence Disprove or Prove the Bible?" http://www.biblearchaeology.org/post/2009/01/jericho-does-the-evidence-disprove-or-prove-the-bible.aspx Last visited 3.1.2019

Notice I didn't say any of these finds *confirms* the biblical record. From a historical perspective, the Bible should be received as a reliable historical source, at least as reliable as the silver scrolls, the Tel Dan Stele and other archeological finds. People like to say that Archeology confirms the Bible. I think that statement is incomplete. The Bible often confirms archeology. Further, the Bible provides an interpretive framework for archeological findings.[78] To dismiss the Bible as a viable resource, as some historians do, strikes me as circular reasoning and intellectually irresponsible. The Bible gives accurate history.

(5) Accurate Prophecy

The Bible is remarkably accurate when it tells us about the past, but its accuracy is mind-blowing when it talks about the future. Our fifth witness is the fact that the Bible gives us accurate prophecy. Now, we should notice that prophecy is more than foretelling the future. To prophesy is to speak the Word of the Lord. Sometimes this includes foretelling the future, but not always. However, when the Bible does predict the future, it does so with astonishing precision. "The best way to predict your future is to create it." I'm told that Abraham Lincoln said that. God does it. God can predict the future because He knows what He is going to do. As Isaiah 46:9c-10 says, *I am God, and there is none like me, declaring the end from the beginning and from ancient*

---

[78] For dozens more examples, see "Historical Accuracy of the Bible ... Silencing the Skeptics with Archeology" https://www.youtube.com/watch?time_continue=824&v=LdSEx DE8EsU Last visited 3.1.2019

times things not yet done, saying, 'My counsel shall stand, and I will accomplish all my purpose.' And as Amos 3:7 says, *Surely the Sovereign LORD does nothing without revealing his plan to his servants the prophets.* There are more prophecies in the Bible than we could ever examine in this brief section. Some of those prophecies still await fulfillment, but others have come true in High Def detail. Let's explore some examples.

In Deuteronomy 28:36-37, Moses warned the young nation of Israel what would happen if they turned away from their mission, which was to bless all nations by remaining faithful to the Lord. He said, *The LORD will bring you and your king whom you set over you to a nation that neither you nor your fathers have known. And there you shall serve other gods of wood and stone. And you shall become a horror, a proverb, and a byword among all the peoples where the LORD will lead you away.* At the time of Moses, Israel didn't have a king. That didn't happen until more than 400 years later. And about 400 years after that, this poignant prophecy came true. God's people were conquered and carried off to captivity in Babylon.

The Babylonian Captivity wasn't the final chapter in Judah's history, however. God also showed the prophets that there would be a time of restoration. Through Isaiah, God said, *Thus says the LORD, your Redeemer who formed you from the womb: "I am the LORD, who made all things, ... who says of Cyrus, 'He is my shepherd, and he shall fulfill all my purpose'; saying of Jerusalem, 'She shall be built,' and of the temple, 'Your foundation shall be laid'"* (Isaiah 44:24, 28). The details of this prophecy are amazing. If we read the

Bible in a straightforward manner, Isaiah wrote about 200 years before Cyrus. Yet right on cue, just as God's Word decreed, a man named Cyrus was born, became the head of the Persian Empire, took over the Babylonian Empire and released God's people to rebuild Jerusalem and the Temple. What laser-like accuracy!

The book of Daniel bubbles over with a number of remarkable prophecies that predict the future. Let's just consider Daniel 8. Using vivid symbols of a mighty ram, a ferocious goat and peculiar horns, it foretells the rise of the Medio-Persian empire (ca. 539-330 BCE), its fall to the Greeks under Alexander the Great (330 BCE), the fourfold division of Alexander's empire among his generals, Cassander, Lysimachus, Ptolemy and Selecus (333 BCE), and the prideful pogrom executed against God's people by Antiochus IV, who considered himself an epiphany of the god Zeus (215-164 BCE). [79] I've filled in the names and dates from what actually happened in history, so take a moment to read Daniel 8 and, now that you know the historical facts, see how powerfully Daniel's prophecy predicts what really came to pass.

Now, skeptics will claim that these predictions were all retrospective. Moses didn't write Deuteronomy, they say. It was written during the reign of King Josiah, not long before

---

[79] For more detail see "Fulfilled Prophecy (Daniel 7-8) Evidence for the Bible pt3" by Mike Winger
https://www.youtube.com/watch?v=VfQCgNLV6Rw&t=425s Last visited 3.1.2019. Also "Defending Daniel, Evidence for the Bible pt 4" by Mike Winger
https://www.youtube.com/watch?v=5z4c4DxTHhE Last visited 3.1.2019

the Babylonian Captivity. By then Babylon was on the rise and that tragedy was more easily predictable. Further, they assert, Deuteronomy was edited during the captivity itself. So of course, the writer/editor knew that time of exile would come. He was living in the exile, according to the skeptics. Similarly, skeptics insist, it was not Isaiah of Jerusalem who spoke or wrote those words about Cyrus in Isaiah 44. The first thirty-nine chapters of Isaiah are mostly recognized as authentic. They're attributed to Isaiah of Jerusalem, the one who received his call in the year that King Uzziah died (Isaiah 6:1). These thirty-nine chapters predominantly warn Jerusalem about impending disaster and call the people to repent. In chapter 40, however, the tone changes and promises of comfort and restoration prevail. But rather than recognize these oracles as predictive prophecy addressed to a future generation, many scholars insist that chapters 40-66 of Isaiah were penned by one or more authors who wrote *after* the exile. These postulated authors are called Deutero-Isaiah and Trito-Isaiah (Second Isaiah and Third Isaiah). These pseudonymous imitators simply tagged their works onto the real Isaiah's writings. When the legendary Deutero-Isaiah allegedly penned Isaiah 44, Cyrus was already a person of past history. And Daniel? They say that book wasn't written until the middle of the second century BCE, after the events it "predicted" were already in the history books.

Why do skeptics have such a hard time believing that these prophecies were spoken before the incidents they describe took place? Precisely because the prophecies are so, well, precise. My own friend and teacher, Sib Towner, said this about Daniel 8:

"We need to assume that the vision as a whole is a prophecy after the fact. Why? Because human beings are unable accurately to predict future events centuries in advance and to say that Daniel could do so, even on the basis of a symbolic revelation vouchsafed to him by God and interpreted by an angel, is to fly in the face of the certainties of human nature. So what we have here is in fact not a road map of the future laid down in the sixth century B.C. but an interpretation of the events of the author's own time, 167-164 BC."[80]

What Dr. Towner said about the prophecies in Daniel is typical of the skeptical scholastic view of predictive prophecy in general. Skeptics assume their conclusion before they even start to think about the issue. They assume that human beings can never foretell the future. Therefore, when we hear stories of God revealing the future to His servants, those stories are automatically dismissed as false fables. The Bible's prophecies are so pinpoint accurate that, whenever possible, skeptics claim that they weren't prophesies at all. That is to say the prophets did not foretell the future but rehashed the past. Skeptics suppose the Bible's prophecies are literally too good to be true. But true they are. That's how accurate the Bible's prophecies are.

The Bible's prophecies are most spectacular, however, when they talk about Jesus Christ. He, you remember, is the main character of the whole story. Hundreds of years before He

---

[80] W. Sibley Towner, *Daniel* in the series *Interpretation: A Bible Commentary for Preaching and Teaching* © John Knox Press, 1984, p. 115

came into the world as a human being, the Bible prophesied that He would be born of a Virgin (Isaiah 7:14, see Mathew 1:22-23, Luke 1:34) in the town of Bethlehem (Micah 5:2, see Matthew 2:5-6, Luke 2:4-5). It also foretells His ministry of teaching, preaching (Isaiah 61:1-2, see Luke 4:17-21) and healing (Malachi 4:2, see Matthew 4:24 and many places in the Gospels). There are more than a hundred Old Testament predictions about Jesus.

Among the Old Testament prophecies about Jesus, those which tell of His crucifixion and resurrection are particularly stunning. Read the last two chapters of Matthew, Mark and Luke and the last three chapters of John, then read Isaiah 53, written about 800 years before Jesus was born. Also read Psalm 22, written around 1,000 BCE. Jesus quoted the first verse of this psalm in Matthew 27:46. By crying out the opening words of this familiar song, which all the people who heard Him had sung in worship just as we sing "Amazing Grace," Jesus called their attention to the whole psalm. In quoting those nine powerful words, *My God, my God, why have you forsaken me?* It was as if He cried, "Look! See all the prophecies in that psalm that are coming true before your very eyes! See them wag their heads and mock. See them pierce my hands and feet. See them gamble over my clothing and all the rest. All this is happening, just as the prophecies proclaimed." Like all of Scripture, the psalm points to Him.

It's important to recognize that this is the way Jesus interpreted Scripture both before and after His resurrection. For example, in Mark 8:31 we read, *And he began to teach them that the Son of Man must suffer many things and be rejected by the elders and the chief priests and the scribes and be killed, and after three days rise again.* After those prophecies were fulfilled, Luke 24:25-27 tells us this about the risen Jesus, *And he said to them, "O foolish ones, and slow of heart to believe all that the prophets have spoken! Was it not necessary that the Christ should suffer these things and enter into his glory?" And beginning with Moses and all the Prophets, he interpreted to them in all the Scriptures the things concerning himself.*

Some will object that the Gospel writers made up the details of Jesus' life, death and resurrection to fit the prophecies. Once again, however, the only reason for such a high level of skepticism is the that the prophecies are so astoundingly accurate. Further, if the Gospel writers fabricated facts to fit their theological agendas, the Gospel can't be trusted in any way. If the facts about Jesus are really fiction, then He is not the fulfillment of God's promises. He is not the hope of the world. In that case, there is no hope for the world after all.

Obviously, the Gospel writers highlight many prophecies that were actually fulfilled in Christ. They underline things that really happened. But that doesn't mean they are spinning yarns. In fact, the sympathetic reader can sense the amazement and feel the excitement the Gospel writers must have experienced when they pointed out the accuracy of Old Testament prophecies as they recount the life, death and resurrection of Jesus.

We recognize the Bible as the Word of God because it presents us with accurate prophecies, many of which have already been fulfilled. But here's something really remarkable. The word of the Lord is so deep that the prophets themselves didn't fully understand the meaning of the words they spoke and wrote. In 1 Peter 1:10-12 we read, *Concerning this salvation, the prophets, who spoke of the grace that was to come to you, searched intently and with the greatest care, trying to find out the time and circumstances to which the Spirit of Christ in them was pointing when he predicted the sufferings of the Messiah and the glories that would follow. It was revealed to them that they were not serving themselves but you, when they spoke of the things that have now been told you by those who have preached the gospel to you by the Holy Spirit sent from heaven. Even angels long to look into these things.* The true prophets wrote beyond their human understanding! The Bible is not just another human book. We know this because it is far more profound than its human writers were able to grasp. They wrote what God guided them to write without fully comprehending what it meant. The Bible gives us incredibly accurate prophecy because, like the rest of Scripture, those prophecies were breathed by God.

(6) Changed Lives

Our sixth witness is a bit more practical and down to earth. Reading the Bible changes people's lives. Let's look at a classic example. You may know the story of St. Augustine. Though he was raised by a Christian mother who prayed for him every day, Augustine didn't have much interest in the things of Christ. He searched for life's meaning in other venues. For a while he became a member of a popular cult called the Manichees, but he eventually rejected their teaching as vapid. He indulged his sexual appetites to the degree that he had a child with his mistress, rejected her for a maiden he wanted to marry, but since he couldn't remain faithful to his fiancé, that relationship fell apart. For a while he dabbled in his mother's religion, but considered himself too sophisticated for Christianity, at least as he viewed it at that time. Augustine had a great mind, so he dedicated himself to intellectual pursuits and advanced his academic career, but none of these things brought peace to his restless heart.

One day when Augustine was alone in the garden of a Christian friend, he heard a strange, singsong chant that sounded like the voice of a child. The chant said, in the Latin of his day, *"Tolle, lege, tolle lege"* which means, "take and read." His friend had left a Bible portion nearby, so Augustine picked it up, opened it at random, and started reading. The first passage his eyes fell upon was Romans 13:13-14, *Let us walk properly as in the daytime, not in orgies and drunkenness, not in sexual immorality and sensuality, not in quarreling and jealousy. But put on the Lord Jesus Christ, and make no provision for the flesh, to gratify its desires.* It was as if those verses had been written specifically for him! Augustine opened his life to Christ, and everything changed. He quickly went and told his mother what had happened.[81] As he grew in his faith he became one of the most effective preachers and influential writers in history. His profound spiritual insights still impact us today. While there were many factors leading up to this pivotal event, it was reading the Bible with an open mind and a searching heart that changed Augustine's life, and to no small degree, changed history.

---

[81] Augustine, *Confessions* Book 8, Chapter 12

That classic example is far from an isolated incident. The same thing happens again and again, even nowadays. Have you ever been in a hotel room and opened the nightstand drawer? If so, chances are good that you found a *Gideons Bible*. Since 1908 Gideons International has placed over two billion Bibles or Bible portions in motel, hotel, hospital rooms, jail cells and other places.[82] They do this because they know the Bible's power to change lives. In their own words, "We believe distributing copies of God's Word plants powerful seeds God can use according to His own timing (1 Corinthians 3:6), allows many to read the truth for themselves (John 8:32), provides a lasting witness (Hebrews 4:12), and makes it easier for those we reach to boldly spread the Good News (2 Timothy 2:2)."[83]

They are clearly right. Among the innumerable people whose lives have been changed by reading a Gideons Bible are Bernie Dymet[84] and Ravi Zacharias.[85] Bernie, who is now the CEO of Christianityworks in Australia, and whose Bible broadcasts reach more than 40,000,000 listeners, was dissuaded from a suicide attempt by reading a Gideons Bible in his hotel room while on a business trip to Brisbane.

---

[82] "Gideons Distribute Two Billionth Scripture," http://blog.gideons.org/2015/04/two-billion/ (Last visited 3.1.2019)
[83] "The Gideons International: About Us" https://www.gideons.org/about (Last visited 3.1.2019)
[84] "How a Gideon Bible Changed My Life," https://www.youtube.com/watch?v=GuBbKC-0-oM Last visited 3.1.2019
[85] "Ravi Zacharias short testimony," https://www.youtube.com/watch?v=cHRMb3to_HU Last visited 3.1.2019

Seventeen-year-old Ravi Zacharias had already tried to take his life when God encountered him through a Gideons Bible in his hospital room in India. Today Ravi is one of the leading Christian teachers and apologists in the world, speaking at college campuses through Ravi Zacharias Ministries and publishing very helpful books and videos on understanding the Christian faith. These men's lives were changed through reading the Bible (thanks to the Gideons), and with a mighty ripple effect, God has used them to change the lives of many others.[86]

There is life-changing power in God's Word. Once, after a controversial teaching, many people who had been following Jesus deserted Him. *So Jesus said to the twelve, "Do you want to go away as well?" Simon Peter answered him, "Lord, to whom shall we go? You have the words of eternal life"* (John 6:67-68). Peter understood exactly what we've been discussing. Like myriads of people through the centuries, Peter understood and experienced the reality that God's Word changes lives.

Even the Beatles understood this phenomenon to some degree. They wrote,

> "Rocky Raccoon, he fell back in his room only to find Gideon's Bible.
>
> Gideon checked out, and he left it no doubt to help with good Rocky's revival."[87]

---

[86] For more testimonies see *The Gideons International: Blog* https://www.gideons.org/blog Last visited 3.1.2019
[87] John Lennon and Paul McCartney, "Rocky Raccoon" 1968

While these playful lyrics express a very cheeky pun, they point to a valuable reality. God often uses the Bible to give new life, and to renew abundant life in those who read it. Reading the Bible changes lives. The nasty rumors we've been examining discourage people from reading the Bible. They prompt people to leave their Bibles on their shelves or shut up somewhere in a drawer. But we would do well to follow the advice Augustine heard. *Tolle lege.* Take and read. It can bring revival. It can change your life.

(7) Spiritual Growth

Further, this life change is not a "one-and-done" deal. Reading the Bible can not only transform faithless people into joyful, purposeful believers, as it did with the individuals we just met, it also helps believers grow in our faith. In fact, reading the Bible is an indispensable practice for genuine spiritual growth. Consider the last words the Apostle Peter wrote to other Christians. *But grow in the grace and knowledge of our Lord and Savior Jesus Christ. To him be the glory both now and to the day of eternity. Amen* (2 Peter 3:18). Like all living things, followers of Jesus are either growing or dying. There is no such thing as status quo.

So how do we grow? First, we openly and gratefully acknowledge that spiritual growth is always a work of the Holy Spirit in our lives. As 2 Corinthians 3:18 tells us, *And we all, who with unveiled faces contemplate the Lord's glory, are being transformed into his image with ever-increasing glory, which comes from the Lord, who is the Spirit* (NIV). Chew on that amazing verse for a moment. We grow with ever-increasing glory. We can expect to be more magnificent today than we were yesterday, and more splendorous tomorrow than we are today. Most astonishingly, the end result of this continual progression is that we are transformed into the very image of Christ! The goal of our growth is nothing less than Christ-likeness. (See also Romans 8:29.) This, of course, is something we could never achieve on our own. It's the work of the Holy Spirit in our lives.

Nevertheless, we also have a role to play in our growth, in our progress toward Christ-likeness. Psalm 1 talks about the person who delights in the Scriptures and meditates on them day and night. Verse 3 observes, *That person is like a tree planted by streams of water, which yields its fruit in season and whose leaf does not wither—whatever they do prospers* (Psalm 1:3 NIV). God's Word nourishes our spirits and makes us flourish. It is food for our faith. Remember what Jesus Himself said when He faced temptation to settle for less than what God intended for Him, He answered, *It is written, "Man shall not live by bread alone, but by every word that comes from the mouth of God."* (Matthew 4:4 quoting Deuteronomy 8:3)

This process of growing in Christ-likeness is called sanctification. The night before He gave His life for you and me, Jesus prayed these words about us, *"Sanctify them in the truth; your word is truth"* (John 17:17). The Apostle Paul said in Romans 12:2, *Do not be conformed to this world, but be transformed by the renewal of your mind, that by testing you may discern what is the will of God, what is good and acceptable and perfect.* Transformation comes by the renewal of our minds. Can you think of a better way to renew your mind than to read and meditate on the Bible? I cannot.

If you want to get a good glimpse at the promises of spiritual treasure and growth that are made to those who deeply read the Scriptures, take a look at Psalm 119. Read all 176 verses. In fact, I encourage you to read it every day for a week. See how to live a pure life (verses 9-11). Learn how to be wiser than your enemies, your teachers and your elders (verses 98-100). Discover where you can find divine guidance (verse 105) and comfort (verses 50-52). All those promises and more are found just in Psalm 119, and they're all for you! The Bible helps believers grow spiritually.

Of course, the point is not just to read the Bible and think about it, but to apply it to our lives. James 1:23-25 says, *For if anyone is a hearer* [and we could add "or reader"] *of the word and not a doer, he is like a man who looks intently at his natural face in a mirror. For he looks at himself and goes away and at once forgets what he was like. But the one who looks into the perfect law, the law of liberty, and perseveres, being no hearer who forgets but a doer who acts, he will be blessed in his doing.* Jesus taught something similar in Matthew 7:24-27.

We started this chapter by looking at 2 Timothy 3:16, *All Scripture is breathed out by God and profitable for teaching, for reproof, for correction, and for training in righteousness.* The Bible shows us God's will and God's ways (teaching). It points out where we are wrong (reproof) and shows us what is right (correction). It guides us in a lifestyle of right relationships with God and others (training and righteousness). Further, the purpose of Scripture is made clear in the next verse, 2 Timothy 3:17, *that the man of God may be complete, equipped for every good work.* Christian men and women grow toward completion. We grow toward Christ-likeness. God breathed out His Word to help us do that, but if we never read the God-breathed Scriptures, then God just wasted His breath.

To help write this chapter I asked my Facebook friends, "How has the Bible changed your life? And/or how have you seen it change the lives of others?" I got some great responses.

> ➢ Pam said, "I read every morning, my devotions and then reference the verses, it makes me try 'n' do better, be a better person than yesterday! Try to forgive others for hurting me and taking advantage of my kindness!"

> ➢ Cindy agreed, saying "Daily reading, particularly with references, start to give you context and depth of faith."

> ➢ Stephen stated, "I grew up in a Christian home, but didn't understand the fullness of the gospel of justification by faith alone through Christ alone, until reading and journaling through Romans in my thirties with a friend."

> ➢ Gayle added, "The Bible constantly amazes me. How can a book be so old, yet so timely? So many different books, yet one connected book? So simple, yet so layered with meaning?"

> ➢ Aaron replied, "I witnessed a divided Session [a board of elders] become united over the course of six months as they committed themselves to prayer and the study of Scripture."

➢ Renee responded, "I have so many stories! My brother used to worship the devil and I saw all kinds of weird things. My mom's best friend told me about rebuking demons. It was so weird! Eons later, I read the gospels and sure enough, that's how they react to Jesus! As I read the gospels, I noticed that Jesus also cast out sickness like He did to the demons. I tried it. I've heard a sermon about casting out sickness as well. I tried it. It couldn't make me any worse off. I had retinopathy, which is irreversible, but it's completely gone! Although now, I'm having troublesome symptoms in my eyes. Ugh…. I need some help!"

➢ Donna summed it all up when she said, "To be fair - how hasn't it? My whole life is changed by the Bible and God."

Not long ago I encouraged the congregation I serve to read Psalm 32 in preparation for Communion the following Sunday. Saturday night before I went to bed, I opened my Bible app and reviewed that chapter. As soon as I got through verse 1, which says, *Blessed is the one whose transgression is forgiven, whose sin is covered,* the Spirit spoke to my heart and said, "Rod, that's you!" Wow! I was filled with joy. I mean, I already knew that Jesus Christ has covered my sin and forgiven my transgression. I proclaim that truth every Sunday in one form or another. But reading that verse that night led to an encounter with God that not only strengthened me, it sent my spirit soaring.

We live in a complex world and face difficult issues. It's easy to let the moods and morals of our culture pull us off track and derail our spiritual growth. Spending time in the Bible on a frequent, daily basis is an absolute necessity if we want to rise above our surroundings and become more like Jesus Christ. The Bible helps us grow spiritually.

(8) Confirmed by Experience (and Vice Versa)

Our eighth witness is the fact that the teachings of the Bible are often confirmed by experience. On one level this is closely related to the previous witness. People believe what the Bible says, put it into practice and, voila! What the Bible says comes true. Their lives are changed. They experience spiritual growth. They find themselves with more purpose, more hope, more joy, more faith, more love and so on. But that isn't the only way our experiences confirm the Bible. When we walk by faith we see again and again how true-to-life the Bible is.

Let me show you what I mean. Rarely do I preach from the pulpit. Most of the time I stand on the floor amid the congregation. I tend to move around a bit. One Sunday I was making a point that it is wrong to use the Scriptures as a weapon to beat up people with whom we disagree. As I said that, I struck one of the worshippers on the shoulder with my Bible. It wasn't much more than a tap, but as soon I did it, I realized that this man was a first-time guest at the church. What was I thinking? Surely he would leave and never come back. Later, however, I discovered that the man came in with chronic shoulder pain that had tormented him for years. When I hit him with my Bible, the pain went away! It hasn't come back, and the man became an active member of our congregation.

That event reminds me of stories we find in the book of Acts. In Acts 5:15-16 we read that people *even carried out the sick into the streets and laid them on cots and mats, that as Peter came by at least his shadow might fall on some of them. The people also gathered from the towns around Jerusalem, bringing the sick and those afflicted with unclean spirits, and they were all healed.* Likewise Acts 19:12 tells us *that even handkerchiefs or aprons that had touched* [Paul's] *skin were carried away to the sick, and their diseases left them and the evil spirits came out of them.* Now, my point isn't that I'm on a level with Peter or Paul, or even that an imitation leather-bound Bible has intrinsic healing power, any more than shadows or handkerchiefs have such power. The point is that God still works in miraculous ways today. What we read about in the Bible we sometimes experience today.

We already saw this in Renee's testimony a few paragraphs ago. In the name of Jesus, she cast out sickness and her retinopathy disappeared. (We continue to pray for the troublesome symptoms she's experiencing now.) In Chapter Eight I'll share several similar stories, but you get the idea. We experience some of the very things described in Scripture. Our experience confirms the Bible.

We read this in 2 Peter 1:19, which says, *And we have the prophetic word more fully confirmed, to which you will do well to pay attention as to a lamp shining in a dark place, until the day dawns and the morning star rises in your hearts.* Peter is talking about an experience he shared with James and John, when, at the "Transfiguration of Jesus," these three apostles got a first-hand peek of Christ in the fullness of His glory. They also heard the very voice of God. (1 Peter 1:16-21, see also Matthew 17:1-8.) That experience confirms the prophetic word. Experience confirms Scripture.

But hold on a moment. Remember how in Chapter Four we saw how helpful it is to compare translations? This is another verse where that is true. Where the ESV says *we have the prophetic word more fully confirmed*, the NIV says, *We also have the prophetic message as something completely reliable*. That's a bit different. In the ESV, the word is confirmed by experience while in the NIV the message is reliable on its own. It needs no confirmation. The KJV is even stronger when it says, *We have also a more sure word of prophecy*. Here the prophetic word is not just reliable independent of experience, it is actually *more sure* than experience. God's word is even more certain than the remarkable experience the apostles had on the Mount of Transfiguration. Perhaps the Greek could be understood the way the ESV expresses it, but the word is βεβαιότερον (bebaioteron). That is a comparative adjective, meaning something is "more certain." "Made more certain" would be a passive verb, βεβαιωθεντα (bebaiothenta).[88] But that isn't the word the Spirit chose. Samuel Cox explains the verse this way, "Peter knew a sounder basis for faith than that of signs and wonders. He had seen our Lord Jesus Christ receive honor and glory from God the Father in the holy mount; he

---

[88] Thanks to Professor Mike Glodo for helping me sort through the Greek grammar and pointing me to Michael Green's *2 Peter and Jude: An Introduction and Commentary, vol. 18, Tyndale New Testament Commentaries* (Downers Grove, IL: InterVarsity Press, 1987), 108.

had been dazzled and carried out of himself by visions and voices from heaven; but nevertheless, even with his memory and heart throbbing with recollections of that divine scene, he says, 'we have something surer still in the prophetic word' ... It was not the miracles of Christ by which he came to know Jesus, but the word of Christ as interpreted by the Spirit of Christ."[89]

Many people tend to think that if the Bible fits their experience, they'll believe the Bible. In fact, I once asked a group of fellow pastors this question: If you come across a situation where the Bible says one thing and your experience teaches you something else, which do you tend to believe? All five of them said they would believe their experience. That's backwards. We should say that if our experience fits the Bible, then we'll believe our experience.

Moses gave us a remarkable warning about valuing experience above God's Word. In Deuteronomy 13:1-3, he says:

> "If a prophet or a dreamer of dreams arises among you and gives you a sign or a wonder, and the sign or wonder that he tells you comes to pass, and if he says, 'Let us go after other gods,' which you have not known, 'and let us serve them,' you shall not listen to the words of that prophet or that dreamer of dreams. For the LORD your God is testing you, to know whether you love the LORD your God with all your heart and with all your soul."

---

[89] Cited in Kenneth S. Wuest, *In These Last Days* © 1954 by Wm. B. Erdmans Publishing Company (Grand Rapids)

If miraculous experiences seem to "confirm" something that is contrary to the plain teaching of Scripture, (for example, Deuteronomy 5:7, *"You shall have no other gods before me"*) the experience is to be rejected rather than God's Word.

One of the hottest controversies in Christian theology today is the debate between cessationists and continuationists. Cessationists claim that God stopped working (most) miracles after the age of the Apostles. In other words, miracles have ceased. Continuationists interpret the fact that Jesus Christ is the same yesterday, today and forever (Hebrews 13:8) to support the idea that miracles continue to happen today, just as they did in Bible times. You may have guessed by now that I write from a continuationist perspective. An accusation that cessationists often level against us continuationists is that we value experience above revelation. (That idea would fit with the ESV interpretation of 2 Peter 1:19.) Like Rene Descartes, the philosopher of radical doubt, cessationists rightly point out that human experiences, even spiritual experiences, are subjective and deceptive. They can trick us.

Let me clear up that accusation right now. I, for one, emphatically do not value experience above revelation. The same is true of my continuationist (sometimes called charismatic) friends. We insist that Scripture trumps experience every time. Period. Scripture alone is our guide to faith and practice, and our spiritual experiences need to be subjected to and evaluated in light of the Bible. Scripture is the grid through which we can decipher experience. It is the lens though which we interpret reality. It defines our worldview. The Bible helps us understand things like instantly healed shoulders, restored retinae and other remarkable phenomena. Further, even if the people we mentioned were never healed, the Bible would still be true. Experience is subject to Scripture, and any experience, or any interpretation of experience that is contrary to Scripture, we insist, is to be rejected out of hand.

So, on the one hand, Scripture is frequently confirmed by the experiences of the faithful. Far more importantly, however, Christian experience is confirmed by Scripture. Christian experience and supernatural works of the Holy Spirit are phenomenal and exciting. But *we have also a more sure word of prophecy.* The Bible confirms our experience.

Our last two witnesses are a bit different from the first eight, and even weightier. However, I find each of the above witnesses credible and convincing that the Bible is more than just another book. It is nothing less than the unique word of God. Some people, however, will not believe regardless of what evidence is presented. That has always been the case, and I suppose it always will. In John 12:28-30 we find a public conversation between Jesus and His Father. The Father spoke audibly to His Son so that everyone could hear. And everyone did hear, but not everyone believed. Some said it thundered. Funny how the "thunder" sounded exactly like a heavenly endorsement of Jesus. But no matter what evidence comes to the fore, some people simply refuse to believe.

(9) Live It to Believe It

The ninth witness to the Bible's authenticity comes from the words of Jesus Himself. As He does so often when we truly pay attention, Jesus shocks us. He turns our expectations upside down. In John 7:17 the Lord says, *"If anyone's will is to do God's will, he will know whether the teaching is from God or whether I am speaking on my own authority."* Read that again. Jesus says just the opposite of what we want to say. We want to say, "Prove to me that this teaching is from God, then maybe I'll consider doing what it says. Show me its majesty and harmony. Convince me that it's one sweeping story. Demonstrate that its history and its prophecies are accurate. Let me see how it changes lives and promotes spiritual growth. Explain how it is confirmed by real life experience. Do all that, then I might do what it says. I make no promises, but I might." As a matter of fact, on some level many readers have been saying that to themselves while reading this chapter. "Go ahead, Rod. Convince me." But Jesus says that's backwards. First, we set our wills on doing God's will, then, Jesus says, we can know whether His teaching comes from God. Once we've made up our minds to follow it, only then can we know if it is true.

That's a problem for many people. Some are scared of God's will. They remember that when Jesus prayed, *Nevertheless, not my will, but yours, be done* (Luke 22:42), He wound up wounded and crucified. They ignore the fact that the crucifixion was the means by which God gave Jesus the name which is above all names and made Him the Lord of all the world (Philippians 2:9-11). They see God's will as something suspect, dangerous, maybe even something to be avoided. So, they shy away from it. They forget that when we are transformed by the renewing of our minds we prove that God's will is good, perfect and pleasing – to God and to us (Romans 12:2). If we want to know whether the teaching of Jesus, and by extension the whole canon of Scripture, comes from God, the first indispensable step is to desire to do God's will. Tomes have been written about the reliability of the Bible. Tons of pages and countless sages have presented powerful arguments about the veracity of Scripture. You can probably tell, I love reading and hearing those discussions. However, if the nature of Scripture as God's Word is nothing more than an interesting academic question for you, Jesus says you'll never know the answer. You'll never know the truth. You have to do it to get it. You have to live it to believe it. If your will is to do God's will, then, and only then, can you know that the teaching comes from God.

This presses us to ask the question, "How can I come to the place where I will God's will?" "How can I want what God wants?" Philippians 2:13 gives a beautiful answer when it promises, *for it is God who works in you, both to will and to work for his good pleasure.* That leads us to our tenth and final witness.

(10) God Is My Witness

The tenth and most irrefutable witness to the validity of the Scriptures is God Himself. The Lord testifies to the truth of Scripture. When the risen Jesus first appeared to two of His disciples on the road to Emmaus, He explained the Scriptures to them. Though their hearts burned within them, they couldn't understand what they were hearing. In Luke 24:45, however, we're told, *Then he opened their minds to understand the Scriptures.* This seems to be a deeper work than the extensive teaching He did during His ministry as a mortal or even as he walked with them on the road. These disciples had surely heard Him teach about the Scriptures countless times, but it was only when He *opened their minds* that they finally got the message.

Now that Jesus has ascended into Heaven, the Holy Spirit continues that same work for us today. Read these remarkable verses. 1 Corinthians 2:12-14 says:

> *Now we have received not the spirit of the world, but the Spirit who is from God, that we might understand the things freely given us by God. And we impart this in words not taught by human wisdom but taught by the Spirit, interpreting spiritual truths to those who are spiritual. The natural person does not accept the things of the Spirit of God, for they are folly to him, and he is not able to understand them because they are spiritually discerned.*

The Spirit enables us to understand the Scriptures as well as everything that God gives us. Without this witness of the Holy Spirit, spiritual truth strikes us as foolish. The truth of Scripture seems impossible and irrational. Don't you experience that to be true? Don't you know people who think that the very idea that there is a God-breathed book is ridiculous? In their presumed intellectual superiority, they explain away the Bible's extraordinary unity, harmony, accuracy and other characteristics we've discussed in this chapter. These poor souls can't help it. They cannot do otherwise. It's the Spirit who makes spiritual truth clear to us. It's the Spirit who opens our minds to understand. Apart from the Spirit, the Bible wouldn't speak so profoundly to any of us.

The Spirit teaches us many things. For example, Romans 8:16 points out, *The Spirit himself bears witness with our spirit that we are children of God.* Similarly, the Spirit testifies about the validity of the Bible. Earlier in this chapter we read answer 4 in the Westminster Larger Catechism. You recall that it says, "... but the Spirit of God bearing witness by and with the Scriptures in the heart of man, is alone able fully to persuade it that they are the very word of God."[90] God's Spirit convinces our hearts. He is the ultimate and irrefutable witness to the truth of Scripture.

I know this creates an unfair advantage. When we try to explain the truth of Scripture to a person who has not been taught by the Holy Spirit, it is like trying to demonstrate to a color-blind person that orange is a shade between yellow and red, or that green is a hue between yellow and blue. The person may be able to repeat your description and even grasp the general concept, but the reality that is so obvious to you and me is sadly beyond his or her reach. It's the same way with people who can't see the beauty of the Bible. We can never convince them. Of course, we can and should continue to share what we know. Who knows? You or I might just be the instrument the Holy Spirit uses to persuade someone. He used the first draft of this manuscript to change

---

[90] The Larger Catechism, Q 4 *Confessional Standards of ECO: A Covenant Order of Evangelical Presbyterians,* Westminster Shorter Catechism Q 4 https://www.eco-pres.org/static/media/uploads/eco_confessional_standards_digital_12.11.18.pdf p. 103 Last visited 3.1.2019

the mind of at least one person, and I pray that He uses this book to convince many more. Maybe even you, if you do not yet believe. Still, the Spirit is the One who opens minds.

The same Spirit who inspired the Scriptures, the same Spirit who carried the prophets as they spoke and wrote is the One who opens our minds to understand the Bible. So, when we read the Bible, whether to preach or teach or simply for our own spiritual growth, we need to rely on the Spirit to guide us. Some things will be difficult to understand and apply, but we can count on the Holy Spirit to give us wisdom beyond our own intelligence.

Here we encounter a bit of a tightrope and realize a need for balance. We could plunge into error on either side. In Chapter One I talked about the amazing arsenal of Bible study tools available today, and how foolish it would be to ignore the vast wealth of knowledge at our fingertips. I invited you to take advantage of these tools to study the Scriptures deeply, and I don't back away from that for a moment. However, the arsenal can be dangerous. We can rely so heavily on human-made instruments to interpret the Bible that we neglect the Holy Spirit who inspired the Bible. Educated preachers and Bible teachers are especially prone to this prideful free fall. Let's use the tools skillfully, but let's always prayerfully ask the Spirit to guide us. Then let's listen attentively to what He has to say about His Word.

Of course, we have to ask how we can be sure that what we've heard is actually from the Spirit of God. How can we *test the spirits to see whether they are from God* (I John 4:1)? I've heard some pretty fanciful interpretations of the Bible in my day. How can we be confident that we're hearing the Spirit rightly?

I enjoy the blessing of being associated with a group called Presbyterian Reformed Ministries International. More than any other organization I know, PRMI is committed to hearing and following the Holy Spirit. In order to maintain balance, this ministry has devised a four-step process of discernment that is extremely helpful. There are four questions, which can help us distinguish the Spirit's voice from any other, including our own. The questions are easily applicable when we sense the Spirit guiding our understanding of Scripture. Ask these questions about insights you believe the Spirit has given you from the Bible.

1. *Does it give glory to Jesus Christ in the present or the future?* Often our schemes and interpretations glorify ourselves or our causes, or they advance our agendas. The work of the Holy Spirit will always bring glory to Jesus. An insight that is more self-serving than Christ-glorifying probably came from our own psyches or some other source.

2. *Is it consistent with the intentions and character of God as revealed in Scripture?* In the next chapter we will see that a crucial rule of biblical interpretation is that Scripture interprets Scripture. The Holy Spirit is a consistent Author. What He tells us about this or that passage of Scripture will dovetail beautifully with what He teaches elsewhere in the Bible. If it doesn't, we can be sure the guidance was not from Him.

3. *Do other people who are born again and filled with the Holy Spirit have a confirming witness?* Check your insights with other believers in your church or circle of friends. In Bible study, this is where commentaries, sermons and other similar resources can be invaluable. Have other godly women and men discovered the same truth you've been shown? As we have seen in digging deeply into the meaning of particular verses, sometimes commentators and translators disagree on certain details. Nobody, it seems, gets everything right. However, if no one at all ratifies your insight, you might carefully question whether your wisdom was from the Spirit.

4. *Is there confirmation in objectively verifiable events or facts?*[91] We just discussed how experience confirms the Bible and the Bible confirms experience. Consider whether your insights on Scripture fit with reality as you experience it. Remain open to the possibility that God's Word will expand your perception of reality.

With these safeguards in place we reduce the risk of stumbling and plummeting into pure subjectivism by attributing to the Spirit supposed insights He never gave. With these safeguards in place we are free to open ourselves to the guidance of the Spirit when we come to His Word. When we do, we discover that the Holy Spirit's testimony is conclusive. He is the star witness to the truth of Scripture.

---

[91] See Brad Long, Paul Stokes, Cindy Strickler in *Growing the Church in the Power of the Holy Spirit* Zondervan © 2009 by Zeb Bradford Long, Paul Stokes, and Cindy Strickler pp, 177-183

A Priceless Treasure

Is the Bible just another book? Can we believe that nasty rumor? Not for a second. The Bible is a priceless treasure. Consider the words of Psalm 19:7-10:

> *The law of the LORD is perfect, refreshing the soul. The statutes of the LORD are trustworthy, making wise the simple. The precepts of the LORD are right, giving joy to the heart. The commands of the LORD are radiant, giving light to the eyes. The fear of the LORD is pure, enduring forever. The decrees of the LORD are firm, and all of them are righteous. They are more precious than gold, than much pure gold; they are sweeter than honey, than honey from the honeycomb* (NIV).

Does your soul ever need refreshing? Do you ever want more wisdom? Would your heart benefit from greater joy? Your eyes from clearer light? Do you want something more precious than money? You'll find it in the Bible.

Jesus said, *You search the Scriptures because you think that in them you have eternal life; and it is they that bear witness about me* (John 5:39). Do you want to get to know the most wonderful Person who ever lived? Do you want to deepen your relationship with perfect love incarnate? Do you want to know God in a more profound way? That's what the Bible is for. He's what the Bible is about.

I feel sorry for people who neglect the Bible. I pity the people who don't believe it, don't read it, and don't live it. The Bible is not just another book. It's a priceless treasure. It alone is

God-breathed. It's the inspired Word of God.

Chapter Six

Herman Who?

Humpty Dumpty

"'When I use a word,' Humpty Dumpty said in rather a scornful tone, 'it means just what I choose it to mean — neither more nor less.'

"'The question is,' said Alice, 'whether you can make words mean so many different things.'

"'The question is,' said Humpty Dumpty, 'which is to be master — that's all.'"[92]

---

[92] Lewis Carol *Through the Looking Glass* 1934 Chapter 6 p. 205

Some people, it seems, take the same attitude toward the Bible that the egg-man took to words in Lewis Carol's *Through the Looking Glass.* They make Scripture say all sorts of things. For example, in the mid-twentieth century, the very popular theologian (if there can be such a thing) Paul Tillich taught that Jesus did not physically rise from the dead. Rather the resurrection is the symbol that the New Being of which Christ was the bearer did not die with him.[93] In other words, it's as if the disciples were sitting around one night after the crucifixion, maybe polishing off the leftover Passover wine, and one of them said, "Hey guys, Jesus isn't really dead! We still have everything he taught us and all he gave us. It's just as if he rose from the grave." Thus the "symbol" of the resurrection was born.

More recently Marcus Borg, a prominent member in a group of Bible scholars known as the "Jesus Seminar" said something very similar. "Jesus Lives. By that I mean simply that his followers continue to experience him after his death."[94] The disciples had visions and non-visionary experiences of Christ's presence. We may do the same today, but when the New Testament was being written, according to Borg, Jesus' corpse was already rotting in his tomb.

You see, Tillich, Borg and many others know that dead people stay dead. People of this stripe, including many clergy, want to say the Bible is somehow true, but they can't admit anything as preposterous as the literal bodily

---

[93] See especially Paul Tillich, *Systematic Theology vol. II Existence and the Christ* © 1957 by the University of Chicago, pp. 159-161

[94] "The Resurrection Debate: Crossan and Borg vs. White and Renihan" https://www.youtube.com/watch?v=waiM136MeuU Last visited 3.1.2019

resurrection of Jesus (not to mention walking on water, feeding multitudes, healing the sick and all the other miracles). So, they try to invent a way to have their cake and eat it too. They try to interpret the Bible in a way that fits their truncated worldview.

In stark contrast, the Apostle Paul said:

> But if there is no resurrection of the dead, then not even Christ has been raised. And if Christ has not been raised, then our preaching is in vain and your faith is in vain. We are even found to be misrepresenting God, because we testified about God that he raised Christ, whom he did not raise if it is true that the dead are not raised. For if the dead are not raised, not even Christ has been raised. And if Christ has not been raised, your faith is futile and you are still in your sins. Then those also who have fallen asleep in Christ have perished. If in Christ we have hope in this life only, we are of all people most to be pitied. But in fact Christ has been raised from the dead, the firstfruits of those who have fallen asleep" (1 Corinthians 15:13-20).

A straightforward reading of this passage clearly teaches not only that Jesus really, physically rose from the dead, but that this fact is crucial to authentic faith. Yet there are some who say, in a rather scornful tone, "When I read the Bible, it means just what I choose it to mean – neither more nor less."

This phenomenon of trying to make the Bible say more or less than it actually says is nothing new. For centuries before the Protestant Reformation, the "allegorical method of interpretation" was very popular. In an allegory, different parts of a story, speech or piece of writing represent something else. The practice of reading Scripture allegorically supposedly allowed interpreters to find the deeper, spiritual meaning of a passage. As Luther, Calvin and other Reformers rightly recognized, the problem with the allegorical method is that there are no controls, no anchors. The scope of interpretation is as wide as the commentator's imagination. The Reformers insisted on reading the plain sense of Scripture because, by interpreting a Bible passage as an allegory, one can make any passage say nearly anything.

Let's look at an example. Remember Jesus' famous story of the Good Samaritan in Luke 10:25-37? In the early centuries of the Christian Era, many believers, from St. Irenaeus to St. Augustine and even St. Thomas Aquinas, interpreted the passage something like this. Seeing the story as an allegory, each element of the parable stands for something else. The traveler who is headed from Jerusalem to Jericho is Adam, humanity, "Everyman." He is you and I on our journey through life. As we travel, we are assaulted, stripped and robbed by the enemies of our soul like the world, the flesh, and the devil. We are left for dead in our sins. A priest and a Levite – representing the Old Testament religion apart from Christ, and perhaps paganism or Philosophy – pass by us but offer no real help. Finally, thank God, a Samaritan comes along. This rejected outcast represents none other than Jesus Christ. When He throws us on his donkey that demonstrates how Christ took our sins upon Himself. He carries us to a nearby inn – representing the Church. He commands that we be cared for there at His expense until He returns. The two coins He gives to ensure our welfare are the Sacraments of Baptism and the Lord's Supper. Or maybe they are the commands to love God and love our neighbor. Jesus will then make all things right when He comes back for us in glory.[95]

Each element of this interpretation is thrilling and true. Every interpretive detail presents a beautiful biblical aspect of God's work in salvation. There's only one problem. This doesn't seem to be what Jesus' parable was about. Unlike what we encountered with people like Tillich and Borg, this interpretation agrees with the overall teaching of Scripture, but like the modern views, this ancient interpretation says the passage means just what the interpreters choose it to mean, not what it actually says. When we read the passage in a straightforward manner we see that Jesus wasn't laying out the plan of salvation, He was answering one question, "Who is my neighbor" (Luke 10:29)? Jesus' answer is that the way to love our neighbors is to care for their needs.

It's tempting sometimes to make the Bible say more than it means or less than it means. We want to put words into God's mouth, as it were. People fall into that trap more than you might think. I bet you do it sometimes without even knowing it. I bet I do, too. When we take that misstep, however, the Bible becomes merely a reflection of our own ideas. It loses its power to teach, rebuke, correct and train us (2 Timothy 3:16). The question is, of course, whether you can make the Bible mean so many different things. The question is, which is to be master?

---

95 See Mariottini, Claude "Allegorizing the Parables" https://claudemariottini.com/2013/07/02/allegorizing-the-parables/ Last visited 3.1.2019

Times Change

Maybe you've heard the saying, "The Bible says it, I believe it, that settles it." I like that. I wish matters were that simple. The problem is, however, that there are verses that don't mean the same thing now that they meant when they were written, or verses that are hard to apply if we take them at face value. Take the tenth commandment, for example. Exodus 20:17 says, *You shall not covet your neighbor's house. You shall not covet your neighbor's wife, or his male or female servant, his ox or donkey, or anything that belongs to your neighbor* (NIV). Okay, be honest. When was the last time you coveted your neighbor's donkey? House? Maybe. Spouse or employee? Maybe. But ox or donkey? Probably not. Now, I know there are exceptions. I live with one. Our house is in a rural development. We pass a couple ranches every time we drive into town. In the pasture of one of those ranches, there among the cows, is the cutest donkey you'll ever see. My wife breaks the tenth commandment on a regular basis. Actually, she says she doesn't covet the donkey because, she insists, it's *her* donkey! You can pray with me for her. Most of us, however, rarely struggle with undue attachment to our neighbor's mule. So, does that part of the commandment not apply to us? Is God's Word irrelevant? So long as we don't hanker after our neighbor's donkey, is it okay to crave her Escalade? The Bible doesn't say anything about Cadillacs. See? Times change.

Let's try a more serious example. Several times, starting in Deuteronomy, the Bible says that God's people are to worship in the place of His choice. *But you shall seek the place that the LORD your God will choose out of all your tribes to put his name and make his habitation there. There you shall go, and there you shall bring your burnt offerings and your sacrifices, your tithes and the contribution that you present, your vow offerings, your freewill offerings, and the firstborn of your herd and of your flock* (Deuteronomy 12:5-6). That chosen place turns out to be Jerusalem, particularly the Temple Mount. For centuries the Jews worshipped there. A fascinating study would be to trace the history of worship on Mount Moriah, where Abraham prepared to offer Isaac (Genesis 22:2), where David bought the threshing floor from Ornan so he could offer costly sacrifice (1 Chronicles 21:18, 24), where Solomon built the temple (2 Chronicles 3:1) and where Hezekiah (2 Chronicles 30:1) and Josiah (2 Chronicles 35:18) invited all of Judah and Israel to come and worship. This is the same spot where the temple was rebuilt after the Babylonian Exile (Ezra 5:15, 6:14-15) and expanded by King Herod. This is the place where Jesus was dedicated (Luke 2:27), where He taught (Luke 2:46, Matthew 26:55, John 18:20 etc.), and healed (Matthew 21:14). It was the very ground that Jesus cleansed (John 2:13-17, Mark 11:15-17 etc.).

Today, however, Christians and Jews cannot worship there, except for one portion of the ruins of a wall. The temple was obliterated by Rome in 70 CE and today the Temple Mount is strictly controlled by Muslims. Furthermore, God's people now live on every continent and for many of us, Jerusalem is hard to reach. I've had the privilege to travel to Jerusalem twice so far and to worship and pray at the "western wall," but I'm sixty-four years old. I may not get to go again. Some people never get to go. Yet this is the place where God told

His people to worship. The Bible says it and I believe it, but what do we do now? See? Times change.

Another example. God told His people to worship Him with their "firstfruits." Exodus 23:19 says, *The best of the first fruits of your ground you shall bring into the house of the* LORD *your God.* Some version of this directive is repeated more than 15 times in the Old Testament. What are first fruits? They're just what they sound like. The first and finest portion of every crop was to be dedicated and given to the Lord. Wheat, wine, wool, olive oil, honey.[96] Not the leftovers, the first fruits of the crop belong to God. But here's the problem, I don't have any crops. Maybe you're a gardener so you have some first fruits to offer. Maybe you're a farmer, so you have lots of first fruits to give, but you're the exception in our society. Further, how are you going to give the first fruits? We've already seen how daunting it would be to deliver those offerings to the house of the Lord in Jerusalem. And if you bring turnips and tomatoes to your local church, what are they going to do with all those groceries? Maybe they can share some with the poor or the church staff, and that's good. But you can't pay the light bill in carrots. In an agricultural society like ancient Israel the giving of first fruits was a beautiful practice instituted by God, but in our modern culture, it's hard to apply. Again, the Bible says it and I believe it, but how do we pull that off? Times change.

Furthermore, we understand some things about the universe differently now from how the Bible writers understood them.

---

96 "Firstfruits" https://www.biblestudytools.com/lexicons/hebrew/nas/reshiyth. html Last visited 3.1.2019

David wondered, when he considered the heavens, the moon and the stars which God put in place, what are human beings that God should care for us (Psalm 8:3-4)? Solomon, his son, prayerfully proclaimed that heaven and the highest heavens could not contain God (2 Kings 8:27). Both were right, but neither David nor Solomon in all his wisdom had any idea of the overwhelming truth their prayers declared. It would have been impossible for them to grasp the immensity of the Universe. They did not have access even to Galileo's telescope. Today we have tools like the Hubble spacecraft, which hurtles through the final frontier sending home breathtaking photos that expand our meager comprehension of one tiny galactic corner of God's infinite Creation. What David and Solomon declared was true, and the Holy Spirit Who inspired them understood those words better than we do today. Still, the words meant exponentially more than those who spoke them could begin to understand. God said it and I believe it, but the more I understand it, the more it blows my mind. Those words mean even more now than when they were first written or prayed.

On a more mundane level, units of measurement have morphed over time. In Bible times people measured distance in cubits and reeds, not inches, feet or meters. They measured weight in shekels and minas, not grams, ounces or pounds. Liquids came in homers and baths. Dried goods were meted out in omers and kors. The first hour of the day was what we call 6 AM and the eleventh hour was our 5 PM. A talent was the monetary worth of a heavy load of silver or gold and a denarius was an average day's pay.[97] When we

---

[97] For a more complete table see https://biblehub.com/weights-and-measures/ Last visited 3.1.2019

read these measurements in the Bible, we often find them confusing, or we have no idea what they mean. This is especially true with money because value is so variable. As I said, a denarius was an average day's pay. Even in my life time the average wage a worker gets per day has varied greatly. When I was a young teen my dad made $200 per week. I remember because he said he couldn't afford to buy me a $300 Gretsch Country Gentleman guitar. I, of course, knew he could buy it in just two weeks and have $100 left over for groceries, mortgage and all the rest! I couldn't understand his priorities. By contrast, today a carpenter gets paid six or eight times my dad's hourly income, and a new Country Gentleman goes for about $3,000. If the value of a dollar has fluctuated that much in half a century, how can we express the worth of ancient monetary measures? It's tricky to express ancient measures, especially for money, by modern standards. Even on such a mundane plane, things change over time.

Herman Who?

How, then, can we relate things that were written in very different cultures to our situation? What value can ancient biblical texts offer us today? That question points to another nasty rumor about the Bible. People say the Bible was written so long ago, in cultures so different from ours, that it can't possibly say anything meaningful to us today.

If you haven't already met, allow me to introduce you to hermeneutics. Sounds like the name of somebody's cousin, doesn't it? But hermeneutics isn't a who, it's a what.

Hermeneutics is the art and science people use to understand what is said in one context and apply it appropriately to another context. The name comes from the Greek word *hermeneuo* (ἑρμηνεύω) which means to translate or interpret. We find a derivative of this word in the story where the risen Jesus explains the meaning of the Scriptures to two of His disciples. *And beginning with Moses and all the Prophets, he interpreted* (διερμηνεύω) *to them in all the Scriptures the things concerning himself* (Luke 24:27). Jesus applied the ancient writings of the Old Testament to the new, post-resurrection context in which His disciples suddenly lived. He did hermeneutics. While this discipline can be used with any piece of literature or unit of meaning, it most commonly pertains to study of the Bible. How do we appropriately apply the teachings of the Bible to our context? Let me emphasize that "appropriately" is an important word in this question. Hermeneutics is not a way for us to make the Bible say things the Spirit never intended when He inspired the Scriptures. We want to discern what the Spirit really said and how it applies to us. To do this, we need some hermeneutical tools. Without the use of good hermeneutical tools, we can, following the example of Humpty Dumpty, make any passage of Scripture mean just what we choose it to mean – neither more nor less. When that happens, the passage means nothing at all. By the way, that's another nasty rumor. Since people often twist the Scriptures to serve their own purposes, skeptics allege that the Bible has nothing to teach us. How can we trust the Bible when we see people make it a mere reflection of their private prejudices? Hermeneutics helps us steer clear of that trap.

Three Questions

Three hermeneutical questions will guide us in interpreting a passage. What does the passage say? What did the passage mean to its original target audience? What does the passage mean to us today? The third question is really the hermeneutical question, but if we don't answer the first two, we set ourselves up to have a great fall.

(1) What Does It Say?

What does the passage say? It's amazing how often people can hear or read a message, think they know what it says, and entirely miss the point. That happened to me recently. My family met at my favorite restaurant[98] to celebrate my birthday. It's a rustic seafood place on the inner coastal water-way. No fancy dishes, just delicious fish, crab, shrimp and so on. Tragically, the jalapeño cheese grits are off my diet. Still, it's a great place to celebrate. My daughter and son-in-law, Jessi and Luis, were expecting their first child, our first grandbaby. (I'll spare you the details on how adorable little Liliana turned out to be.) It was a delightful gathering, even before the "big moment," which I ruined. What big moment? Just before we ordered supper, my son and daughter-in-law gave me a very touching birthday card. In it my son wrote,

> "Dear Dad, Happy birthday. We are so blessed to have a father like you in our lives. A father who is

---

[98] Our Deck Down Under in Daytona Beach Shores. If you go, tell them Rod sent you!
https://www.ourdeckdu.com Last visited 3.1.2019

spiritually wise, loves courageously and teaches generously. You have always been a great role model for us all and we know you'll be a great Papa to Liliana ... *and* the newest addition to our family.

Love Mike, Sarah, Baron, Skye [our grandpuppies] *and Baby Pinder.*" (Italics added.)

Wasn't that nice? But I didn't catch the full significance of what the card said. Somehow, I failed to read the most important words, the ones I italicized. I was moved by Mike's beautiful tribute. (The boy can write.) I was also a little distracted by the server coming at that moment to ask what we wanted to eat. But all excuses aside, I didn't get the main point he was trying to make. The card said that Mike and Sarah are expecting a baby, too! Alas, I was oblivious to announcement. To my children's disappointment, I calmly passed the card on to my wife, who obviously has better reading comprehension skills than I do. As she read it she exclaimed, "What? Really?" The next thing I knew she was out of her chair, hugging Mike and Sarah. I was sitting there saying, "What did I miss? What did I miss?" My children had announced that our second grand daughter, Arebella, was already in the oven. (She is as lovable as Lil, and this book is dedicated to the two of them, with the prayer that their generation will know and love God's Word.) But I missed the grand announcement. Now mind you, I have two advanced degrees in interpreting texts. I do it for a living. But I missed the message of Mike and Sarah's text by about a galaxy. By ignoring four little words, by assuming I already knew what the text said, I let the good news sneak right past me, in plain sight.

We can make the same mistake with the Bible. When you read a passage, read it carefully and ask yourself, "What does this passage say?" Try to set aside your doctrinal presuppositions, your philosophical prejudices, your societal constructs. Forget what your pastor said it means, what your Sunday School teacher said it means, what your professor said it means, what you hope it means, what you're afraid it might mean. Just read the passage. What does it say?

(2) What Did It Mean?

Next, we ask what the passage meant to its original target audience. In one sense, when we're reading the Bible, we're reading someone else's mail. Paul didn't write the book of Titus to you or me. He wrote it to Titus. Isaiah was prophesying directly to the people of Jerusalem in the eighth century BCE. You and I weren't even born. Therefore, before we ask what a passage means to us we need to try to understand what it meant to the people who first read and heard it. Let's look at some examples.

Jesus tells about a man who went away and entrusted his property to his servants, and He says, *To one he gave five talents, to another two, to another one, to each according to his ability* (Matthew 25:15). That doesn't mean that the first servant received the ability to play the saxophone, write poetry, paint portraits, build houses and dance ballet while the second servant could only strum the guitar and sing. A talent, you remember, was a measure of money. The original audience would have known that and, to them, the parable would have been about what the servants did with someone else's money.

Again, when Jesus told that story about the poor man who was assaulted on his way from Jerusalem to Jericho (Luke 10:25-37), His original hearers would have been familiar with that treacherous road. They would have also understood the historical background of Samaritans and why the Jews demeaned them as an inferior race. Jesus' original hearers would have been scandalized that a Samaritan, of all people, followed God's law to love one's neighbor while the revered priest and Levite were disobedient. They would have felt the shocking impact of that story in ways that later interpreters missed. We understand a passage better when we can grasp what it meant to the original target audience. This is the step of interpretation where Bible commentaries and historical notes in various study Bibles are most helpful.

(3) What Does It Mean?

Once we've got a grip on what the passage says and what it meant back then, we aren't finished by a long stretch. In fact, now the good part begins. You see, the original target audience isn't the *only* target audience. The Bible was written not just for them, but for you and me, too. When we read the Bible, we may be reading someone else's mail, but that correspondence has been openly published for our benefit, for our direction and growth. Romans 15:4 says, *For whatever was written in former days was written for our instruction, that through endurance and through the encouragement of the Scriptures we might have hope.* Paul may have written privately to Titus, Isaiah might have preached particularly to the people of Jerusalem, but in their words, in all the words of Scripture, the Holy Spirit also speaks personally to you and me.

So, now we have to ask what the passage means to us today. What it means today may be different in some ways from what it meant originally, as we will soon see. Nevertheless, what a passage means today will always be consistent with what the passage actually says and what it meant to the original target audience. These are twin anchors for our modern understanding. These are the two legs on which our hermeneutic stands upright.

Now that we've got the big picture of the hermeneutical process, let's go back and fill in a few helpful details. Ponderous tomes have been written on this subject and we won't be able to address every issue, but a few simple guidelines will help us as we read the Bible and apply it to our lives today.

Plain Sense

Some well-intentioned people say we should always interpret the Bible literally. I do not think that word means what they think it means. I understand their intention, and I appreciate their passion for Scriptural truth, but a strictly literal approach to Scripture raises some real problems. Consider, for example, Psalm 91:4. It says, *He will cover you with his feathers, and under his wings you will find refuge; his faithfulness will be your shield and rampart* (NIV). That verse talks about God's feathers and wings, but does the psalmist *mean* that God has plumage and wings in a literal sense, like some sort of cosmic chicken? Further, is His faithfulness literally a shield? If so, is it round or rectangular? Wooden? Bronze? How big? When we try to interpret that verse literally, we run into problems. Worse, we miss the powerful point it is making about God's protection of His people.

In Matthew 5:29-30 Jesus famously commanded, *"If your right eye causes you to sin, tear it out and throw it away. For it is better that you lose one of your members than that your whole body be thrown into hell. And if your right hand causes you to sin, cut it off and throw it away. For it is better that you lose one of your members than that your whole body go into hell"*. Do you suppose the Master really wants every person who ever looks lustfully at someone else to perform a self-eyeball-ectomy? Should everyone whose hand touches or gestures something it shouldn't make herself an amputee? Again, a strictly literal approach leads to problems.

Now look at John 10. Drawing on a rich image from the Old Testament, Jesus speaks of Himself as the Good Shepherd. But what is His point? Does He want to teach us that, in addition to working as a carpenter and a teacher, He is also literally a keeper of rams, lambs and ewes? And if He is literally a shepherd, are we literally four-legged, wooly mammals? Bah! Humbug. Further, how can He literally be both a Shepherd and a Lamb, which He is called dozens of times (John 1:29, Revelation 5, 6, 7 etc.)? As a matter of fact, John 10:6 makes it perfectly clear how we should read this passage. *This figure of speech Jesus used with them, but they did not understand what he was saying to them.* Jesus was using a figure of speech. Precisely, it was a metaphor. We would be silly to interpret a figure of speech literally. We would be going against the Teacher's true intentions if we read that passage as anything other than a figure of speech.

Of course, some things in the Bible are meant to be taken literally. John 3:16 really means that *God so loved the world, that he gave his only Son, that whoever believes in him should not perish but have eternal life.* And if you, dear reader, have never put your trust in God's Son, I encourage you to set aside the study of hermeneutics for a moment and simply place your trust in Him. Trust Him for everything, in every aspect of your life, now and forever. There's no metaphor here. It's literally true.

In other places, however, there are figures of speech, poetry, parables, metaphors and other literary forms. Each passage needs to be read and understood as the kind of literature, the kind of speech-form it is. Suppose I were to say to you, "A priest, a rabbi and a minister walked into a bar ..." You would not ask whether the priest was a Jesuit or a Franciscan, whether the rabbi was Orthodox or Reform, or whether the minister was a Presbyterian or a Baptist – and if he was a Baptist, what was he doing in a bar anyway? No, you'd recognize that I was starting to tell a joke, and you would interpret what I said accordingly. It's the same way with the Bible. Some things are presented literally and should be interpreted literally. Other things are figures of speech (poems, parables, allegories, metaphors). They should be interpreted figuratively.

So, when we read the parable of the Good Samaritan, which we've already visited twice in this chapter (Luke 10:25-37), we will miss the point if we get caught up in literal details such as whether the traveler had a wife and children, what time of day or season of year it was when he made his journey, where was the inn? The story would lose its punch. The point about loving our neighbor would be blunted. Let the parable be a parable.

This perspective is called reading the "plain sense" of Scripture. It's what I've had in mind when I've talked about reading the Bible "in a straightforward manner." Read an imperative as an imperative. *Let no corrupting talk come out of your mouths, but only such as is good for building up, as fits the occasion, that it may give grace to those who hear* (Ephesians 4:29). That verse says, meant, and means that we should guard our words and use them for good. *Flee sexual immorality* (1 Corinthians 6:18) says, meant, and means that we should get as far as we can from sensual sin. However, we should read a metaphor as a metaphor. Psalm 23:1 uses a familiar metaphor when it says, *The LORD is my shepherd ...* That meant and means that the Lord guides, provides and cares for us. Read a parable like a parable. Read an allegory like an allegory. Read hyperbole as hyperbole and so on.

Reluctantly, we have to admit that this approach can leave some ambiguities. We might not always be certain what the plain sense of a passage is. Is the particular passage you're studying literal or figurative? There may be disagreement. Some, for example, will insist that the Creation story in Genesis 1 is poetic, so we shouldn't believe the whole Universe came about in six literal days. Others will take the repeated phrase, *and there was evening and there was morning* (Genesis 1:5, 8, 13, 19, 23, 31) to mean that each day was a twenty-four-hour period. In that case all that exists was fashioned in 144 hours. On the one hand, therefore, reading the plain sense of Scripture doesn't solve every problem or answer every question because readers may dispute what the plain sense is. Other principles will help guide us closer to appropriate interpretation. On the other hand, we've seen the ridiculous conclusions we'd be forced to draw if we interpreted the Bible literally in every passage. What we really want to discern is the plain sense of the passage.

Some outrageous and silly alternative methods of reading Scripture have been proposed. In 1997 Michael Drosnin came out with a bestselling book, *The Bible Code*.[99] Using a scheme called "Equidistant Letter Sequences" the Bible Code methodology picks every tenth letter of the Hebrew text of the Old Testament (or every fifth letter, or seventh letter or the letters on a diagonal line when a page is arranged in a certain way etc.) and discovers hidden messages in the text. That's a pretty fanciful way of reading the Bible. I promise you'll get a lot more out of the Bible by interpreting the plain sense of Scripture.

It's the Principle of the Thing

In addition to reading the plain sense of Scripture, it's important to discern the principle that's being taught in a passage. The principle being taught can be more important than the specifics that are mentioned. Again, perhaps not

---

[99] See Thomas, Dave "Hidden Messages and the Bible Code" https://www.csicop.org/si/show/hidden_messages_and_the_bible_code
Last visited 3.1.2019

many of us will be tempted to covet our neighbor's donkey, but the principle against coveting is what the commandment really teaches. That principle applies to cars and guitars and jobs and salaries and all kinds of other attractive baubles. The verse isn't just about donkeys. It's the principle of the thing that counts.

The Bible itself uses this hermeneutical method. Deuteronomy 25:4 says, *You shall not muzzle an ox when it is treading out the grain.* In its original context the verse meant exactly what it says. Literally. Farmers should let oxen graze as they thresh corn, wheat and similar crops by walking over the stalks. Not even animals should be expected to work for free. However, the apostle Paul applies that verse to his current and very different situation in 1 Corinthians 9:9. *For it is written in the Law of Moses, "You shall not muzzle an ox when it treads out the grain." Is it for oxen that God is concerned?* He quotes it again in 1 Timothy 5:18. *For the Scripture says, "You shall not muzzle an ox when it treads out the grain," and, "The laborer deserves his wages."* Now for the record, I do believe that God is concerned about oxen as He is for all creatures great and small. Nevertheless, the contexts of these two verses make it clear that Paul's hermeneutic in these passages is to take the principle taught about oxen in Deuteronomy and apply it to preachers. Paul uses the principle taught in Deuteronomy 25:4 to show that it's right for preachers to be compensated for their work. We could extend that insight to secretaries, janitors, musicians, educators, writers and other workers. Paul applies the verse from Deuteronomy to fortify the maxims he states in 1 Corinthians 9:14, *In the same way, the Lord commanded that those who proclaim the gospel should get their living by the gospel* and Galatians 6:6, *Let the one who is taught the word share all good things with the one who teaches.* Now, I am not opposed to volunteer ministry. Neither was Paul. The point, however, is that while the plain sense of Deuteronomy 25:4 pertains literally to farmers who thresh with oxen, the principle applies to everyone who employs people to work. Particularly, Paul applies it to churches. Having served nearly four decades as a pastor, I greatly appreciate the apostle's point, even if the preacher/ox comparison he chose is less than flattering! In any event, it's the principle of the thing that counts.

Another example. In His most famous sermon, Jesus said, *"But when you fast, anoint your head and wash your face, that your fasting may not be seen by others but by your Father who is in secret. And your Father who sees in secret will reward you"* (Matthew 6:17-18). In passing, notice that Jesus said *when you fast*, not if you fast. Fasting is a sorely neglected aspect of prayer and an underused weapon of spiritual warfare. For our purposes, we need to recognize that Jesus is talking about literal fasting, that is, occasionally abstaining from food for a period of time. He assumes that his followers will practice fasting from time to time. In that regard the plain sense of the passage is the literal sense. It should be applied literally. But what about this business of anointing one's head and washing one's face?

When I was a kid it was common for men to put oil on their heads. They did this in order to style their hair and keep every strand in place. I can still smell the scent of good ol' Vitalis. It felt like baby oil when you rubbed it on your hands to apply to your scalp. If a guy wanted to wear his hair in a "duck tail" in the back or split the front with a "spit curl" (and who didn't?), Vitalis was the way to go. If your hair was shorter, Butch Wax was the grooming goop for you. For a slightly more natural but still slick look, a little dab of Brylcreem would do ya. Then times changed. A few years later, men and boys would use hair spray or styling mousse for the popular "dry look." By that time, guys who still used oily products were known as "greasers." Nowadays I really don't know what kinds of hair products men use. For me "bad hair day" has become a contradiction in terms. An oxymoron. At sixty-four years of age, as I remember my hair days, they were all good.

But let's get back to hermeneutics. When Jesus told people to anoint their heads and wash their faces when they fasted, His point was that they should not allow themselves to look shabby in order to call attention to the fact that they were fasting. In 1950's America, His words would have applied literally. If you see the Fonz without grease in his hair, you know something's wrong. In 2019, however, this conversation could take place:

> Mary: Hi John. I notice your hair is slick and oily this morning, though it's usually dry and natural. What's up?
>
> John: Oh, I'm fasting today, and Jesus said we should anoint our heads when we fast. So, I want everyone to know that I'm doing exactly what Jesus told us to do, because I am a paragon of piety.

In fact, John would be doing exactly the opposite of what Jesus told us to do. The Lord's point was not about Butch Wax or Brylcreem, His point was that we should not draw attention to ourselves when we fast. If I were to anoint my hairless pate when I fast, I would glisten like a golden globe. Even astronauts on the space station would know I was up to something unusual. Jesus meant that we shouldn't publicize our piety. If we apply what He said literally in this case, we could be doing the exact opposite of what He intended. It's the principle that counts.

Now we can go back to firstfuits. Most of us can't give literal firstfruits to God because we don't grow our own food, but we can still dedicate to God the first and best of what we produce. We can give to God "off the top" so to speak. Even if we can't follow the exact words of Scripture, we can still apply the principle.

Similarly, we saw that when Jesus told the parable of the talents He was talking about money. We are right to apply that parable literally and invest our material possessions in advancing God's kingdom. But when we apply the principle as well as the literal meaning, we see that it is very appropriate for us to use our abilities to play the saxophone, write poetry, paint portraits, build houses, dance ballet, play guitar, sing and any other skills we may have to the glory of God. Those talents are also entrusted to us by God.

By the same token, while I've never met anyone who has popped out an eye or hacked off a hand to prevent lust or inappropriate behavior, no matter how much they insist on interpreting the Bible literally, that doesn't mean Jesus' words don't apply to us at all. Self-mutilation would miss the Master's point. Chances are it wouldn't solve the problem anyway. Once you've gouged out your right eye, the other would soon have to follow. Even then, the lust problem would likely remain. Principally, Jesus was telling us how dreadfully dangerous lust is and urging us to stay away from it at all costs. The principle still applies.

I've never said "Raca" to my brother or sister (Matthew 6:22 NIV and several translations), but I understand that the Lord doesn't want us to insult other people. I've never met a Samaritan, but I grasp the truth that the One who, with His blood, ransomed people from every tribe, language, people and nation (see Revelation 5:9) doesn't want us to look down on people who are racially different from ourselves. He wants us to love them as He does. It's the principle of the thing that counts.

In 2 Chronicles 29:5 Hezekiah calls the people to sanctify themselves, then take out all the rubbish from the holy place in the temple. This is a good word for our lives. The literal Temple is not standing right now, but we can apply the principle. The holy place of your life and mine gets gunked up from time to time. The spiritual space where we experience intimacy with God often gets filled with clutter. We need to clean it out with repentance, confession, rededication, and drawing near to God. Hezekiah was talking about the actual temple in Jerusalem, but the principle applies to our lives. Your body is a temple. So is mine (1 Corinthians 6:18-19). (It's okay if you need to set this book aside for a moment and do some temple cleansing right now. We'll be here when you get back.)

Sometimes when we apply the Bible to our present-day situation, we have to look beyond the historical prescription to the eternal principle. When we do, we find that God's

Word is as alive today as it ever was. You and I can hear the Lord speaking to us just as He spoke to people long ago.

Scripture Interprets Scripture

One September evening I decided to indulge my family with bacon-wrapped scallops. I had tasted this delicacy at a restaurant and wanted to make it at home. We don't usually cook aromatic seafood inside the house, so I figured I'd prepare my culinary delight on the grill. Though I had never made this entree before, I gave it an intrepid try. The first step was to parboil the bacon so it would be partially pre-cooked and easy to wrap around the scallops. I wrapped. I skewered. I seasoned. My mouth watered at the thought of what was coming. When I put the meat on the grill, however, the bacon started dripping grease. Suddenly the whole grill erupted in flames. I feared for the safety of my house. I feared for the safety of my eyebrows. "Pat, help!" I shouted. My wife came running with water. We doused the fire. We were safe. And the scallops? Char-broiled to perfection! Now I know the secret of preparing that delicious dish. It includes a three-alarm fire. Next time I'll keep the water bottle close by.

Why am I telling you about bacon-wrapped scallops in a book about the Bible? Maybe you remember that the Bible forbids the eating of pork (Leviticus 11:7, Deuteronomy 14:8). It also prohibits eating shellfish (Leviticus 11:10-11, Deuteronomy 14:10). So, if I think it's important to follow the teachings of the Bible, and you know I do, why do I think it's okay to eat bacon wrapped scallops?

This leads us to our third hermeneutical guideline. Scripture interprets Scripture. The Westminster Confession of Faith puts it this way:

> "The infallible rule of interpretation of Scripture is the Scripture itself: and therefore, when there is a question about the true and full sense of any Scripture (which is not manifold, but one), it must be searched and known by other places that speak more clearly."[100]

In other words, we need to listen to the whole symphony of Scripture, not just a few select sound-bites. Just as we saw in Chapter Five, ideas that at first seem to clash in ear-stabbing dissonance can create lush harmony when played in the context of a full chord. Similarly, each note of Scripture must be considered in the total harmony of the whole score. The entire opus defines the meaning of each bar. In the same way, the entirety of the Bible defines the meaning of each passage.

In Mark 7:18-19 we find Jesus saying, *"Then are you also without understanding? Do you not see that whatever goes into a person from outside cannot defile him, since it enters not his heart but his stomach, and is expelled?" (Thus he declared all foods clean.)* In that parenthetical aside, we're told that Jesus reinterpreted the Old Testament laws about clean or "kosher" food. This interpretation was reinforced years later when the apostle Peter had a vision of a banquet of non-kosher foods being lowered on a sheet. He was told to

---

[100] Westminster Confession of Faith Ch. 1 sec.IX. https://www.eco-pres.org/static/media/uploads/eco_confessional_standards_digit al_12.11.18.pdf p. 53 Last visited 3.1.2019

eat it, but the apostle refused because he had always obeyed the Old Testament dietary restrictions. However, a voice from heaven answered him, *"Do not call anything impure that God has made clean"* (Acts 10:15, 11:9). This happened three times. If you're familiar with that story you know that the main message of the vision was about racial prejudice more than it was about eating habits, but the point was made through declaring pork, shellfish and other forbidden foods to be acceptable. Bacon-wrapped scallops are now on the menu. Yum! If I had read only Leviticus and Deuteronomy, I would have had to grill snapper or trout, or disobey Scripture. However, when we let Scripture interpret Scripture we get a fuller picture. Remember that Jesus is the fulfilment of the Old Testament promises. So, if He declares all foods clean, all foods are clean. Scripture interprets Scripture.

Similarly, remember the problems we encountered when we saw that Deuteronomy 12:5-6 said God's people should only worship at the Temple in Jerusalem? Sadly, most of us cannot worship there regularly. When we let Scripture interpret Scripture, however, we discover a beautiful way out of that impasse. In the fourth chapter of John we find Jesus having a controversial conversation with a Samaritan woman. In what seems like an attempt to avoid dealing with deeper spiritual issues, the woman tries to start a theological debate. (People often use theology as subterfuge to distract from spiritual matters.) She points out that Samaritans say God should be worshipped on Mount Gerizim while Jews insist that He is to be worshipped in Jerusalem. As He often does so amazingly well, Jesus cuts through the theological malarkey and says," *"Woman, believe me, the hour is coming when neither on this mountain nor in Jerusalem will you worship the Father. ... But the hour is coming, and is now here, when the true worshipers will worship the Father in spirit and truth, for the Father is seeking such people to worship him. God is spirit, and those who worship him must worship in spirit and truth"* (John 4:21, 23-24). Now, Jesus says, the issue is not where we worship but how we worship. I may never get to Jerusalem again. Some of us may never visit there at all. It doesn't matter. The right way to worship God now is to worship Him in Spirit and in truth. We can do that anywhere. You can do that right where you are. In fact, I hope you are doing it now. We come to understand that freeing truth when we let Scripture interpret Scripture.

This guideline does not mean that the New Testament renders everything in the Old Testament null and void. Many times, in fact the New Testament reiterates what is said in the Old. Nor is this just a comparison between the Old Testament and the New. Rather, when any part of Scripture speaks more clearly than another, the clearer teaching interprets the obscure one. Likewise, when one passage presents the fulfillment of an earlier teaching, the later passage takes precedence. We no longer expect the Messiah to be born in Bethlehem (Micah 5:2) or to come and suffer for our sins (Isaiah 53). Those promises have been fulfilled in Jesus. In the same way, things like the dietary laws and the mandate to worship in Jerusalem foreshadowed the uniqueness and holiness of Christ. Now that Jesus has come and filled out those shadows, those particular requirements have lost their substance. Their purpose was to point us to Christ. As Galatians 3:24 says, *the Law has become our tutor to lead us to Christ* (NASB). There are places where the Bible gives the authoritative interpretation of other passages of Scripture. This is especially true in the teachings of Jesus. Scripture interprets Scripture.

The Rule of Love

In 1562 Pastor Heinrich Bullinger wrote a comprehensive document to help the churches of Switzerland express their faith in that era. That document is called *The Second Helvetic Confession*. In it, Bullinger says:

> "But we hold that the interpretation of the Scripture to be orthodox and genuine which is gleaned from the Scriptures themselves (from the nature of the language in which they were written, likewise according to the circumstances in which they were set down, and expounded in the light of like and unlike passages and of many and clearer passages) and which agree with the rule of faith and love, and contributes much to the glory of God and man's salvation."[101]

This statement lines up nicely with our guidelines about reading the plain sense of a passage and letting Scripture interpret Scripture, but here Pastor Bullinger introduces some guidelines that are too often overlooked: the rule of faith, the rule of love and the glory of God. The rule of faith

---

[101] "The Second Helvetic Confession: Chapter II, Of the Interpreting the Holy Scripture." https://www.ccel.org/creeds/helvetic.htm Last visited 3.1.2019

essentially means that our understanding of a passage of Scripture should be biblically orthodox. It should correspond with the message of Scripture as the people of God have understood it through the centuries. If our interpretation falls far outside the lines of biblical orthodoxy, it violates the rule of faith. Similarly, any interpretation that does not contribute to the glory of God and the salvation of people is contrary to the message and purpose of the Bible. That interpretation can be dismissed. The guideline I'd really like to lift up, however, is the rule of love.

We find this important hermeneutical principle at least a millennium before Bullinger. In *On Christian Teaching,* St. Augustine said, "So anyone who thinks that he has understood the divine scriptures or any part of them, but cannot by his understanding build up this double love of God and neighbor, has not yet succeeded in understanding them."[102] The Bible is about love, and if we don't grasp love, we don't understand the Bible.

In Chapter Nine we will explore how the message of the entire Bible is summed up by 1 John 4:19, *We love because* [God] *first loved us.* The Bible is the love story of God and people. That love story reaches its climax in Jesus Christ, the main character of Scripture. Jesus said that the commandments to love God with all one's being and to love one's neighbor as oneself encapsulate the Law and the prophets (Matthew 22:37-40). That is, the whole Old Testament culminates in those commandments. They are

---

[102] Augustine, *On Christian Teaching,* Translation and editorial material © R. P. H. Green 1997, Oxford University Press Inc. New York, Book One XXXVI, p. 27

also foundational to the New Testament. Even more relevant, God is love (I John 4:8, 16). So, any valid interpretation of God's Word must be consistent with the loving nature of God.

This guideline makes us ask the question, what is love? Too often people confuse love with things like pleasantness, permissiveness, amicability. If you love someone, people think that means you encourage your loved one to pursue his goals and desires. If you love someone, you try never to cause her pain or even discomfort. If we apply that understanding of love to the biblical hermeneutics, the rule of love means we have to reject any interpretation of Scripture that makes people feel uncomfortable or restricts them from being, doing or having whatever they want. Any decent parent immediately recognizes that definition of love to be too shallow and cheap. We make our children eat veggies, take baths, go to bed, do chores and homework and all sorts of things they don't want to do, and we do these things precisely because we love them. My wife loves me, so she discourages me from eating candy and carrot cake and other evil goodies because those foods would exacerbate my diabetes.

One of the greatest thinkers ever was St. Thomas Aquinas. He once said, "Further, to love a man is to wish him good things ... Now, to all our neighbors we wish an equal good, viz. everlasting life."[103] We could paraphrase that to say that

---

[103] Aquinas, Thomas *Summa Theologica* II II 26 http://www.scottmsullivan.com/AquinasWorks/summa/SS/SS026.html#SSQ26OUTP1 Last visited 3.1.2019 (I understand that this

to love someone is to desire that person's greatest good. To love someone is to want what is best for that person. Sometimes that means indulgence but sometimes it means restriction. Sometimes such love is pleasant and other times it can be hard. Always, however, love aims for the highest benefit of the person we love. That's how God loves us. He always seeks our highest good, especially eternal life.[104] As someone has said, God loves us the way we are, and He loves us too much to leave us that way.

This understanding of love fits with what 2 Timothy 3:16-17 tells us about how Scripture functions in the life of the believer. You remember, *All Scripture is breathed out by God and profitable for teaching, for reproof, for correction, and for training in righteousness, that the man of God may be complete, equipped for every good work.* God's Word teaches us, rebukes us, corrects us and trains us in righteousness precisely because God desires our greatest good. He loves us. Sometimes that teaching, rebuking, correcting, and training can be unpleasant or downright excruciating. As Hebrews 12:11 says, *For the moment all discipline seems painful rather than pleasant, but later it yields the peaceful fruit of righteousness to those who have been trained by it.* The word translated "discipline" is *paideia* (παιδεία). It's a word that pertains to raising children. The same word is translated "training" in 2 Timothy 3:16. It could be rendered "correction" (see CEV) or

---

is listed in one of Thomas' "objections," but he ends up affirming it in his reply.)

[104] For more on the nature of love, see my video "Fish Love?" at https://www.youtube.com/watch?v=Z6VTfusDUkk&feature=yout u.be

"chastening" (KJV). However you translate it, the result of that discipline, that training, is good fruit. Discipline, *paideia,* is for the benefit and blessing of the person being trained. And what is the motive of this training? Hebrews 12:6 tells us. *For the Lord disciplines the one he loves, and chastises every son whom he receives.* The risen, glorified Jesus makes the same point when He says, *"Those whom I love, I reprove and discipline, so be zealous and repent"* (Revelation 3:19). Any valid interpretation of Scripture will help people grow toward their highest good, whether that growth is immediately enjoyable or not. The rule of love guides us to that interpretation of Scripture which contributes to the greatest good of God's people. The rule of love is the guideline that helps us be sure that our understanding of Scripture is consistent with the loving purpose of God's Word.

Three Controversial Examples

So, we have these hermeneutical guidelines or parameters for applying the Bible's teaching to our current situation.

> ➤ We ask what the passage says, meant, and means.
> ➤ We read the plain sense of Scripture.
> ➤ We look for overriding principles that endure through changing times.
> ➤ We let Scripture interpret Scripture.
> ➤ We make sure our interpretations follow the rule of love.

Now let's apply those guidelines to three topics that have been controversial in the life of the Church. Two of them are still being debated though one is pretty much settled in our culture. What does the Bible say about slavery, the place of women, and human sexuality? How can these guidelines we've studied help us rightly apply Scripture's teachings to our lives?

(1) Let My People Go (Slavery)

Robert Lewis Dabney taught at my alma mater, Union Theological Seminary in Virginia (now Union Presbyterian Seminary), though more than a century before I arrived. He was a brilliant, sincere and godly man who, in the pre-Civil War South, argued from the Bible that slavery was God's will. It's easy to see where he got that idea. Ephesians 6:5-9 says:

> *Slaves, obey your earthly masters with respect and fear, and with sincerity of heart, just as you would obey Christ. Obey them not only to win their favor when their eye is on you, but as slaves of Christ, doing the will of God from your heart. Serve wholeheartedly, as if you were serving the Lord, not people, because you know that the Lord will reward each one for whatever good they do, whether they are slave or free. And masters, treat your slaves in the same way. Do not threaten them, since you know that he who is both their Master and yours is in heaven, and there is no favoritism with him (NIV).*

Similarly, Colossians 3:22 says, *Slaves, obey your earthly masters in everything; and do it, not only when their eye is on you and to curry their favor, but with sincerity of heart and reverence for the Lord* (NIV). How could slaves obey their masters or masters treat their slaves well if slavery were abolished? Dr. Dabney, and many people like him, read and applied the plain sense of Scripture. They understood what these passages said. They thought they knew what they meant to Paul's target audience, and they assumed that the verses meant the same thing to 19th Century America.

However, when we let Scripture interpret Scripture we find a different strand from the one Dabney emphasized. Paul's letter to Philemon was written to encourage Philemon to forgive Onesimus, Philemon's slave. Onesimus had run away to help Paul while the apostle was in prison. Even more, Paul tries to persuade Philemon not just to forgive his slave, but to set Onesimus free. Paul urged Philemon to receive Onesimus as a brother instead of a slave (Philemon 16). By the same token 1 Corinthians 7:21 says to slaves, *Were you a slave when you were called? Don't let it trouble you— although if you can gain your freedom, do so* (NIV).

Slavery was a social reality in the first century. The Bible acknowledges that, but the Bible does not sanction slavery. In fact, standing against that cultural reality, the Bible calls masters to free their slaves and encourages slaves to get their freedom if they can. The Bible never says that slavery is good. In fact, Galatians 3:28 shows us that God's Kingdom soars above slavery when it declares, *There is neither Jew nor Greek, there is neither slave nor free, there is no male and female, for you are all one in Christ Jesus.*

The Bible doesn't endorse slavery, though it recognizes it as part of the flawed cultural landscape of the time. Paul was speaking to a particular historical situation when he said, *Slaves, obey your earthly masters in everything.* Slavery is not good, but if you have to be a slave, be a good one. You and I, however, are not slaves. We don't own slaves. We live in a cultural situation where slavery is illegal. So those words don't apply directly to us any more than the commandment against coveting your neighbor's donkey. Less. But that doesn't render this passage meaningless to you and me. Read the whole paragraph in Colossians that talks about slaves.

> *Slaves, obey your earthly masters in everything; and do it, not only when their eye is on you and to curry their favor, but with sincerity of heart and reverence for the Lord. Whatever you do, work at it with all your heart, as working for the Lord, not for human masters, since you know that you will receive an inheritance from the Lord as a reward. It is the Lord Christ you are serving* (Colossians 3:22-24 NIV).

Here we find a rich principle that applies to us regardless of the fact that we are not slaves. Whatever we do, we are serving the Lord Christ, not just our earthly employers, companies, clients or customers. Are you a doctor or lawyer? Work at it with all your heart. You're serving Christ. Are you a CEO or a mechanic? Work at it with all your heart. You're serving Christ. Are you an entrepreneur or an educator? A student or a sales clerk? A builder or a banker? A musician or a movie maker? Put everything you've got into your work. Ultimately, you work for the Lord Christ. The principle applies to us in a powerful way.

Further, when Galatians 3:28 says, *There is neither Jew nor Greek, there is neither slave nor free, there is no male and female, for you are all one in Christ Jesus,* it's teaching us that our differences don't really make any difference. Doctors aren't higher beings than ditch-diggers. Those who are skilled at working with their hands aren't more valuable than those who work with words. We have a robust tendency to look for reasons to look down on other people. We try so hard to find evidence that we're better than others. But the fact of the matter is that we are all precious to Christ. When we see things from His perspective, all our attempts at ranking and rating people melt away like the wicked witch of the West. Believers are all one in Christ. That's an eternal principle that is true in any historical situation.

Robert Lewis Dabney's reading of Scripture seems to have been colored by his own cultural context. I could make the same mistake. So could you. For this reason, we always need to be humble in our understanding of Scripture. We are wise if we are always willing to learn. We should continually expect the Bible to teach, rebuke, correct and train us in righteousness.

(2) A Woman's Place

A more current controversy has to do with the role of women in the church and in society. What does the Bible say about that, and how does it apply to us today?[105] In 1 Corinthians 14:33b-35 Paul writes, *As in all the churches of the saints, the women should keep silent in the churches. For*

---

[105] For a detailed treatment of the issue of the role of women in the New Testament church, and for an excellent model of responsible hermeneutics, see the articles by Kenneth E. Baily in *Theology Matters*, Vol 6 No 1 Jan/Feb 2000 http://www.theologymatters.com/JanFeb001.PDF Last visited 3.1.2019

they are not permitted to speak, but should be in submission, as the Law also says. If there is anything they desire to learn, let them ask their husbands at home. For it is shameful for a woman to speak in church. Because of these and a few similar verses some Christians say it is wrong for women to be pastors – or elders or deacons for that matter. And we can see why. The plain sense of these verses seems to say that women shouldn't speak in church. It's hard to imagine a pastor who stays silent in church (though some people might like to try).

However, are these verses like the ones we just read about slavery? Do they apply to that historical situation but not to us today? After all, they were written to a male dominated society. They were written in a time when women weren't allowed to be educated or hold positions of civic leadership or in many cases even to own property. In fact, women were seen as property themselves. We live in a different situation today. Women can hold pretty much any job a man can hold, and they should receive equal pay for equal work. Women are free to take loans and start their own companies and even run for public office. My primary doctor is a woman. I've studied and served under the capable leadership of some very competent women. Should they still be silenced in the church?

Now understand, we must not simply say that the historical situation has changed so we can ignore what the Bible says. We can't say that Scripture's teaching doesn't apply to our culture because we like our culture better. Our culture might be wrong. There are many ways in which our culture should be corrected by Scripture. But we can and should ask whether there are other parts of Scripture that shed additional light on these and similar verses. In fact, there are. We've already seen Galatians 3:28, *There is neither Jew nor Greek, there is neither slave nor free, there is no male and female, for you are all one in Christ Jesus.* That never meant, of course, that there are no anatomical distinctions between Christian women and Christian men, but it does mean that in Christ, unity is more important than hierarchy. Neither male dominance nor female dominance is a Christian value.

Further, Acts 2:17-18 says:

> *"And in the last days it shall be", God declares, "that I will pour out my Spirit on all flesh, and your sons and your daughters shall prophesy, and your young men shall see visions, and your old men shall dream dreams; even on my male servants and female servants in those days I will pour out my Spirit, and they shall prophesy.*

These verses are not only a quotation of Joel 2:28-29 but also a hermeneutical declaration that Joel's prophecy is fulfilled in the Church. Now of course, if God empowers our daughters to prophesy, if God's Spirit impels both men *and women* to speak His message, well, they can't very well prophesy and be quiet at the same time, can they? Besides, in both the Old and New Testaments we see women like Miriam (Exodus 15:20), Deborah (Judges 4-5), Priscilla (Acts 18:26), the four daughters of Philip (Acts 21:9) and other women speaking and leading according to God's will. So, some Christians say that the injunction for women to keep silent in the church was addressed to a particular culture and shouldn't be applied to women of today. In fact, there is evidence that these pronouncements were addressed to specific and temporary cultural situations in particular churches. When we let Scripture interpret Scripture, some would say we see that restricting women is as outdated as slavery. Those Christians freely ordain women as pastors and officers in the church, and they do so because they believe that's what the Scripture teaches.

At this point we have to admit something very sad. Some people refuse to ordain women out of a sexist ideology. They are male chauvinists and they just use Scripture to enforce their own prejudice. Likewise, some people are feminists and they want to ordain women regardless of what the Bible may teach. They, too, use Scripture to advance their own agenda. Both parties are practicing Humpty Dumpty hermeneutics. Both parties are twisting the Scriptures to make them say what they want them to say. When we do that, the Bible becomes meaningless. It becomes a blank screen on which we project our own preconceptions and presumptions. When we do that, we rob the Bible of its authority as the Word of God and turn it into an arsenal to help us bully others into doing and thinking what we want. God, forgive us.

In contrast to that unhappy reality, I know brothers and sisters who do not practice the ordination of women because they sincerely want to be obedient to what Scripture teaches. *The women should keep silent in the churches.* As they see it, that's God's final word on the matter. I also know sisters and brothers – and I am one of them – who believe that, when we look at the full scope of Scripture, we see that God's Spirit empowers both men and women to proclaim His message.

And while there have been historical situations in which women were to keep quiet, and while there conceivably could be situations where men ought to be silenced, God pours out His Spirit on both men and women, both our sons and daughters. Both are to proclaim His message. Those who believe this don't hesitate to ordain women and men, and they are confident that they (we) are doing so in obedience to Scripture.

You probably have Christian friends who don't agree with me on that issue. You may not agree with me, but that underscores a very important lesson. We need to be humble in our reading of Scripture. We need to recognize that others may see something in their reading of Scripture that we don't see. We need to expect the Spirit to show us exciting things we've never noticed before. In other words, we must be willing to change our minds. So, we need to be respectful of those who see things in the Bible differently from how we may see them. No Christian can ignore what the Bible teaches, but no Christian has a monopoly on biblical truth. It is essential that we read the Bible with open hearts and minds.

Further, I want to point out something that isn't often mentioned when people debate about women in ministry. *God declares, that I will pour out my Spirit on all flesh, and your sons and your daughters shall prophesy* (Acts 2:17). Sometimes we focus only on the last part of that declaration, but the first half is even more important. Therefore, I believe it is scriptural to ordain a woman or a man only if God's Spirit has been poured out on that person. It is indisputably more important for a Christian leader to have the Holy Spirit than to have a Y chromosome. Sometimes we forget that. I would have a hard time refusing to ordain a woman who is empowered to preach or lead by God's Holy Spirit, but it is a tragedy when we ordain or follow a man or a woman who does not have the power of the Holy Spirit at work in his or her life.

(3) You Can't Help Who You Love

The third controversy we'll consider has to do with human sexuality. For centuries the people of God have understood the Bible to say and mean that sexual activity should be enjoyed only within the safe boundaries of marriage between a man and a woman. Some, however, would say that this old-fashioned idea no longer applies in our culture, which is much "freer" and sexually open. They trace the following trajectory. Two centuries ago we thought the Bible endorsed slavery, but now we all know better. After that, people continued to believe that the Scriptures legitimated male dominance and superiority, but now some of us know better. The next step is to recognize that the old restrictions on sexual expression are outmoded and, like slavery, should be abolished.

People who think this way often call themselves "progressives." Progressivism is a school of thought that grows out of the dialectic philosophy of G.W.F. Hegel.[106] It's

---

[106] Hegel (1770-1831) was a German Philosopher who basically taught that history progresses when "thesis" (the status quo) is confronted by "antithesis" (an alternative). This conflict yields a new "synthesis," which is by nature better than the old thesis. The synthesis in turn becomes the new thesis which is itself confronted

an elaborate evolutionary theory of how the world is constantly getting better. Is this philosophy true? On the one hand, no one can sanely deny that real progress happens. For example, I'm writing this book on a laptop computer with access to research resources far more extensive and easier to use than what anyone would have found in the stacks of the greatest libraries of the 20ᵗʰ century. When I was in college (which wasn't *all* that long ago), writing this way was not only impossible but unimaginable. Progress really does happen and we should celebrate it. We've come a long way, baby.

The weakness of Progressivism as a philosophy, however, is its tendency to assume that *all* change is progress. Anything that replaces the old must be an improvement. That assumption is simply false. Some change is deterioration. Decay. For example, we are capable of many things, from cell phones to space travel, that would have blown the minds of the people who built the pyramids and the Acropolis. Nevertheless, those ancients knew things about engineering that we have literally forgotten and cannot duplicate. Not all change is progress. It is true that we have come to a better understanding of what the Scripture says about slavery than R.L. Dabney was able to grasp. I believe we have also come to a deeper understanding about the role of women than was common 50 years ago. In these cases, I believe the "newer" views are better. They are better, however, not because we have improved upon the Bible or progressed beyond God's Word, but because we have rediscovered more about the Bible's original teaching. So, it does not automatically follow

---

and replaced by something better still. So the world is always making progress.

that because those two changes were improvements, all changes are really progress. We changed our views on slavery and the roles of women because of a growing understanding of what the Bible always said, not because we made the Scriptures say something new. Does the Bible warrant a similar change when it comes to our views of human sexuality and sexual expression?

We heard two different voices about slavery in the Bible. When we listened to them in harmony, we changed our tune. We likewise hear two different voices on the role of women. I think the dominant motif is that the Spirit of God empowers sons *and* daughters for ministry. *Let the women keep silence in the churches* is an enriching counterpoint that enhances the beauty of the dominant theme. So now we have to ask whether we hear a similar blend of melodies when it comes to sexuality.

To be sure the Bible gives us a smorgasbord of examples of sexual expression. In sacred history, God worked through prostitutes, concubines, adulterers, polygamists, all kinds of people with a wide variety of practices and preferences. He accomplished His purposes through them. However, while God uses such a sordid assortment of imperfect characters, none of their loose sexual practices is approved by God. Jesus encapsulated the Scriptures' teaching on sexuality when He said, *"But from the beginning of creation, 'God made them male and female.' 'Therefore a man shall leave his father and mother and hold fast to his wife, and the two shall become one flesh.' So they are no longer two but one flesh"* (Mark 10:6-9). It is true that because of the hardness of our hearts, God graciously endures our departures from

His plan (Matthew 19:8), but He never calls us to any of those divergences. The only counterpoint I can think of to this theme of sex within marriage is Paul's commendation of celibacy in 1 Corinthians 7. There simply is no verse equivalent to *if you can gain your freedom, do so* regarding slavery or *your sons and daughters will prophesy* regarding the role of women. Chastity and marriage, those are the melody and counter-melody the Bible gives us when it comes to sexuality. Anything else is out of biblical bounds.

Consider the Greek word *pornea* (πορνεία). This term occurs twenty-five times in the New Testament.[107] It has been translated "fornication," "unchastity" or more commonly nowadays, "sexual immorality." It comes from the same root as *porneuo* (πορνεύω) which means "to commit fornication" and occurs eight times; *porne* (πόρνη) which means "prostitute" and occurs twelve times; and *pornos* (πόρνος), which means "fornicator" and shows up ten times. Sexual immorality, *pornea*, is always prohibited or condemned. The same is true of the related words. (Obviously, we derive our word "pornography" from the same Greek root.) Because *porne* means "prostitute," some might be tempted to argue that *pornea* really only refers to prostitution, but when 1 Corinthians 5:1 uses this word to describe a sexual relationship between a man and his step mother, it's clear that the meaning of the word is broader than simply engaging in a wanton commercial transaction. "Sexual immorality" is best understood as any sexual expression beyond the borders of a one-flesh marriage between a

---

[107] One can find all the references at *Strong's Concordance sv 4202 pornea* at https://biblehub.com/greek/4202.htm Last visited 3.1.2019

woman and a man. No form of sexual immorality is ever endorsed by Scripture. In fact, when the apostles wrote to new Gentile believers and explained that the Old Testament dietary laws were already fulfilled and not to be enforced (so we can eat those bacon-wrapped scallops), all believers were still instructed to abstain from sexual immorality (Acts 15:20, 29). At the time the New Testament was written, the Greco-Roman world was clearly decadent by Jewish/Christian standards. It was at least as sexually permissive as our society. Faithful monogamy between a man and a woman was far from the norm. The Bible's teaching was even more counter-cultural then than it is today. Still, the Bible is unrelenting in its call to *flee from sexual immorality* (1 Corinthians 6:18).

Some will want to argue that, because of the rule of love, we should not restrict sexual expression to heterosexual marriage. Instead, we should lovingly encourage people to enjoy whatever sexual expressions fulfill their inclinations. I understand fully how the Bible's teaching can feel restrictive to someone whose desires may run in a different direction.[108] Remember, however, that biblical love is not primarily permissive. Biblical love wills the greatest good for people. Love wants God's will for His precious children. God loves those who struggle with various forms of sexual immorality as much as He loves the rest of us sinners. For all of us, biblical love teaches us, rebukes us, corrects us and trains us

---

[108] See Goeke, Mike "Offended" http://www.oneby1.org/testimony-offended.cfm for the true story of a man whose family and friends loved him enough to confront him about sexual immorality.

in righteousness. Biblical love disciplines us for our highest good.

There's a popular slogan nowadays, "You can't help who you love." It's catchy, but is it true? The Bible tells us many times whom to love. *Love God* (Deuteronomy 6:5, Matthew 22:37). *Love your neighbor* (Leviticus 19:18, Matthew 22:39, Romans 13:9 etc.). *Love one another* (John 13:34-35, 15:12, 17). *Love your wives* (Ephesians 5:28, Colossians 3:19). *Love your enemies* (Matthew 5:44, Luke 6:27, 35). If we can't control which people we love and which people we don't, then those commands make no sense. Of course, the slogan intends something different by "love." It means something more like "You can't help whom you find sexually attractive." That might be true, though even there I think we have more control than the catchphrase assumes. However, what people seem to infer as a logical conclusion of the mantra is that it's impossible to restrict what people you'll join in sexual activity. "You can't help who you love" is interpreted to mean, "You can't control who you have sex with." When we state it that way, we see how misleading the motto really is. Some people exercise that control regularly! I personally am not genetically inclined toward monogamy. Nevertheless, I have practiced it (at least outwardly) since my wedding day. Why? Not because it has always been easy. Not because I don't empathize with people who struggle to stay inside the banks of this refreshing stream. I do. I understand the conflict. Nevertheless, I practice monogamy because God's loving Word tells me to do so. As a result, I experience the continual deepening of that rich, complex one-flesh reality that God designed. At various times over the decades I could have given into my non-monogamous inclinations. Had I done so, I would have marred the gift of God and deprived myself of tremendous joy. By applying the rule of love to my understanding of Scripture I allowed Scripture to discipline me (at least in that area), and the benefits are wonderful. Applying the rule of love to human sexuality, I compassionately encourage people in our society to follow the Bible's clear, unequivocal teaching on sexuality, even if that involves discipline and sacrifice. Even if it means denying some of our inclinations and desires. Steering sexual expression along the straight path of monogamous marriage between a man and a woman may be challenging, but it leads to our highest good in that area of life.

In pre-marriage counselling, I always encourage couples to practice abstinence until their wedding day, even if they have previously been sexually active. I remember one couple in their forties who were already living together. When I made that suggestion, actually when I offered them that gift, he moved to the couch. In their last session with me before the wedding he came in and said, "Preacher, I almost stumbled this week." "Tell me about it," I replied. "Well," he recounted, "one night I went to her room to tuck her in for the night. The lighting was perfect, the mood was right, she was beautiful, and I was tempted. But then I looked down at her and saw your face!" That would have stopped me, too. I told him so, and we laughed. However, I encourage couples to practice abstinence as an act of joyful compliance with God's will, a recognition that His will is good, and as a foundation for the godly covenant they are about to enter. I know it's counter-cultural, but many couples have been grateful for that guidance.

Our culture is moving toward more and more sexual laxity. To many, sexual expression enveloped in what is called traditional marriage seems too constricting. As the culture changes, I see many progressive Christians falling into the same snare that trapped R.L. Dabney. To a far greater degree than Dabney ever considered, they are letting the current cultural trends dominate and correct (or corrupt) their reading of Scripture. Though there is no biblical endorsement of sexual expression outside the covenant of marriage between a man and a woman, many disciples and denominations are looking for ways to justify divergent practices. Good hermeneutics recognizes that we must take things the other way around. Scripture corrects our culture. Otherwise we make the Bible mean just what we want it to mean, neither more nor less.

The More Things Change …

Dr. Tim Keller has argued that today's culture has become so much like the Greco-Roman culture that, almost without hermeneutic, the Book of Acts is now the Mission Manual for the Church.[109] I found that insight intriguing. The good doctor demurred too much on whether the supernatural manifestations we see in the Book of Acts should be expected today, but that raises another point we should consider when it comes to hermeneutics. What do we do with all the amazing supernatural events recorded in the Bible? Do

---

[109] See Keller's remarks to 2012 Fellowship of Presbyterians Gathering in Colorado Springs. https://vimeo.com/50785140 Last visited 3.1.2019

miracles have an expiration date, or should we expect to experience such signs and wonders today? In Chapter Five we talked about the differences between cessationists (who believe many miracles have ceased) and continuationists (who believe God works and empowers today the same as He did in Bible times). Your beliefs about how God works today will have a decisive impact on your hermeneutics. For example, Paul says, *Now I want you all to speak in tongues, but even more to prophesy* (1 Corinthians 14:5a). Does that apply to us directly today, or was that injunction limited to a particular place and time?

Cessationists insist, "that was then and this is now." Things change, including the way God acts in the world. Today, they say, we no longer have nor need spiritual gifts like tongues, prophecy, miraculous healings and so on. Further, our worldview is very different from that of the Bible writers. Take, for example, the many New Testament stories about demons being cast out. How do those stories apply to us today? Should we even believe in demons? New Testament scholar Joseph Fitzmeyer says this about the demon stories in the Bible. "It might be best to speak of 'demon sickness.' It is a form of protological thinking which cannot ascribe physical or psychic disorders to proper secondary causes that makes ancient writers attribute them to beings of an intermediate spirit-world."[110] From Father Fitzmeyer's Progressive perspective, the ancient Bible writers were too naïve and unsophisticated on spiritual matters. They didn't

---

[110] Joseph Fitzmeyer, *The Gospel According to Luke I-IX, Anchor Bible volume 28* ©1981 by Doubleday & Company Inc. p.545

know what we know about psychology and mental illness. So, they talked about people being afflicted by demons. Nowadays we know better. But do we really? Is the Bible telling the literal truth when it talks about unclean spirits? If there actually were demons then, where are they now? Did the Bible describe a reality that existed once upon a time but has somehow faded away?

Continuationists, on the other hand, contend, "the more things change, the more they stay the same." A continuationist hermeneutic would leave open the possibility that some people might be greatly helped by having demons cast out of them. It would also say that Jesus still gives His followers the power to perform that ministry. A cessationist hermeneutic would be more likely to limit possible remedies to various forms of counseling and therapy. This is an important difference, especially if someone might really need victory over an evil spirit.

However, it isn't only the problem of the demonic that's at stake. Many issues are on the table. For example, if a person needs physical or emotional healing, how we will care and pray for such a person is a hermeneutical issue. The Bible says Jesus healed the sick. Back then it meant Jesus healed the sick, but what does it mean today? Does God still heal apart from the practice of modern medicine? If someone is sick, should we *call for the elders of the church, and let them pray over him, anointing him with oil in the name of the Lord* (James 5:13)? Or have we progressed beyond that primitive, "protological" practice?

In Chapter Eight I will talk about many phenomena that I've heard of and experienced in which God acted in miraculous ways. I'll share experiences that sound a lot like events described in the New Testament. Healings, dreams, visions, prophecies and more will be discussed. For now, I'll add to the few but remarkable examples already mentioned in Chapter Five (section 8) by pointing to the phenomenon of thousands of Muslims coming to faith in Jesus Christ through dreams and visions of Jesus.[111] These modern stories remind us of the dreams of both Josephs (Genesis 37:5, Matthew 1:20, 2:13, 19) and the vision of Saul of Tarsus. (Acts 9:3-8, 26:19) We have mountains of convincing evidence that God still works in supernatural ways, just as He did in Bible times. Are fraudulent or exaggerated claims ever made? Probably. Are there ever prayers for healing that do not lead to the result we desire? Far more than I would like to see. But there are also countless examples of God working in today's world just as He did in the New Testament era.

Sometimes, sadly, people are blind to the valid evidence because of their presuppositions, their worldview. We saw that with Joseph Fitzmeyer's treatment of the Bible's message about demonic deliverance. We see it when disciples are doubtful about asking God for healing. We see it often with our cessationist brothers and sisters. How tragic. The Bible still means what it meant more often than some are ready to admit. The more things change, the more they stay the same. Or better, no matter how things change, God

---

[111] See, for example, the beautiful story in the blog of Mateen Elass, "Do You Believe in Prayer? Then Pray." November 19, 2018 https://mateenelass.wordpress.com/2018/11/19/do-you-believe-in-prayer-then-pray/?fbclid=IwAR3pFUTc2YA2AsAHJJPfV8bl1c4PkwzpdBZA9PJ1T0ofWYOHSH7UVPczqVw Last visited 11.30.18

remains the same. When we restrict mighty acts of the eternal God to the early ages of Christianity, we are adding an unnecessary hermeneutical level that blocks us from enjoying and experiencing the Christian life to the fullest.

Ask the Author

By far the most important factor in applying the Scriptures to our situation is having a conversation with the Author. I have a fun photo of myself sitting at a table in the Tel Aviv airport reading a book called *Dream Discoveries* by Barbara Braun Koob.[112] What makes the picture comical is that Barb, the author, is sitting right next to me. I could be talking directly to my friend. I could be deepening our friendship. Instead, I'm just reading her book. Of course, reading her book is part of developing our relationship, but it isn't the whole thing. I'm afraid there are many Christians who do to the Holy Spirit what I was doing to Barb in that shot. We read His book but ignore His presence.

The word for Spirit in the Hebrew Old Testament is *ruah* (רוּחַ). It also means wind and breath. The Greek word for Spirit in the New Testament is *pneuma* (πνεῦμα). It too can mean wind or breath. When we say all Scripture is God-breathed (2 Timothy 3:16), we are declaring that Scripture is the work of the Holy Spirit. It is Spirit inspired. It was the

---

[112] Koob, Barbara *Dream Discoveries: Learn to Hope and Dream with Purpose* © 2016 by Barbara Koob.
https://www.amazon.com/Dream-Discoveries-Learn-Hope-Purpose/dp/1943217270/ref=la_B01DOAXMTS_1_1?s=books&ie=UTF8&qid=1463282140&sr=1-1

Spirit who "carried along" the human writers (2 Peter 1:21). As the Nicene Creed says, the Holy Spirit "spoke through the prophets." So, when we want a deeper understanding of what the Bible means for us today, the best tactic is simply to ask the Author. No, we cannot interrogate Matthew or Malachi, Moses, David or Paul, but we can seek guidance and wisdom from the Holy Spirit.

Yes, we will study each passage in its context and ask what it says and what it meant to the original target audience. We will consider the plain sense of Scripture, let Scripture interpret Scripture, apply the rule of love and all that. But unless we ask the Holy Spirit to explain and apply the Bible's message to our hearts and lives, we are simply engaging in a futile intellectual exercise. When it comes to hermeneutics, Proverbs 3:5 is supremely relevant. *Trust in the Lord with all your heart, and do not lean on your own understanding.*

So, read and interpret the Bible prayerfully. Ask the Holy Spirit to make the meaning clear to you. By all means, apply the four discernment questions we explored at the end of Chapter Five. As you interpret and apply the Bible, ask whether your understanding brings glory to Jesus Christ in the present and in the future. Does it fit with the character of God as revealed in the rest of Scripture? Do other Spirit-filled believers bear witness to your interpretation, and is there confirmation in verifiable events or facts? Strive to be sure that you are hearing from the Lord instead of relying on your own understanding or reading Scripture through your own cultural lenses. When we do those things, the Bible is unleashed to teach us, rebuke us, correct us and train us in righteousness. After all, when we read the Word, it means just what God chooses it to mean – neither more nor less.

Chapter Seven

On The Contrary

The Down-Side of the Teeter-Totter

Have you ever noticed how, when somebody's down on you, you can't do anything right in his or her eyes? You've probably experienced that pain personally. I've been on both sides of that fulcrum. My wife is a wonderful person and I'm blessed to share life with her. Sometimes, however, we go through rough patches. There are short seasons when it seems to me she's just being inconsiderate or even mean. From her perspective, I'm just in a bad mood. Hypersensitive. Maybe she's right about me, maybe I'm right about her. It might be a little of both. In any event, during those spells, nearly everything she does offends me.

I've been on the other end of that see-saw, too. As a pastor I've enjoyed long periods when all my efforts were appreciated and fruitful. I love when that happens. Unfortunately, there have also been heart-breaking times when it feels like my every action is opposed and every motive is misjudged. I've learned from this experience to try never to judge the intentions of others because, when people try to guess at my motives, they're almost always wrong. I'm not perfect by any means, but I'm usually innocent of their indictments against my intentions. That downside of the teeter-totter is no fun. Sometimes people find fault with you, no matter what you do.

There are people who seem to have a similar negative attitude toward the Bible. They look for fault where none exists. Another nasty rumor we often hear is that we can't trust the Bible because it's full of contradictions. Is that true? Are there genuine discrepancies, or are people just looking for a fight? Let's take a look at some of those alleged contradictions and see if the accusations are fair. Are there real problems, or are people just trying to find fault?

The White House

We've already looked at some of the supposed biblical discrepancies. In Chapter Three we agreed that, since Ahaziah could not have been born two years before the birth of his father, the text which said Ahaziah became king at age twenty-two reflects the correct reading. In Chapter Five we examined the apparent inconsistency between Jesus telling his disciples not to tell anyone that He was the Christ (Matthew 16:20) and His command to preach the Gospel to the whole world (Matthew 28:19-20). There we discovered that the difference was really a matter of plot development. In the earlier part of the story it was too soon to reveal the whole truth, but after Jesus' death and resurrection were accomplished, the time was right to proclaim Him to all the world. There was no contradiction, just fulfillment. Development. When we filled in the other notes of the chord, the dissonance became harmony. When we learned the rest of the story, the tension was resolved. All the elements fit.

In order for two statements to be contradictory, it has to be the case that both can't be true. If one is true the other must be false, and vice versa. If there is a way for both statements to be true, there is no contradiction. Let me share a fun bit of family lore. When I was growing up my dad worked most weekends to make ends meet. Once, when he had a weekend off, we started painting our house. We covered the southern and eastern walls in gleaming white. The next several weekends Dad had to work again. Then we had an opportunity to go fishing. Then he worked again, and so on. By the time he got around to painting the rest of the house, my mom had decided she wanted a different color. So, the northern and western walls were painted pale green. We'd paint the rest green later. Someday. Meanwhile a young man on the high school football team became interested in my sister. When he wanted to pick her up for a date he asked, "What color is your house?" Now, if she had said, "Green," she'd have told the truth, if he had been coming from the north. If she had said "White," that would have been true, too, provided he was coming from the opposite direction. No contradiction either way. He just needed to know the whole story. Wisely, my sister answered her suitor with a question. "Which direction will you be coming from?" He found the house, they went on their first date and, three weeks before I wrote this chapter they celebrated their 50th wedding anniversary. It all started when he picked her up at that gleaming white house. Or was it green? Both descriptions would be true.

A lot of the supposed contradictions in the Bible are like that. When you take the whole story into account, when you fairly consider all the facts, the tensions dissolve. Again, if two statements are said to be contradictory but both can be true, that isn't a real contradiction. In this chapter we'll look at several instances where the Scriptures are alleged to be inconsistent. The accusations are so numerous it would be impossible to deal with them all,[113] but we'll explore several that I think will instruct and encourage us.

---

[113] For more details, I highly recommend three videos on this topic by Mike Winger.
"FULL of Contradictions!" pt1: Evidence for the Bible pt18
https://www.youtube.com/watch?v=OA-4eQN16no&t=1s
13 Bible Contradictions refuted: Evidence for the Bible pt19
https://www.youtube.com/watch?v=uoLYyyqijfU&t=1983s
Biggest Bible Contradictions: Evidence for the Bible pt20
https://www.youtube.com/watch?v=7zS4VgFDf8s All Last visited 3.1.2019

A Redeemed Robber

Take, for example, the story about the two criminals who were crucified with Jesus. Matthew tells us that, as they hung on their respective crosses, both robbers reviled the Lord (Matthew 27:44). Luke, on the other hand, says that one thief turned to Jesus for salvation (Luke 23:42). So, which is it? Were both criminals against Jesus, or did one rail at Him while the other found redemption? Is this a bona fide contradiction, or is someone just trying to find fault with the Bible? Can both accounts be true? Certainly. Isn't it possible to imagine that one thief started out opposed to Jesus but later changed his mind? The three men suffered together for three hours. During that time both criminals faced their mortality head on. Both wrongdoers also watched how Jesus suffered with character, courage, faith and even forgiveness. Is it hard to conclude that, as he dealt with the ultimate questions of life for the last time, one of the robbers had a change of heart and turned to the Christ, who was right beside him? Isn't it more astonishing that the other criminal did *not* have a change of heart? At one point both criminals insulted Jesus. Matthew told the truth. Later, however, one of them repented. He changed his mind. He changed his heart. Listen to the beautiful story as Luke tells it.

> One of the criminals who were hanged railed at him, saying, "Are you not the Christ? Save yourself and us!" But the other rebuked him, saying, "Do you not fear God, since you are under the same sentence of condemnation? And we indeed justly, for we are receiving the due reward of our deeds; but this man has done nothing wrong." And he said, "Jesus,

remember me when you come into your kingdom." And he said to him, "Truly, I say to you, today you will be with me in paradise" (Luke 23:39-43).

What astoundingly good news! Clearly both robbers had lived sinful lives. Matthew points out that *both* of them reviled Jesus. As Luke tells the story, however, we see that it is never too late for someone to turn to Christ. Even in the last hours of his dissolute life, even after blatant blasphemy against the Son of God, one robber turned to Jesus, and that day joined Him in paradise. Some of the people who spread these nasty rumors about the Bible are like those reviling robbers. They hurl insults at the Lord. My prayer is that they too will change their hearts and minds about Jesus. The sooner the better. When they do, that won't be a contradiction but a joyful development, a fulfillment. A completion.

Again, we see a case where what some call a contradiction is really just a matter of one part of the Bible filling in details that aren't mentioned in another place. As we said in Chapter Six, Scripture interprets Scripture. To be sure, each writer is sounding a distinctive theological or spiritual note, and that note needs to be heard in its own voice. One passage might be different from another, but that does not necessarily make the two contradictory. Both facts can be true. Both tones can be part of the same rich chord. When it comes to the Gospels, no one Gospel tells the whole story. You remember that John told us, *Now Jesus did many other signs in the presence of the disciples, which are not written in this book; but these are written so that you may believe that*

Jesus is the Christ, the Son of God, and that by believing you may have life in his name (John 20:30-31). He also said, *Now there are also many other things that Jesus did. Were every one of them to be written, I suppose that the world itself could not contain the books that would be written* (John 21:25). So, it isn't the least bit surprising to find that one writer shares details another doesn't mention. No one writer could tell it all. What is true of the Gospels in this regard is true of the rest of Scripture.

Blessed Are the Poor ...?

It's sometimes pointed out that, according to Matthew 5:3 Jesus preached, *"Blessed are the poor in spirit, for theirs is the kingdom of heaven"* while in Luke 6:20 He only says, *"Blessed are you who are poor, for yours is the kingdom of God."* Is it *poor in spirit*, or just *poor*? That's a big difference. Poverty of spirit is different from plain old penury. One is a character trait, the other is an economic situation. So, what did Jesus really say? Which condition does He call blessed? Again, we should ask if it's possible for both statements to be true. Is it possible that Jesus said both? We might suggest that Matthew simply included a phrase that Luke left out, "in spirit." In this case, however, that isn't just filling in a detail. Those two words change the meaning of the teaching drastically. These really are two different statements. But do they form an actual contradiction? Could Jesus have said both? Again, when we read the Bible at face value, we see that these statements were made on two different occasions. In Matthew Jesus was teaching from a mountain (Matthew 5:1). In Luke He was speaking on a "level place" (Luke 6:17). Jesus was an itinerate preacher. He proclaimed the Kingdom of God from place to place. No doubt He presented the same material in different locations. However, it isn't surprising that no two sermons were identical. Many churches nowadays have multiple services each weekend. We did that at the church I serve for a while. I preached *roughly* the same sermon at each of three services, but no two sermons were ever exactly the same. Jesus had an important message to share. The most important message of all time, as a matter of fact. So of course, He repeated Himself so everyone could hear the truth. Sometimes, however, different contexts called for different applications, different emphases. What was needed on the mountain was a message about spiritual poverty. What was called for on the plain was sermon on scarcity. So, Jesus preached both. The sermons were similar in structure with appropriate variations in content. Matthew and Luke both told the truth. There is no contradiction. No need to find fault. A good number of the so-called discrepancies in the Gospels fade away when we remember the itinerate nature of Jesus' preaching ministry.

Did Jesus Get the Bible Wrong?

Another favorite inconsistency for critics is found in some translations of Mark 2:26.[114] In the New Revised Standard

---

[114] Andrew Wilson offers a fascinating explanation of this verse with some profound implications in his 2015 *Christianity Today* article "When Jesus Got the Bible Wrong" https://www.christianitytoday.com/ct/2015/september/when-jesus-got-bible-

Version of that verse we hear Jesus tell us how David *entered the house of God, when Abiathar was high priest, and ate the bread of the Presence, which it is not lawful for any but the priests to eat, and he gave some to his companions.* Where's the conflict? According to 1 Samuel 21:1-9, Abiathar was not the high priest when this event took place. His father, Ahimelech held that holy office at the time. As a matter of fact, David's eating the consecrated bread was the event that led to Ahimelech's vengeful execution by King Saul. Abiathar became high priest in his father's place. So, this may be far worse than a mere contradiction, it might be an example of Jesus being confused about the Bible.

You probably noticed that I said the inconsistency is found in *some translations* of the Bible. NRSV, RSV and a few others have Jesus say something like "when Abiathar was high priest." The ESV translates the phrase, *in the time of Abiathar the high priest.* That's a bit different. NIV and the majority of translations agree with ESV. There's no real contradiction if we use that translation. David and his men *did* eat the bread of the Presence in the *days* of Abiathar. Abiathar was not high priest yet, but he was alive. In fact, he may have witnessed the incident (1 Samuel 22:20-21).

So which translation of Mark 2:26 is correct? The decision can't be made on grammar alone. It depends on how one interprets a slippery preposition. The Greek word *epi* (ἐπὶ) has a wide range of meaning. It can mean "on," "upon," "above," "before," "beyond," "concerning" and many other things. That isn't really peculiar. In English the same

wrong.html?share=7ZtKUxgDLLX49u3%2fO36UbjjiAC4mNs2L Last visited 3.1.2019 preposition can have different meanings as well. "I left my cell phone on the table," "I left my cell phone on overnight," "I sent you a message on your cell phone" and "Someday I'll write an article on cell phones." In all four cases "on" means something different. *Epi* (ἐπὶ) is like that. The Greek verse of Mark 2:26 literally says, "he entered into the house of God *epi* (ἐπὶ) Abiathar high priest." That's it. *Epi* Abiathar. In English that makes no sense. He entered the house of God *on* Abiathar? *Upon* Abiathar? Was he ridding piggy-back? Translators have to fill in some specifics. The Greek could even mean "in the passage about Abiathar." So grammatically the NRSV translation is as good as the ESV. If people want to find a contradiction here they can, depending on the translation they choose. But there are very good translation options that avoid the conflict. Most translations take the non-contradictory route.

Bartimaeus and Company

Or how about this example? Matthew 20:29-34 tells the story of how Jesus healed two blind men near Jericho when they cried *Lord, have mercy on us, Son of David* (verses 30 and 31)*!* We find the same story in Mark 10:46-52, but this time only one blind man is mentioned. His name is Bartimaeus. So, did Jesus heal one blind man or two? Some critics say the two stories are contradictory. But do we really have a contradiction in these two passages? Isn't it easy to see how both can be true? Matthew reports that two men received their sight. Mark only mentions one, but gives us his name.[115] If Jesus healed Bartimaeus *and* a companion, there's no contradiction at all. Why should we doubt that Jesus healed Bartimaeus even though Matthew doesn't specify the blind man's name? Why should we doubt that two men were healed, though Mark only mentions one? Both can be true, and I believe they are. No contradiction, just different emphasis.

Adam and Eve

So far, all the so-called contradictions we've looked at are found in the Gospels. However, such allegations are leveled against the Bible from its very beginning. Critics like to point out that there are two creation stories in Genesis. The fact that there are two separate sagas is itself taken to be an indictment by some. Further, there are indeed differences between the stories. As we've learned by now, however, differences don't have to be contradictions.

I first noticed the variances when I was in my mid-teens, though I'm sure I didn't catch all the fine points. I had recently realized that believing in Jesus meant I needed to commit my life to following Him, so I began reading the Bible. As a child I rarely went to Sunday school and my family didn't attend church at that time. Consequently, my Bible reading skills weren't very sophisticated. (Such skills

---

[115] For an explanation of a different detail in Luke, see Winger, Mike,
"FULL of Contradictions!" pt1: Evidence for the Bible pt18, starting at 13:15 https://www.youtube.com/watch?v=OA-4eQN16n0&t=1s Last visited 3.1.2019

develop with practice.) Nevertheless, I naturally (or maybe I should say supernaturally) started with the assumption that the Bible is true. I believed what I read. Given that presupposition, it was clear to me that the story in Genesis 2 makes perfect sense when we realize that this passage simply zooms in on some details of Genesis 1. The second story is kind of like an instant replay of the first, highlighting some important points. Five decades and three theological degrees later, I still think that paradigm works, though I understand the details far better today.

Of course, people who read Genesis 1 and 2 as poetry aren't worried about contradictions. Both stories reveal profound, beautiful, spiritual truths about God's creation, and those pronouncements are complementary. However, even for those of us who want to approach the text more literally, the second Creation story doesn't contradict the first, it simply highlights some details. There is no contradiction. [116]

Before we go on, let's stop and take in some of those beautiful spiritual truths in the opening chapters of the Bible. First, both stories tell us that the world in which we live is the intentional creation of God. My wife and I enjoy watching nature programs. We marvel at the majesty, the intricacy, the vastness, the colorful, exquisite splendor of what our Father has made. About the time we are almost spellbound in awe, however, the narrator will comment on how this species or that formation randomly evolved. It

---

[116] For a more detailed treatment of supposed contradictions in Genesis 1 and 2, see the appendix to this chapter.

always breaks our hearts. What a pitiful perspective to have on the glorious gallery of the greatest of Artists. Both Creation stories in Genesis tell us that the cosmos is not a fluke of happenstance, it is the handiwork of God. They also tell us that human beings are the climax of creation. Many people think of themselves as the arbitrary outcome of an accidental process. If that's your presupposition, you inevitably conclude that existence is inherently meaningless. Genesis, however, tells you that you are the masterpiece in God's gallery. As a matter of fact, you are His self-portrait. Genesis 1:27 declares,

So God created man in his own image,

in the image of God he created him;

male and female he created them.

If you ever struggle with issues of self-worth, meditate on that verse. Contemplate the fact that you are designed and custom-made as a replica of God! You are the apex of His handiwork. That's one of the primary points of the first creation story.

The second creation story provides an indispensable balance to that great truth. Genesis 2:7 says, *then the LORD God formed the man of dust from the ground and breathed into his nostrils the breath of life, and the man became a living creature.* Yes, you and I are created in God's image, but we are not God. We were fashioned from dirt. The Hebrew word for "man" is *Adam* (אָדָם). The Hebrew word for "ground" is *Adamah* (אֲדָמָה). We were made with an earthly nature. In the purest sense of the word, we are organic. We are dust. Yet we are not *merely* dust. God Himself blew the breath of life into the body of Adam. God is the Giver of life, and we need Him to sustain us. These two creation stories together protect us from both hubris and despair, both pride and existential angst. The first story reassures us that we are made in God's image. The second soberly reminds us that we are dust. We are God's masterpiece, sculpted from earthen clay.

Further, the second creation story tells us that we are not solitary creatures. *Then the LORD God said, "It is not good that the man should be alone; I will make him a helper fit for him* (Genesis 2:18). We should note that the Hebrew word for "helper" is *ezer* (עֵזֶר). It's the same word that is used to describe God in several places, like Psalm 33:20, *Our soul waits for the LORD; he is our help and our shield.* So, the word does not denote any sense of inferiority or subordination. Woman is not man's lovely assistant. Men and women are compatible. Partners. In verses 21-22 we see that the woman is made from man. So, Adam and Eve, the man and woman, need each other. When Adam meets Eve, he is like a child on Christmas morning. Excitedly he exclaims,

This at last is bone of my bones

and flesh of my flesh;

she shall be called Woman,

because she was taken out of Man (Genesis 2:23).

It is together that man and woman are created in the image of God. *...in the image of God he created him; male and female he created them* (Genesis 1:27). Man is not the image of God by himself. Neither is woman. They are created for one another.

There is so much more for us to learn from the two creation stories in Genesis, but we cannot go into all of it now. We can point out, however, that the two stories do not contradict one another. Rather they complete and enrich one another, like Adam and Eve.

Do You Hear What I Hear?

One of the most dramatic stories in the Bible is the report of the conversion of Saul of Tarsus from being a sworn enemy of all things Christian to becoming an apostle of Jesus Christ. In fact, after that event, he even started using his Greek name, Paul. Paul did more to propagate faith in Christ than anyone else in the New Testament. You remember the story from Acts 9. Saul is on his way to Damascus to persecute Christians there. He has just supervised the fatal stoning of Stephen (Acts 7:58, 8:1) and seems to have a similar agenda in mind for believers who have fled to Syria. Luke recounts the incident like this:

> *Now as he went on his way, he approached Damascus, and suddenly a light from heaven shone around him. And falling to the ground, he heard a voice saying to him, "Saul, Saul, why are you persecuting me?" And he said, "Who are you, Lord?" And he said, "I am Jesus, whom you are persecuting. But rise and enter the city, and you will be told what you are to do." The men who were traveling with him stood speechless, hearing the voice but seeing no one.*

> *Saul rose from the ground, and although his eyes were opened, he saw nothing. So they led him by the hand and brought him into Damascus* (Acts 9:3-8).

What a powerful conversion story! Like the thief on the cross, whom we met a moment ago, Saul experienced a dramatic change of heart and mind.

There is a problem with this passage however. We find another possible Bible contradiction in Acts 22, when we hear Paul's own testimony about the experience. The apparent discrepancies show up best, once again, in the NRSV. In that translation of Acts 9:7, Luke, the author of Acts, narrates, *The men who were traveling with him* (Saul/Paul) *stood speechless because they heard the voice but saw no one.* However, in Acts 22 Luke recounts Paul's own version of the story. As Paul tells it, he says, *Now those who were with me saw the light but did not hear the voice of the one who was speaking to me* (Acts 22:9 NRSV). Did you catch the differences? What did these people see and hear? It differs. In Acts 9:7 Saul's companions heard the voice but saw no one. In Acts 22:9 they saw the light but didn't hear the voice. Is this an irreconcilable difference? Do we have here a real contradiction? I can think of two possible explanations.

Not long ago I was visiting my friend Joe, who is a few years younger than I. We got to talking about physical fitness and I boasted that, when I was in seminary, I used to run five miles every day, and I could easily run ten miles any time I wanted. As I thought about it, however, I realized I needed to correct that statement. In fact, I ran two miles every day and could go five miles any time I wanted. I don't think I ever had a ten-mile run. The saying is really true: The older I get the better I was. My memory tricked me.

Could something similar have happened to Paul? Perhaps what really *happened* on the road to Damascus is that his co-travelers heard the voice but didn't see anyone, but what Paul actually *said* years later was that his entourage saw the light but did not hear the voice. If for some unforeseeable reason, you were to write a factual chronicle of my life, you would have to report that when I was twenty-four years old I ran two miles every day and occasionally ran five, but when I was sixty-four years old I *said* the distances were five and ten miles respectively. For you to say otherwise would be to falsify the record. Likewise, as Luke shares the story of Paul's life, he truthfully tells in Acts 9 what actually happened on the Damascus Road. In Acts 22 he tells, just as truthfully, what Paul said about that event years later. Luke was a very good and very careful writer. It is unlikely that he would have left a mistake like that uncorrected in his manuscript. It's entirely possible that he told the truth both times. In fact, it's likely. There's no contradiction.

There is another solution, however. Again, it has to do with translation. Look again at the two supposedly conflicting verses, this time in the ESV.

Acts 9:7 *The men who were traveling with him stood speechless, hearing the voice but seeing no one.*

Acts 22:9 *Now those who were with me saw the light but did not understand the voice of the one who was speaking to me.*

Translated this way, there is no necessary conflict about what Saul's escorts saw. Acts 22:9 says they saw the light. Act 9:7 only asserts that they saw no one. They could have seen the light and nothing more.

That leaves the question of what Paul's posse heard. The Greek word translated "heard" in Acts 9:7 and "understood" in the ESV of Acts 22:9 is *akouo* (ἀκούω). You won't be surprised to learn that it can mean "hear" or "understand." Jesus Himself drew on this double meaning in Matthew 13:13 when He said, *"This is why I speak to them in parables, because seeing they do not see, and hearing they do not hear, nor do they understand"* (Matthew 13:13). We use the word both ways in English, too. A lecturing parent might ask a child, "Do you hear me?" The parent knows the sound waves are striking the child's eardrums. The question really being asked is, "Do you understand me?" I can't help but think of that story in John 12 where a voice from heaven speaks articulately to Jesus, but *the crowd that stood there and heard it said that it had thundered* (John 12:29). The crowd heard the sound but missed the message. That could be what happened to those other travelers on the way to Damascus. There are a couple of ways in which both Acts 9:7 and Acts 22:9 can be true. In that case, there is no contradiction. The nasty rumor is becoming more and more dubious.

Sitting or Serving?

In Chapter Six we had some fun exploring Jesus' famous parable of the Good Samaritan. You remember, a certain man encounters calamity on the road. His pitiful condition is ignored by two publicly pious people, a priest and a Levite. However, a despised Samaritan cares for the man, showing him love and mercy. Jesus drives the point of His parable home when He commands, *You go, and do likewise.* Serve like the Samaritan. To follow Jesus means to care for others in love. The Christian life is a life of active service.

On the other hand, there's a beautiful story about Jesus visiting the home Martha and her sister, Mary. During the visit, Martha bustles about serving everyone. While she cooks and cleans and works her patience to a frayed, frazzled end, her sister is sitting at Jesus' feet. Mary is listening to Jesus, learning from Him, giving Him her undivided attention. Finally, Martha gets so fed up she blurts out, *"Lord, do you not care that my sister has left me to serve alone? Tell her then to help me."* We just saw that the Christian life is a life of active service. Surely Jesus will take Martha's side. But the Lord answered her, *"Martha, Martha, you are anxious and troubled about many things, but one thing is necessary. Mary has chosen the good portion, which will not be taken away from her."* Martha pours herself into service. Martha is meeting practical needs, but Jesus says that it's better to sit at His feet. That's the good portion. To sit at Jesus feet means to learn from Him as a disciple. Today we "sit at Jesus feet" through practices like Bible reading, prayer, study, contemplation, worship, and other acts of devotion. The Marthas of the world can serve all they want, but in this story, Jesus seems to prefer His disciples learn from Him in attentive devotion.

Do these two stories create a contradiction about how

Christians should live? The parable of the Good Samaritan stresses practical service. The story of Martha and Mary points to the importance of piety, sitting at Jesus' feet. So, which did Jesus say? Which does He want from His followers? Action or devotion?

You may have noticed I've departed from my usual practice of telling you where Bible quotations come from. So far, I haven't given you any Scripture references for these two stories. That's because both stories come from the same chapter, Luke 10. Luke 10:25-37 is the parable of the Good Samaritan and Luke 10:38-42 is the story of Martha and Mary. Neither story appears anywhere else in Scripture, and the two passages are next door neighbors. Luke doesn't even try to give the impression that these stories are told in chronological order. Luke is a competent historian, but here he isn't interested in Jesus' itinerary. Luke's agenda is purely spiritual. As I've already mentioned, Luke was a careful, purposeful writer. The Holy Spirit is even more purposeful. At His inspiration, Luke put these two stories back to back so we could not read one without the other. The Christian life consists of both devotion and service, sitting at Jesus' feet and caring for those around us. There is no contradiction. There's no real tension. Service and devotion. The balanced Christian life needs both. You shouldn't have one without the other.

I hope that reading this book is an act of devotion for you. If these chapters help you sit at the feet of Jesus and learn, that's wonderful. If they encourage you to read, meditate on and apply the Scriptures regularly, that's even better. That's my dream as I type these words. But there's more. When you finish reading, give this book so someone who is diligently engaged in meeting people's needs in the name of Jesus, someone with a servant's heart. Service oriented people need to read this, too. They require time at Jesus' feet. Meanwhile, you go and help someone in need. Visit someone sick or lonely. Help wash some dishes. Feed someone who is hungry. Tutor or teach a class. Devotion is the good portion and it should not be taken away from us, but Jesus also commands us to serve. Both are needed. Both are true.

The Devil Made Me Do It

We've saved the most shocking problem for last. 2 Samuel 24 and 1 Chronicles 21 each describe an incident in which King David took a census of the people of Israel and Judah. In both stories David repented after he had taken the census and, in order to ward off a plague from the Lord, David purchased the threshing floor of a certain Jebusite as a place of sacrifice. This is the chosen spot where Solomon later built the temple. 2 Samuel says the Jebusite was named Araunah while 1 Chronicles calls him Ornan, but that isn't the discrepancy that we need to deal with. Many people go by two names, particularly in the Bible. The stunning difference between the stories is in the source of David's motive for taking the census in the first place.

2 Samuel 24:1 says, *Again the anger of the LORD was kindled against Israel, and he incited David against them, saying, "Go, number Israel and Judah.* Those of us who bristle against the idea of the Lord being angry are very uncomfortable with this verse because it plainly says that

God prompted David to take the census. We might be more at ease with 1 Chronicles 21:1, *Then Satan stood against Israel and incited David to number Israel.* Why did David take the census? The devil made him do it! At least according to Chronicles. But that raises another difficulty, doesn't it? Could there be any greater contradiction than to say in one place that Satan provoked an event and to say in another that God caused it? "The Lord incited." "Satan incited." Is there any way both statements can be true?

We find a surprising answer in the first two chapters of the book of Job. There we see an assembly, a divine council meeting in heaven. And guess who takes a break from his travels to and fro on the earth to attend this meeting. Satan. God asks if Satan has noticed what a righteous man Job is. Satan replies that Job is only good because God has blessed him abundantly. However, the devil bets that, in the face of tragedy, Job would turn his back on God. So, the Lord gives Satan permission to assault all that Job treasures. Job loses everything, his children, his vast wealth, all but his health. And his integrity. So, Satan goes back to God and ups the ante. He makes the diabolical suggestion that, if Job faces physical suffering, surely then he will turn his back on God. Once again God grants Satan limited permission. He can afflict Job but not take his life.

In this age when the prosperity gospel has permeated the thinking of many Western Christians, it's hard to fathom that the Lord would allow Satan to attack a righteous person. We see godly people suffer every day and hear of our brothers and sisters being persecuted and martyred around the world. Nevertheless, the idea that God might do anything we find unpleasant strikes us as terribly wrong. When we think a little more deeply, however, we realize that we've been missing an extremely important point. While it is troubling to recognize that God might grant the devil permission to assault the righteous, the good news is that the devil cannot do anything without getting God's clearance first. Satan himself is God's subordinate. Though the devil is in active rebellion against God, the Lord tells Satan that he can go so far and no farther. And the devil obeys! When we think about it, that's wonderful news. No matter what may befall us, we are never solely in Satan's hands. Ultimately, even in the depths of our darkest tragedies, God is still in control. Yes, this is an obscure mystery. I prefer those sunny days when God's blessings flow like a bubbling river, when joy wells up in our hearts and spills out on our whole lives. But sometimes, for reasons we can't understand, arid seasons come. When they do, it is comforting to know that even in the driest drought we are ultimately in the hands of a loving God.

God uses evil. He even uses the devil himself to accomplish His ultimate, loving purpose. As Joseph explained to his brothers, who had planned to murder him but instead sold him as a slave, *"As for you, you meant evil against me, but God meant it for good"* (Genesis 50:20). God uses evil for good. In the words of Romans 8:28, *And we know that in all things God works for the good of those who love him, who have been called according to his purpose.* When we acknowledge that Satan is God's subordinate, both stories of David's census make perfect sense, without contradiction. Did Satan incite David, as 1 Chronicles 21:1 says? Yes, but he could only do so at the Lord's behest. Did the Lord incite

David, as 2 Samuel 24:1 says? Yes. And Satan was the flunky who did God's bidding.

Between these two verses it seemed we had a devastating contradiction. When we took a few steps back, however, we discovered there was no conflict at all. On the contrary, we discovered a profound truth about God's power over evil. The dissonance resolved into heart-moving harmony.

Quarks and Quirks

Someone said that theology is for people who find quantum physics too straight-forward. I like that in part because it makes it sound like theologians are smarter than quantum physicists. Well, maybe some theologians are, but I don't count myself in that category. What I really like about that quote, however, is the perception that our understanding of God is not always linear. God is so far above our capacity to understand, there will always be particular uncertainties.[117] Quantum physics has its quarks.[118] Theology has some quirks of its own. Our understanding of God and God's Word cannot be one-dimensional. The Bible is too rich and

---

[117] One of the most familiar principles of Quantum Physics is the Heisenberg Uncertainty Principle, concerning the unpredictability of protons. See "What is the Heisenberg Uncertainty Principle? – Chad Orzel" https://ed.ted.com/lessons/what-is-the-heisenberg-uncertainty-principle-chad-orzel Last visited 3.1.2019

[118] Quarks are subatomic, elementary particles, the building blocks of matter. See Physics Girl, "What Are Quarks? Sugar Edition!" https://www.youtube.com/watch?time_continue=244&v=LraNu_78sCw Last visited 3.1.2019

complex for that. When we take the Bible at face value, when we read the plain sense of Scripture, some things make us scratch our heads in puzzlement. Some things seem paradoxical and push us to seek for deeper wisdom.

In this chapter we've explored places where the Bible seems to contradict itself. In some cases, the contradictions were resolved when we zoomed out and looked at the bigger picture. Other times we saw how legitimate translation choices can make apparent contradictions disappear. Most intriguing to me are those paradoxes that create theological tension. They push us to struggle with our assumptions. They force us to expand our understanding. Often, they produce profound insights into the nature of Scripture, of God, and of His relationship with us.

We all come to Scripture with our own presuppositions. We can't help it. When people come with a preset belief that the Bible is somehow faulty or downright false, they find all kinds of flaws, just as I do with my wife when I'm in a bad mood. Just as antagonists have done with you at times, I'm sure. When you're holding a grudge and looking for a fight, one is easy enough to find. On the other hand, when people approach the Bible with the primary premise that they are dealing with the inspired Word of God, they read Scripture through a clearer lens. When we give God's Word the benefit of the doubt, the doubt starts to diminish and dissolve. To be sure there are people who try to read the Bible without prejudice, with an open mind. They can encounter honest questions. I know. I've grappled personally with some of the polarities discussed in this chapter. I'm grateful that I didn't ignore them because they became for me profound conundrums. As I wrestled with them, they blessed me. They pressed me into a deeper appreciation of and love for God's Word. If the Bible really is God-breathed, then the alleged contradictions aren't there by accident or error. They are there on purpose. They invite us to dig deeper, where we can find buried treasure. There's a nasty rumor going around that we can't believe the Bible because it's full of contradictions. On the contrary, those so-called contradictions can compel us to discover deeper truth.

Addendum to Chapter Seven

More about the Creation

Stories

Critics find more specific conflict in the two creation stories of Genesis 1 and 2 than the ones we considered in the body of this chapter. These differences in detail are claimed to be in the order in which things were created. Genesis 1:11-12 report that plants came into being on the third day of creation. A few verses later, Genesis 1:20-22 tells us that God made sea creatures and birds on the fifth day. On the sixth day he made *the beasts of the earth and the livestock* (Genesis 1:24-25), then culminated His creation by making man and woman in His own image (Genesis 1:26-27). So, the relevant order in Genesis 1 is plants, then animals, then humans.

In Genesis 2, when the creation story is told again, aspects of creation are mentioned in a different order. This is supposed to raise two problems. First, Genesis 2:5-9 could be interpreted to say that God created humans before He created plants. Second, one might infer from Genesis 2:18-20 that God created animals after He created the first man,

Adam. The woman, Eve, was created separately from the man. Again, is this really a contradiction?

The first creation story goes from Genesis 1:1 to Genesis 2:4. Many Bibles start the second story at Genesis 2:4 but I think that verse works better as a summary of what was before. (Remember, ancient manuscripts didn't even put spaces between words, much less clearly mark where new paragraphs began.) The second story starts in verse 5 and focuses on the Garden of Eden. In that place there were no cultivated plants yet because, as Genesis 2:5 says, there were no humans to tend them. Plants existed on earth since the third day, they just weren't yet in what would become the Garden of Eden. That's a solution to the first problem.

The second problem is a matter of translation. We've encountered such matters before. In the NRSV, Genesis 2:19 says, *So out of the ground the LORD God formed every animal of the field and every bird of the air, and brought them to the man to see what he would call them.* That obviously implies that, contrary to Genesis 1:24-28, the animals were created after the man. This translation is grammatically possible and I can see reasons to use it. However, instead of saying *The LORD God formed every animal*, several translations of Genesis 2:19 say, *Out of the ground the LORD had formed every animal.* (ESV. Also NIV, NASB and others.) See the difference? It's in the tense of the verb. The pluperfect or past-perfect tense, "had formed," means the animals were there already, just like we would expect from Genesis 1. The perfect tense, "formed" might imply that God formed the animals on the spot, while the man, Adam, was already there. Which is correct? The Hebrew word is *yitzer* (יִּצֶר), a form of the verb *yatzar* (יָצַר)

meaning to form or fashion. But what form is it? Perfect or past-perfect? You've probably already guessed. It can mean either. Hebrew doesn't distinguish between the two. If you're reading a translation like the ESV, NIV or NASB, you would never suspect that a problem might exist. It's a matter of interpretation, a translation issue. In these perfectly good translations, there is no contradiction, even in the details, between Genesis 2 and Genesis 1. [119]

---

[119] For more information, see "Are Genesis 1 and 2 contradictory?" (Creation Magazine LIVE! 6-05) https://www.youtube.com/watch?time_continue=1387&v=1EKj9 KDPE_w Last visited 3.1.2019

Chapter Eight

Reality Check

Is the Bible True?

Is the Bible true? When I was a young Christian, even after I graduated from seminary, I would have answered that question with a resounding "Yes!" By that I would have meant that if you could write every statement in the Bible on a "truth table," I would have marked a "T" next to each one. According to the "plain sense of Scripture" I would have affirmed the veracity of every statement. The Red Sea parted and made a watery wall with a corridor of dry land. Joshua marched around Jericho and "the walls came tumblin' down." The prophet Jonah was fish food, but only for a time. Jesus took Peter for a stroll on the water. Paul raised a boy from the dead. You name it, I would have affirmed it. However, now I've changed my mind. I would still say yes, the Bible is true, but I wouldn't mean quite the same thing. After more than five decades of trying to follow Christ and nearly forty years of ordained ministry, the truth of the Bible means so much more to me than it did then. The Bible is true in a much more powerful sense. Let me share a few stories, then I'll explain.

Here Am I. Send Me?

When I received a call to the preaching ministry I had in mind that I would go wherever God called me – except to Africa as a missionary. I have no idea why I wasn't willing to do that one thing, but I wasn't. After my first few very happy years as a pastor, however, I sensed the Lord might indeed be calling me to the mission field. Where? Well, Africa, of course. I tried to ignore the idea, but it kept chewing at me. It was inescapable. For example, it seemed that every time I turned on the radio, whatever station I tuned in played the hit song "Africa" by Toto. Three years earlier that wouldn't have been unusual. "Africa" was a number one hit, and I had liked the song a lot when it was popular. However, the song had fallen off the charts by then, and I didn't listen to an "oldies station." As good a song as "Africa" was, it shouldn't have been getting that much air time. Nevertheless, it felt like I couldn't listen to tunes on my way to the grocery store or to make a hospital visit without hearing the haunting chant, "I hear the drums echo in the night ..."

Maybe Someone was trying to tell me something. Finally, I said, "Okay, Lord. You're in charge. I'll go." I wrote the chair of the foreign missions board of the denomination I served at the time and told her I was willing to go anywhere they needed me. I had seen a position open in Cameroon that I thought I might be able to serve well. Can you guess what the missions board said? Nothing. They never even wrote back. But the nagging went away, and my radio play list returned to normal.

I think the Lord was graciously reminding me that *He* is Lord. I'm His servant. I don't get to tell Him where I will serve and where I won't. I believe He spoke to me through that series of incidents. He revealed His will for me to obey. He didn't want me to go to Africa, He wanted me to submit completely to Him: my life, my "career," everything. Some people say God doesn't speak to us nowadays as He did in the Bible. I disagree. This is one of the times He spoke to me. Friends have commented that this story reminds them of the time when God called Abraham to sacrifice his son, Isaac (Genesis 22). I can see the similarities. The point, however, is this. What the Bible says is true. It was true then and it's still true today. God still speaks to His people. Of course, God speaks to us through the Bible, but is that the only way He speaks? In Matthew 28:19-20 Jesus clearly told us to go into all the world and make disciples, but the Bible doesn't say whether Rod Pinder is supposed to move to Cameroon. God provided that specific information in other ways.

A Distressed Dad

Roughly 30 years later God did call me to the mission field in Africa – for a week. In 2014 I went on a mission trip to the Democratic Republic of Congo with Presbyterian Reformed Ministries International. I had been to Egypt and Morocco, but this was my first venture into sub-Saharan Africa. We went to teach the *Dunamis* course, introducing the person and work of the Holy Spirit.[120] I love teaching that course, but I was also excited about the people I would meet and the things I would learn. I wasn't disappointed.

Our team taught for five days. On the fifth day the leadership team broke into pairs to pray for the participants in the workshop. The specific purpose of this prayer session was to ask the Holy Spirit to empower participants with spiritual gifts for ministry. People lined up to receive prayer, laying on of hands, and anointing with oil. My prayer partner was Dr. Omalanga, a wonderful Congolese pastor and professor of Old Testament.

A man whose eyes were fraught with distress came to our prayer station. He asked us to pray for his infant son whose life hung in the balance in the local hospital. Of course, I wanted to pray for the baby, but this time was set aside to pray for empowerment, not healing. (Sometimes when I get focused on an undertaking, it's hard for me to shift my attention.) What to do? Suddenly the right course of action hit me. We prayed for the little boy. How could we refuse?

---

[120] For more information about this insightful, theologically balanced and spiritually powerful course, visit https://www.dunamisinstitute.org. Last visited 3.1.2019

But even more we prayed for the dad. We asked the Spirit to grant him gifts of healing. Then I anointed the father's hands and told him to go to the hospital, lay hands on his son and pray for his healing. It seemed the Lord was leading me to do that, as if it was what He wanted to do.

That was Friday. I didn't see the man on Saturday and wondered if I would ever hear the outcome. Did the dad do what I suggested? Did I hear rightly from the Lord? Was the boy healed? Perhaps I would never know. On Sunday after the conference I was invited to preach at the church where Dr. Omalanga was pastor. In the course of the sermon I shared that story and my prayer that God acted through our simple obedience. After the service I discovered that the dad was in that crowded congregation that morning. He had gone to the hospital and prayed for his son. The baby was home and continuing to improve. Thanks be to God! There was a time when that vignette would have sounded strange to me. It reminds us of the sort of story we would read in the Bible, doesn't it? But it happened in the 21st century.

What We Needed to Hear

On that same Sunday, an elder on the team was asked to preach at another church. Though he is a gifted and dedicated church leader with whom I've served for years, I don't think Dick had ever preached before. Further, he did not have much time to prepare. Nevertheless, he faithfully answered God's call. He worked through his fear and trembling and spoke a bold message about controversial behavior in the congregation, though he did not know much about that church. After worship a member came up to him and said, "I had a vision of you coming to us and telling us exactly what we need to hear. Thank you." Wow! Sounds like the flip side of St. Paul's vision of the man saying, *"Come to Macedonia and help us"* (Acts 16:9-10). It reminds me of Cornelius being told to invite Peter to come and speak at his house (Acts 10:1-6, 30-33). Surprising? Less and less, actually. The more time I spend reading the Bible and trying to live it out, the more I see that the Bible describes reality as it really is. Those things still happen, and not just on mission trips. I could tell you about similar incidents at the congregation I serve in Orlando, Florida and many other churches where people are open minded when it comes to Scripture. Is the Bible true? Can we trust the Bible? Yes, in ways far deeper than we might have imagined.

Dreams and Visions

On a Saturday night in June of 2016 Sandi, another of our elders, was awakened from sleep. In a vision she was looking down on an urban building that was teeming with life, symbolized by birds and butterflies flying around the structure. Though she didn't recognize the scene, she sensed the Lord was calling her to pray. So, she prayed. For hours she prayed. Apparently, she fell asleep, for she said that when she woke up "the scene was still there, but the life was gone." That morning, stumbling toward the kitchen for her first cup of coffee, she was stunned to see that same scene on the television. It was the aerial view of the Pulse night club, where in the early hours of that dark morning, forty-nine people had been murdered and fifty-three injured. Only in heaven will we learn the impact of Sandi's midnight prayers in mitigating that tragic event. Nevertheless, it sounds like the kind of thing we would read about in the Bible.

The Bible is true not only because it is filled with true statements, but also because it gives an accurate description of the world. It teaches us what the world is really like. Joel 2:28-29 records the LORD's declaration, *And it shall come to pass afterward, that I will pour out my Spirit on all flesh; your sons and your daughters shall prophesy, your old men shall dream dreams, and your young men shall see visions. Even on the male and female servants in those days I will pour out my Spirit.* That happened at Pentecost (Acts 2:16-21). It still happens today.

Killing My People

ISIS, the radical Islamic terrorist group, is infamous for brutal murders of those who oppose their views, particularly Christians. Among the many stories of Muslims encountering Jesus Christ in dreams and subsequently coming to faith in Him, [121] there is an amazing and credible report of a former ISIS fighter who had just such an experience. In a dream, Jesus appeared to him and said, "You are killing My people." Yet the man continued his bloodthirsty campaign. One day a Christian whom the terrorist was about to slaughter said to him, "I know you will

---

[121] See, for example, "SHOCKING: ISIS Jihadist Converted to Christianity After Seeing Jesus In A Dream" https://www.youtube.com/watch?time_continue=10&v=90NEOV XiCxk Last visited 3.1.2019 See also chapter six, note 111.

kill me, but I give you my Bible." The Christian was right. The terrorist killed him. Remarkably, however, the persecutor started reading the Scriptures. He then had another dream in which Jesus invited him, "Follow me." We know the story because the former killer sought out a missionary from Youth with a Mission (YWAM) and asked to be discipled, trained as a follower of Christ.[122] The story is not an exact parallel to the conversion of Saul of Tarsus as we read it in the book of Acts, but the similarities are striking. God still works today. The Bible is not only true, it is true to life.

Double for Your Trouble

Elizabeth was a little girl in the church I serve. She moved to Mississippi and grew to be a godly woman there. We've kept in touch by social media. She is happily married to Jason, but they struggled with infertility. After a heartbreaking miscarriage she shared the news with her church family. A member named Mrs. Clara came to Elizabeth and Jason, put her arms around them both then declared that God would give them "double for their trouble." Sometime after that, a

---

[122] "Dreams and Visions of Jesus Are Fueling the Explosive Growth of Christianity in Muslim Nations Worldwide," https://www.charismanews.com/opinion/63635-dreams-and-visions-of-jesus-are-fueling-the-explosive-growth-of-christianity-in-muslim-nations-worldwide Last visited 3.1.2019. See also "Reports: ISIS Jihadist Converts to Christ after Dream," http://www1.cbn.com/cbnnews/world/2015/june/reports-isis-jihadist-converts-to-christ-after-dream Last visited 3.1.2019

preacher from Texarkana[123] came to Elizabeth's church. Elizabeth was suffering from neck pain, so at the appropriate time she went forward for healing. After praying for her neck, the preacher prompted her, "There's more." In response, she explained about the miscarriage and infertility. He prayed for that, too. Three months later, like several barren couples in the Bible, Jason and Elizabeth conceived. As a matter of fact, they conceived twins! Double for their trouble. At this time of writing the two girls are five years old. They are vivacious bundles of energy, personality and joy. They love Jesus and their church family, as well as singing and dancing. Elizabeth writes, "We can't wait to see what God does with them, how He uses them, and how they live their lives for Him. They were His before they were ours." Oh, and Elizabeth's neck? It's completely healed. She has before-and-after x-rays to prove it.

Some people say God doesn't do things now like He did in Bible times. I find that view inconceivable. My experience, like the experience of many Christians, conforms to what the Scriptures teach and describe. In this modern-day story, God spoke a prophetic word through Mrs. Clara, and it came true. He healed Elizabeth's neck miraculously, and the barren woman had a baby, as the preacher prophesied. Two babies, in fact. The Bible really is true.

In Chapter Five, we read how God healed Noel's shoulder with a literal thump from the Bible. We also read how He reversed Renee's retinopathy. More stories could be told and

---

[123] For more information about Tracy Harris Ministries, see http://wp.experiencehim.org/# Last visited 3.1.2019

verified, but I hope these are enough to make the point. [124] God still works among us today. The Bible gives us an accurate description of reality. The Bible is not only true in the sense that it makes valid statements; the Bible is "true to life." It gives a true picture of reality.

A Bad Day at the Office

One Sunday afternoon I was chatting with a buddy from seminary. He asked me how the service had gone that morning. I told him it was horrible. Oh sure, I prayed with a handful of people who recovered completely from various illnesses, but other than that the service was flat. Okay, that didn't really happen to me, but something similar happened to Jesus. Matthew, Mark and Luke all tell us about Jesus visiting His home synagogue in Nazareth. The visit doesn't go well. For some reason the people who watched Him grow up as a boy don't take Jesus seriously as the Son of God. They outright reject Him. Mark tells us, *and he could do no mighty work there, except that he laid his hands on a few sick people and healed them. And he marveled because of their unbelief* (Mark 6:5-6). Now, I think healing four or five sick people is awesome, but for Jesus that was a bad day at the office.

---

[124] See "Dr. Craig Keener, Acts, Lecture 4, Credibility of Miracles," https://yhoo.it/2KPeX87
Last visited 3.1.2019 Keener has produced a 2 volume work, *Miracles: The Crediblity of the New Testament Accounts.* http://bakerpublishinggroup.com/books/miracles/335370.

So why did that happen? Why was Jesus so stymied? Apparently, it was because of the lack of faith of the people. That fits with the fact that we hear Jesus say things like "Your faith has made you well" and "Your faith has saved you" in as many as seven separate instances. There seems to be a connection between people's faith and the Lord's ability to do signs and wonders, to do things that we would call supernatural. When people don't expect the Lord to work, He often doesn't. When we expect Him to act, things are more likely to happen. Paul said to the Galatians, *Does he who supplies the Spirit to you and works miracles among you do so by works of the law, or by hearing with faith* (Galatians 3:5)*?* The answer Paul clearly has in mind is, "faith." God works miracles among His people by faith. It shouldn't surprise us that where faith is low, miracles are few.

A Thorny Issue

Now, we must be very careful here. It is easy to blame people's disbelief for their sickness or misfortune. Sometimes Christians send this toxic message, "You're sick because you don't believe. You're having trouble because you don't trust God. If you had faith, then God would work a miracle for you." Still today we can become like Job's friends who blamed his calamity on his alleged unrighteousness. And still today the Lord declares, *"you have not spoken of me what is right"* (Job 42:7).

Even for people with great faith, miracles don't always happen. In Acts 12 there's an epic account of an angel rescuing the apostle Peter from prison. The angel came into his cell in the dark of night, when Peter was bound with chains and sleeping between two soldiers. Light flooded the room. The chains snapped. Crack! The apostle was set free! Miraculous. However, at the beginning of that same chapter we find a more dismal story. Acts 12:1-2 says, *About that time Herod the king laid violent hands on some who belonged to the church. He killed James the brother of John with the sword.* What? The apostle James had faith just like the apostle Peter. So why didn't an angel deliver James? Why was Peter set free, but James had to die? Why did James not get the same miracle Peter got? Sometimes, even in the Bible, events take a tragic course.

In the 12th chapter of 2 Corinthians the apostle Paul talks about a horrible struggle he experienced. He called it "a thorn in the flesh." There are many speculative theories about what Paul's thorn was. Some think it was a physical malady, like blindness. Others think it was nagging doubt or some persistent temptation. We don't know. But we do know what God did about this problem. Paul tells us, *Three times I pleaded with the Lord about this, that it should leave me. But he said to me, "My grace is sufficient for you, for my power is made perfect in weakness." Therefore I will boast all the more gladly of my weaknesses, so that the power of Christ may rest upon me* (2 Corinthians 12:8-9). Paul had faith. Paul prayed fervently about his problem, but the Lord didn't solve it the way Paul wanted. The Lord didn't take the thorn away.

God works miracles in the Bible, but He doesn't *always* work miracles. God sets captives free, but He doesn't set *all* captives free. God heals people supernaturally, but still people die. No one would try to argue that God didn't rescue James, therefore He must not have rescued Peter either. No one would seriously contend that God didn't take away Paul's thorn, therefore, blind Bartimaeus never received his sight. Yet some argue that way about today. "I didn't get a miracle," they say, "even though I prayed for it. Therefore, I know that miracles don't happen anymore." No. Miracles happen today. God works signs and wonders today just as He did in Bible times. But they don't happen every time we want them to. Our faith creates a fertile field where miracles can flourish, but our faith isn't the only factor. We should never shame people when a miracle doesn't occur, blaming their unbelief (or secretly blaming our own). But we should encourage faith, build faith, and strengthen faith. We can pray, like that distraught father in Mark 9:24, *I believe; help my unbelief.*

Christ a' L'Orange

Most of us only scratch the surface of Christian living. Think of the Kingdom of God as a sweet, succulent orange. Many people never penetrate the orange peel. Their religion is bitter, like biting into the rind of the fruit. They get just enough Jesus to set their teeth on edge. Others who call themselves Christians eat the orange peel as a condiment. They add some of it to their other foods. Jesus is the spice of life. He gives life a little extra zest. Both groups are missing out. The peel isn't the juicy part. It isn't where we find the full flavor and nourishment. The life-giving nutrients are deeper down. The savory sweetness is in the succulent meat. When people try to limit the God of the Bible to what they can manage or understand, they're adding Jesus as a spice to life. They're trying to serve Christ a' l'orange. This is what we do when we let our worldview, our perspective on reality limit how we see God working in the world.[125] When we say "God doesn't do miraculous things anymore," when we say, "That was then and this is now," we try to cram God into a box that won't hold Him. We truncate the Bible's message.

Martin Lloyd Jones gives this profound diagnosis:

> "People come to the New Testament and, instead of taking it as it is, they interpret it in the light of their experience, and so they reduce it. Everything is interpreted in terms of what they have and what they experience. And I believe that this is largely responsible for the condition of the Christian church at this present time. People are so afraid of what they call enthusiasm, and are so afraid of fanaticism, that in order to avoid those they go right over to the other side without facing what is offered in the New Testament. They take what they have and what they are as the norm."[126]

Is the Bible true? Absolutely. But that means so much more than a fundamental affirmation of certain historical facts or

---

[125] For an excellent treatment of worldview and the Bible see Long, Zeb Bradford and McMurry, Douglas, *Collapse of the Brass Heaven: Rebuilding Our Worldview to Embrace the Power of God.* https://www.amazon.com/Collapse-Brass-Heaven-Rebuilding-Worldview/dp/0800792157 © 1994 by Zeb Bradford Long and Douglas McMurry, Published by Chosen Books

[126] Martin Lloyd-Jones, *Joy Unspeakable: Power and Renewal in the Holy Spirit.* Wheaton, IL: Harold Shaw Publishers, 1984, pp. 18-19

spiritual teachings. The Bible also describes the world as it really is. The Bible describes a world in which a loving God is busy, active and in control.

All Christians believe the basics of the Gospel. God created us for a loving relationship with Himself. We turned our back on God by choosing to live life our way instead of His. So, in unfathomable love, God became a human being in Jesus Christ. He died on the cross to take away our sins. He was raised from the dead to win eternal life for all who trust in Him. He ascended into heaven, where He reigns with God the Father. From there He hears our prayers. From there He pours out His Holy Spirit. From there He will return to destroy evil and restore all things to perfection. If you believe that, you are a Christian. If you trust Christ, you are saved. If you follow Him you are His disciple.

All that's true. All that leads to the comfort of forgiveness and the hope of eternal life. All of that can give your life meaning and zest, but it is not the whole story. The Bible teaches all of that, but that isn't all the Bible teaches. The Bible reveals God's worldview. The Bible shows us how God intends life to look and function. That is to say, the Bible shows us what reality really is. Many people believe the Scriptures. I've believed them for a long time. Creation, water into wine, resurrection, healing, prophesy, the whole shebang. But it's one thing to believe the Bible intellectually, it's something very different to live the Bible experientially.

As Matt Chandler said, "Living the book is better than knowing the book."[127]

Another nasty rumor is that the Bible tells us a lot of things that used to be true but aren't any longer. Unfortunately, this rumor is often propagated by people in the church. (Borrowing a phrase from the Harry Potter craze, a friend of mine jokingly calls such believers "muggles." Nothing supernatural happens in their mundane experience.) They say, "God doesn't work supernaturally among us anymore." As a matter of fact, God doesn't work supernaturally among us any less. The Bible describes reality as it really is. Our Father invites us to experience a richer reality, a more multi-dimensional reality. God's Word invites us into a world of greater wonder, of signs and wonders. That's what I now mean when I say the Bible is true. The Bible gives us a reality check.

---

[127] Matt Chandler: Prophecy, tongues, their continuation, and our fears (Convergence, OKC 2017) https://www.youtube.com/watch?v=QFojKyynEI4 Last visited 3.1.2019

Chapter Nine

The Bible in Seven Words

The Whole Thing?

"Pastor," she said with her face crumpled up like a sock puppet, "my problem is I just don't understand the Bible."

"I see," I replied sympathetically. "How many times have you read it?"

"The whole thing?" she asked, this time with her eyebrows hoisted to the middle of her forehead.

"Yes," I echoed, "the whole thing."

"Well, I've never read the whole thing," she sputtered.

"Then I think I know why you don't understand it," I wryly replied.

Okay, I probably could have been a bit more pastoral and tender. I was young in the ministry at that time. But you have to admit I had a point. How can we expect to understand God's Word if we've never read it? Yes, the whole thing. But she had a point, too. Some parts of the Bible are hard to understand. We've just spent seven chapters dealing with some of the difficulties. Besides, the Bible is a massive tome! It's a collection of sixty-six books written over a period of more than 1,500 years about events that happened on three different continents. As we said in Chapter One, reading the Bible gives us ample opportunity to love the Lord with all our minds. Sometimes we have to engage our brains if we want to understand God's Word. We have to think. Yet Christians know that the Bible is the unique, God-breathed Word of the Lord. No other book can guide our lives like the Bible. No other book can give us wisdom and hope like the Bible. No other book can accurately describe reality like the Bible. It may be hard to understand in places, but it proffers eternal wisdom. Isn't that worth the effort?

Break It Down

So, we come to our last nasty rumor. Because parts of the Bible are challenging to comprehend, some say that the Bible is *too* hard to understand. Maybe even impossible. Many people believe that rumor, and so they don't bother reading the Scriptures, at least not much. What a tragedy! That's why it's helpful to have some tools to enrich our understanding. We've looked at tools like tapping into the rich treasure of translations available to us and using good hermeneutical principles. Another very beneficial tool would be a précis of Scripture, an overview of "the whole thing." Something like *Cliffs Notes*. If we had a summary, a schematic, that might help us see the big picture better. Then the context of the big picture could help us understand the individual parts as we read them. In Chapter Five we got a bit of an overview when we talked about the Bible as one story. In an appendix to this chapter, I'll share a longer summary of different sections of the Scriptures. Right now, however, it will help us to see what kinds of writings, what types of literature we find in the Bible.

Bible scholars have identified several different genres: Law, history, poetry, proverbs, prophesy, parables, letters, gospels and more. To be sure, these genres aren't distinctly delineated. There's plenty of overlap among these types. There are wisdom psalms and history psalms. We find psalms and prophecies interjected in the middle of histories and so on. There is a mix, a beautiful interplay of genres in the Bible. For our purposes, however, it will simplify matters to recognize two basic strands in Scripture. There are two primary categories into which every part of the Bible can be sorted. Those two classifications are narrative and instruction, story and teaching. If you like we could call them indicative and imperative. The indicative tells us what happened, the imperative explains what we should do about it. The narrative recounts the story of God's relationship with His people, from creation through alienation, then redemption in Jesus Christ to perfect restoration when Christ returns. The instruction sections teach us how to live in a right relationship with God. That is, instruction tells us how to respond to God's actions in ways that will let us live life to the fullest. Of course, the stories are instructive in themselves. There is still overlap, but this division will help us get a panoramic perspective.

This two-fold paradigm fits with the teaching of the Westminster Shorter Catechism when it declares, "The Scriptures principally teach what man is to believe concerning God, and what duty God requires of man."[128] Essentially, the narratives of Scripture show us, in story form, what we are to believe concerning God[129] while the instruction teaches us how to respond to Him appropriately. If we can find places in the Bible where these two strands are summarized for us, that will help us understand the Bible as

---

[128] *Confessional Standards of ECO: A Covenant Order of Evangelical Presbyterians,* Westminster Shorter Catechism Q 3 https://www.eco-pres.org/static/media/uploads/eco_confessional_standards_digital_12.11.18.pdf p.89 Last visited 1.3.19

[129] Theologians like to say things like, "God is omniscient, God is omnipotent, God is immutable." The Bible also makes a few propositional statements about God, like "God is love (I John 4:8). More often, however, Scripture tends to show us God's character by recounting His deeds.

a whole. But are there passages that encapsulate the Scriptures for us in such a helpful way? Let's see.

Torah

We'll start with instruction. The Hebrew word for instruction is *torah* (תּוֹרָה). You might recognize it as the word that is often translated "law." Passages like Psalm 19:7-14, Psalm 119 and Deuteronomy 4:5-8 make it clear that the purpose of God's *Torah* is not to restrict our lives but to enrich them. *Torah* instructs God's people in the highest possible quality of life. There are civil, ceremonial and dietary laws that apply to particular contexts in ancient Israel. Like the prescription to worship only at the Temple in Jerusalem and the prohibition against bacon wrapped scallops, these requirements have been fulfilled and surpassed in Christ. (See "Scripture Interprets Scripture" in Chapter Five.) There are also moral laws, which are universal in context.

The core of the Old Testament Law is the passage we know as the Ten Commandments. To use the old language of the Shorter Catechism, "The moral law is summarily comprehended in the Ten Commandments."[130] While this passage may be very familiar, I encourage you not to skip or skim it. Read it slowly and meditatively. As you read, think deeply and imagine a society in which people put these

---

[130] *Confessional Standards of ECO: A Covenant Order of Evangelical Presbyterians,* Westminster Shorter Catechism Q 4 https://www.eco-pres.org/static/media/uploads/eco_confessional_standards_digital_12.11.18.pdf p. 93 Last visited 3.1.2019

instructions into practice. How much better would life be without idolatry, adultery and the other things taught against in these verses?

> And God spoke all these words, saying, "I am the LORD your God, who brought you out of the land of Egypt, out of the house of slavery.

> "You shall have no other gods before me.

> "You shall not make for yourself a carved image, or any likeness of anything that is in heaven above, or that is in the earth beneath, or that is in the water under the earth. You shall not bow down to them or serve them, for I the LORD your God am a jealous God, visiting the iniquity of the fathers on the children to the third and the fourth generation of those who hate me, but showing steadfast love to thousands of those who love me and keep my commandments.

> "You shall not take the name of the LORD your God in vain, for the LORD will not hold him guiltless who takes his name in vain.

> "Remember the Sabbath day, to keep it holy. Six days you shall labor, and do all your work, but the seventh day is a Sabbath to the LORD your God. On it you shall not do any work, you, or your son, or your daughter, your male servant, or your female servant, or your livestock, or the sojourner who is within your gates. For in six days the LORD made heaven and earth, the sea, and all that is in them, and rested on

the seventh day. Therefore the LORD blessed the Sabbath day and made it holy.

"Honor your father and your mother, that your days may be long in the land that the LORD your God is giving you.

"You shall not murder.

"You shall not commit adultery.

"You shall not steal.

"You shall not bear false witness against your neighbor.

"You shall not covet your neighbor's house; you shall not covet your neighbor's wife, or his male servant, or his female servant, or his ox, or his donkey, or anything that is your neighbor's" (Exodus 20:1-17).

As a pastor I've counseled and prayed with many people whose lives would have been so much better if they or the people they loved had followed these teachings. My own life would have been better if I had adhered to them more closely.[131] Joy would have been multiplied and pain greatly diminished. The loving God who created us in His image has not left us to our own devices or abandoned us to our desires when it comes to living life to the fullest. He has graciously

---

[131] In line with historic Reformed Theology we could identify three primary uses of God's Law: 1) To order society, 2) To point out our need for a Savior, since no one can perfectly keep God's Law, and so we must be saved by grace through faith in the Savior, 3) To instruct believers how to live a rewarding, holy life that is pleasing to God.

given us His instructions, His *Torah*. The Ten Commandments lift up the *Torah's* most salient points. They are a summary of God's Law.

The Ten Commandments let us rightly perceive life through binocular lenses. The first four commandments tell us how to live in a right relationship with God. Have no other gods before Him. Do not worship idols. Keep His name holy. Set aside the Sabbath day for worship and rest. The last six commandments pertain to how to have right relationships with other people. Show respect to parents. Steer clear of murder, adultery, theft, lying or perjury, and coveting or greed. These point us toward the fulfilling and godly lifestyles our Creator desires for us. When Christians seek guidance on how to live a good life, they invariably turn to the Ten Commandments. Most of the great catechisms contain rich sections explaining and applying this *Torah* to the lives of Jesus' followers.[132]

---

[132] See *Confessional Standards of ECO: A Covenant Order of Evangelical Presbyterians,* The Heidelberg Catechism, Q. 92- 115 (pp. 37-42), The Westminster Shorter Catechism, Q 41-81 (pp. 93-97) The Westminster Larger Catechism, Q 98-148 (pp. 118-131) https://www.eco-pres.org/static/media/uploads/eco_confessional_standards_digital_12.11.18.pdf

For a more modern application see *ECO Constitution: Essential Tenets, Polity and Rules of Discipline,* Essential Tenets: Living in Obedience to the Word of God" III E (p.7-8)

Reader's Digest

The *Torah* is nicely summarized in the Ten Commandments, but what about the narrative strand? Is it ever summarized? Does the Bible ever give us a *Reader's Digest* version of the story? As a matter of fact, there are several passages where the Bible story is at least partially reviewed. The "Historical Psalms" (Psalms 78, 105-107, 114, 135-136) summon people to praise God by recalling His mighty acts through the ages.[133] The great prayer of confession in Nehemiah 9:6-38 is a comprehensive summary of the story of the Old Testament.[134] Hebrews 11:4-38 celebrates the faith of many heroes and heroines of Israel's history. Another comprehensive recap of the Bible story is Stephen's final sermon before his execution (Acts 7:2-53). All of those are worth reading for an overview of the Bible's sweeping saga. We will look now at a summary which Jesus Himself presents in a parable. Look at Matthew 21:33-44:

> *"Hear another parable. There was a master of a house who planted a vineyard and put a fence around it and dug a winepress in it and built a tower and leased it to tenants, and went into another country. When the season for fruit drew near, he sent his servants to the tenants to get his fruit. And*

---

[133] See Kirkland, Geoffery R., "Why Did God Include the 'Historical' Psalms?" - http://vassaloftheking.com/home/180007755/180007755/Images/Why%20did%20God%20include%20the%20the%20Historical%20Psalms.pdf Last visited 3.1.19

[134] For a powerful sermon on this passage, listen to Matt Ferguson, "God is Awesome! We, on the other hand …" http://hillsboropc.org/god_is_awesome_we_on_the_other_hand____ Last visited 3.1.2019

the tenants took his servants and beat one, killed another, and stoned another. Again he sent other servants, more than the first. And they did the same to them. Finally he sent his son to them, saying, 'They will respect my son.' But when the tenants saw the son, they said to themselves, 'This is the heir. Come, let us kill him and have his inheritance.' And they took him and threw him out of the vineyard and killed him. When therefore the owner of the vineyard comes, what will he do to those tenants?" They said to him, "He will put those wretches to a miserable death and let out the vineyard to other tenants who will give him the fruits in their seasons."

Jesus said to them, "Have you never read in the Scriptures:

> *"'The stone that the builders rejected*
>
> *has become the cornerstone;*
>
> *this was the Lord's doing,*
>
> *and it is marvelous in our eyes'?*

"Therefore I tell you, the kingdom of God will be taken away from you and given to a people producing its fruits. And the one who falls on this stone will be broken to pieces; and when it falls on anyone, it will crush him."

A vineyard is a favorite biblical metaphor for Israel. The metaphor comes from a parable told 700 years before Christ by Isaiah (Isaiah 5:1-7). In fact, the prophet explicitly says,

For the vineyard of the Lord of hosts is the house of Israel, and the men of Judah are his pleasant planting (Isaiah 5:7). In His parable Jesus is saying that, throughout Israel's history, God sent prophets to call the people back into a right relationship with Himself, just as the landowner sent servants to the vineyard. But Israel abused the prophets. In another context Jesus lamented, *"O Jerusalem, Jerusalem, the city that kills the prophets and stones those who are sent to it! How often would I have gathered your children together as a hen gathers her brood under her wings, and you were not willing"* (Luke 13:34)! And now, like the landowner, God has sent His Son to His vineyard, but the tenants will kill Him, too. The tenants in the parable clearly represent the religious leaders. That point was not wasted on the leaders of Jesus' day, for Matthew 21:45 tells us, *When the chief priests and the Pharisees heard his parables, they perceived that he was speaking about them.* The Bible is a story of God reaching out in love to His people, but tragically they continue to reject Him. Ultimately God sends His Son, but the Son is also rejected. That's how Jesus summarized the Bible's story. Thank God the story doesn't end there as we will soon see, but the parable is an overview of much of the Bible narrative.

The Great Commandment

So, in passages like the Ten Commandments and the Parable of the Tenants we have summaries of the Bible's instructions and the Bible story. But can we break things down even more than that? Can we narrow the funnel even further? As a matter of fact, we can. In fact, Jesus has already done that for us. In Matthew 22 someone asked Jesus to identify the greatest commandment in the *Torah.* Jesus answered, *"You shall love the Lord your God with all your heart and with all your soul and with all your mind. This is the great and first commandment. And a second is like it: You shall love your neighbor as yourself. On these two commandments depend all the Law and the Prophets"* (Matthew 22:37-40).

Notice the same twin focus we saw in the Ten Commandments. This passage tells us more succinctly yet more fully how to live in a right relationship with God and right relationships with other people. Think of it. If we love God without reservation, will we put other gods before Him? Worship idols? Misuse His name? Will one day a week be too much to devote to fellowship with Him? No, it will be far too little. By the same token, will we murder or steal from those neighbors whom we love? Will we lie to them? Wreck their families and our own by succumbing to our lusts? Will we covet what is theirs? Won't we instead rejoice in their blessings? Love accomplishes, love completes, love satisfies the teachings of Moses and the prophets. Love fulfills the *Torah.* We find this powerful insight repeated several times in the New Testament (Mark 12:29-34, Luke 10:27-28, Romans 13:9-10, Galatians 5:14, James 2:8), but Matthew 22:37-40 gives us a perfect and memorable summary of the Bible's *Torah.* In fact, I encourage you to memorize it.

The Story in a Nutshell

But what about the Bible narrative? What about the story? Is there a verse that encapsulates that as well? Yes. If you know the Bible at all, you are no doubt familiar with the verse I have in mind. In John 3:16 we find the Bible story in a nutshell. *For God so loved the world, that he gave his only Son, that whoever believes in him should not perish but have eternal life.*

So much meaning is packed into that one verse. It presupposes and builds on the whole Bible narrative. God created us in His image for a loving relationship with Himself (Psalm 100:3). Humans, however, turned our backs on the One who made us and loves us (Isaiah 53:6). God could have watched us walk away, but He was not willing to let us go, for He loves us with an everlasting love (Jeremiah 31:3). From all of rebellious humanity, God chose one family, the family of Abraham, through whom He would preserve His truth, through whom He would propagate His blessing (Genesis 12:1-3). Through that family, God would spread His love. Just as God promised, the descendants of Abraham grew into a great nation, the people of Israel (Exodus 1:7, Acts 7:17). God gave His *Torah* to His special people (Exodus 20:1-17). When they grossly violated His law, He sent them prophets to call them back into His love. The people rejected and killed the prophets, but His love never failed. Finally, He sent His Son (Matthew 21:33-44). The Word became flesh and dwelt among us (John 1:14). God Himself became a human being. Jesus taught us the Father's ways and instructed us in godly love. He demonstrated the Spirit's power by working signs and wonders – healing the sick, raising the dead, calming the storm, expelling demons and more (Acts 10:38). He did more than any book could contain (John 21:25). And yes, we killed Him, too, just as He prophesied (Acts 2:23).

But as I said, that isn't the end of the story. His death was the sacrifice that cleanses us from sin (I John 1:7, 4:10 and many other places). Not only that, *But God raised him from the dead, freeing him from the agony of death, because it was impossible for death to keep its hold on him* (Acts 2:24 NIV). He is now at the right hand of the Father in heaven. There He prays, He intercedes for us (Romans 8:34). From there He pours out His Holy Spirit (Acts 2:33) to bring us to faith (1 Corinthians 12:3), to empower us to serve Him and witness for Him (Acts 1:8), to transform us increasingly into His own glorious likeness (2 Corinthians 3:18). From there He will return in glory at the end of the age (Acts 1:11), and He will be known as King of kings and Lord of lords (Revelation 19:16) and He will reign forever and ever (Revelation 22:5).

All of that is behind John 3:16. All of that is summed up in the words, *He gave His only Son.* And He did it out of love. Further, everyone who believes in Him, that is, everyone who trusts Jesus Christ becomes a child of God (John 1:12-13). Our sins are forgiven (Acts 10:43), and our broken relationship with our Father is restored for all eternity. That's what John 3:16 is talking about. *God so loved the world, that he gave his only Son, that whoever believes in him should not perish but have eternal life.* That's the Bible narrative in a nutshell. *That's* the story, and I'm sticking to it.

The Bible in Seven Words

So, we have the message of the whole Bible concentrated in five short verses. Matthew 22:37-40 tells us to love God and love others. That's the *Torah*. John 3:16 tells us why we should live that way: because in sending His Son, God loved the world with sacrificial, saving love. That's the story. But can we break it down further still? Indeed, we can. There is a single verse that summarizes the Bible's whole message in seven simple words: *We love because he first loved us* (1 John 4:19). That's it. Story and *Torah*. Narrative and instruction. Indicative and Imperative. The Bible principally teaches what we are to believe concerning God, namely that He first loved us. And the Bible tells us what duty God requires of us, namely, to love Him and love others. If you can understand 1 John 4:19, you understand the Bible. Everything else is an unpacking of that one verse.

Now this does not mean that once we've memorized 1 John 4:19 we don't need to read the Bible anymore. Quite the contrary, the better we understand that verse the more we will want to know about this God who loves us. We will be all the more eager to learn specifically how to live in His love. We will hunger and thirst for the story and the *Torah*. The reason we were looking for a summary of the Bible was to help us understand "the whole thing." We wanted something like *Cliffs Notes* to help us get the big picture. But *Cliffs Notes*, when used properly, aren't a substitute for great books, they're intended as study guides. In the same way 1 John 4:19 and these other verses, these summaries, are like study guides to help us understand the message of Scripture. They give us a bird's eye view, a satellite snapshot of the Bible's landscape. Now, as we read, study, and meditate on Scripture, we have a broad perspective on where we're going and where we've been.

Living the Bible

If you understand 1 John 4:19, you understand the whole Bible. But remember that powerful statement we quoted from Matt Chandler in Chapter Eight. "It's better to live the Word than to know the Word."[135] The Bible comes to life, not when we understand the theological proposition that God first loved us, but when we *experience* His love. Likewise, the Word of God lives in us, not when we merely comprehend our duty to love God and others, but when we *actually* love Him with every fiber of our being, and when we love our neighbors in our hearts and with our deeds. It's better to live the Word than to know the Word, and we live the Word by living in love.

But how do we do that? How do we experience love and live in love? Ultimately that is the work of the One who inspired the Scriptures in the first place, the Holy Spirit. First, it is the Spirit Who convinces us that God first loved us. Romans 8:16 says, *The Spirit himself bears witness with our spirit that we are children of God.* The Holy Spirit tenderly speaks to our hearts and tells us of God's love for us. Remember, *The natural person does not accept the things of the Spirit of God, for they are folly to him, and he is not able to understand them because they are spiritually discerned* (1 Corinthians 2:14). God's love is spiritually discerned. It is by

---

[135] Matt Chandler: Prophecy, tongues, their continuation, and our fears (Convergence, OKC 2017) https://www.youtube.com/watch?v=QFojKyynEI4 Last visited 3.1.2019

the Spirit of God that we experience the love of God. Immediately before John 3:16 we read the story of Jesus and Nicodemus (John 3:1-15). Whether John 3:16 and the following verses are a part of that story or a commentary on it is a disputed question, but the connection between the two is indisputable. It is significant that in that story Jesus tells Nicodemus, *"Truly, truly, I say to you, unless one is born of water and the Spirit, he cannot enter the kingdom of God"* (John 3:5). We receive eternal life, which is nearly synonymous with saying we enter the kingdom of God, by putting our trust in Jesus. But we really can't do that on our own. It's a matter of being born of the Spirit. The Holy Spirit enables us to know and experience God's love for us.

Likewise, we need the Holy Spirit in order for us to live lives of love. Have you ever tried hard to love someone who is hard to love? The more intensely you try, the more difficult it gets. We can never muster enough love from our own resources. I serve a small but very diverse congregation. One of the highest compliments I ever received was when a member said to me, "God sends us all these difficult people, and you love them. So, we have to love them too." But the good news is, we don't have to love others by our own natural strength. We can love them supernaturally. Romans 5:5 says, *and hope does not put us to shame, because God's love has been poured into our hearts through the Holy Spirit who has been given to us.* We can't live lives of love by our own power. Instead, we become conduits of God's own love. His love flows through us by the Holy Spirit. That's the only way to love our neighbors as we love ourselves (much less to love one another as He loves us, as John says).

There we are. That's the whole Bible in seven words. The Bible isn't impossible to understand. You understand "the whole thing" if you understand this: *We love because He first loved us.* Further, you actually live the Bible's message if, by the power of the Holy Spirit, you live in love.

Addendum to Chapter Nine

A Longer Bible Summary

We love because he first loved us is a succinct summary of the whole Bible, and we just looked at other passages that give us slightly longer summaries. I thought it might be helpful, however, if I offered a somewhat longer overview of the Bible story. The story can be divided into a dozen sections, twelve movements if you will. Let's take a look at each one.

1. Prehistory
The story starts with Creation. In the span of six days, God made everything there is. He simply spoke it into existence. *And God said, "Let there be light," and there was light* (Genesis 1:3). Earth, sun, moon, stars, planets, plants, fish, birds, wild animals, man and woman, God created them all. *And God saw everything that he had made, and behold, it was very good* (Genesis 1:31).

Particularly, God made man and woman in His own image. He created human beings in His likeness and placed them in paradise. God designed them for a beautiful relationship with each other and with Himself. The humans were not satisfied with that, however. They wanted more. They wanted to be like God. So, when the tempter came and enticed them to break the one commandment God had given them, Adam and Eve fell prey to his seduction. They disobeyed their God. Suddenly everything changed. Sin and suffering entered the world. Alienation crept into human relationships. The image of God was marred beyond recognition, and death became the destiny of all living things. Man and woman were banished from paradise and the tempter was warned that one day a woman's Son would crush his crafty head (Genesis 3:15).

From there things went from bad to worse. Wickedness spread across the face of the planet as quickly as the population grew. Finally, God had had enough. *So the LORD said, "I will blot out man whom I have created from the face of the land, man and animals and creeping things and birds of the heavens, for I am sorry that I have made them"* (Genesis 6:7). This was not God's original desire. This is not what the Lord intended when He made everything very good. But sin had polluted the entire enterprise and God was willing to trash everything.

However, there was one man who walked with God. His name was Noah. So, the Lord told Noah to build a huge boat, an ark. Thank God, Noah obeyed. All kinds of animals came to Noah and entered the ark. Noah and his family also went in, as God commanded. Then it started to rain. For the first time ever, it rained. For forty days and forty nights it rained, and rained, and rained, and rained until the earth was covered with water. Every living thing outside the ark drowned. After this flood subsided, God told Noah and his family to repopulate the planet. God then made a covenant with every living creature. This is one of God's many gracious covenants in the Bible. God promised that He would never again destroy the earth with a flood. As a sign, a reminder of His promise, He placed the rainbow in the clouds.

Humankind, however, did not learn its lesson. They did not seek relationship with God. Instead, as the population grew the people desired to "make a name for themselves." The descendants of Adam and Eve still wanted to make themselves equal to God. So, in the land called Babel, they began to build a mighty monument to themselves, a tower all the way to heaven. When God peered down and saw their tiny tower and petty pride, He smashed the tower, mixed up human language, and scattered the people across the face of the earth.

2. Patriarchs

Yet God was not willing to give up on our race. He did not annihilate His rebellious creatures. Instead, He opted for another strategy. This time God chose one man, one family, one nation to be His holy people. They would be His witnesses. They would tell the rest of the world about Him. They would lead people back to their God. So God said to old man Abram, later called Abraham, "... *I will make of you a great nation, and I will bless you and make your name great, so that you will be a blessing. I will bless those who bless you, and him who dishonors you I will curse, and in you all the families of the earth shall be blessed*" (Genesis 12:2-3).

After many years Abraham and his wife, Sarah, finally had a son, Isaac. So great was Abraham's trust in God that he was even willing to sacrifice this precious, promised son to the Lord. But God did not desire that sacrifice and returned Isaac to his father. Isaac and his wife, Rebekah, had two sons, Esau and his younger brother, Jacob. Jacob, who was also called Israel, was quite a character. He tricked his father and brother out of Esau's share of the family inheritance. While he was running away from Esau, Jacob had a dream at a place called Bethel. God promised Israel, as He had promised his grandfather, Abraham, *"...in you and your offspring shall all the families of the earth be blessed"* (Genesis 28:14). Jacob had twelve sons by four different women, and he wrestled with God.

Each of Jacob's sons became the forefather of one of the twelve tribes of Israel, but these sons were not equally prized. Jacob's favorite son was Joseph. Out of bitter jealousy, Joseph's brothers sold him into slavery in Egypt. But God was with Joseph in Egypt, and though he faced severe trials there, ultimately, he prospered. In fact, he became the second most powerful person in the entire nation. Because Joseph was a wise, godly leader, only Egypt had food when drought and famine struck that part of the world. When Jacob's other sons came to Egypt to buy food, they were shocked and terrified to find that the man who controlled their fate was none other than the brother they had betrayed. *But Joseph said to them, "Do not fear, for am I in the place of God? As for you, you meant evil against me, but God meant it for good, to bring it about that many people should be kept alive, as they are today. So do not fear; I will provide for you and your little ones"* (Genesis 50:19-21). So Israel and his descendants moved to Egypt.

3. Exodus and Wilderness

In Egypt, the children of Israel multiplied and grew strong. They became so numerous, in fact, that the new Pharaoh was afraid of them. So, Pharaoh made the Israelites his slaves and ordered that their infant sons be murdered at birth. The children of Israel suffered as Pharaoh's slaves for many years. Yet God did not forget His chosen people. God raised up Moses to deliver the people from slavery. God sent Moses to tell Pharaoh to release the Israelites.

Pharaoh refused, and so God sent plagues on the Egyptians: polluted water, frogs, gnats, flies, livestock disease, boils, hail, locusts, darkness. Still, after all this, Pharaoh would not let God's people go. Finally, God warned Pharaoh that, if he did not acquiesce, the first born in every house of Egypt would die. When Pharaoh remained obstinate, calamity struck. The Lord went through the land and took the life of the firstborn in every family except among the Israelites. At God's command, the people of Israel had marked their homes by putting lamb's blood on the doorposts. When the Lord saw a house that was protected by the blood of the lamb, He passed over that house, and the people were saved. The Israelites escaped that night. Pharaoh chased them to the Red Sea. There God brought about a miraculous victory. The oppressors were destroyed, and God's people were saved and set free.

From the Red Sea, Moses led the people through the desert to Mount Sinai. On the way God provided for their needs in extraordinary ways. When they arrived at Mount Sinai, God called Moses up the mountain. There the Lord gave Moses His *Torah*, His Laws to govern the people. Yet even while Moses was still on the mountaintop with God, the people turned away from the Lord. They made an idol for themselves, a golden calf, and worshiped it. Even then, God did not forsake His people. Instead, He reached out to them in love. He called them to repentance, and again He gave them His Law. Moses built a tabernacle as God had instructed him. There God met with Moses. The Lord led the people through the desert in a pillar of cloud by day and of fire by night. For forty years the Israelites lived in the wilderness. God was with them, though they often murmured and complained.

Moses led the people to the edge of the land that God had promised to Abraham, Isaac, and Jacob, but he did not enter the land with them. Before he died, however, Moses reminded the people of all the Lord had done for them. He reiterated what the Lord had called them to do and be. Moses said to the people:

> *"See, I have set before you today life and good, death and evil. If you obey the commandments of the LORD your God that I command you today, by loving the LORD your God, by walking in his ways, and by keeping his commandments and his statutes and his rules, then you shall live and multiply, and the LORD your God will bless you in the land that you are*

entering to take possession of it. But if your heart turns away, and you will not hear, but are drawn away to worship other gods and serve them, I declare to you today, that you shall surely perish. You shall not live long in the land that you are going over the Jordan to enter and possess. I call heaven and earth to witness against you today, that I have set before you life and death, blessing and curse. Therefore choose life, that you and your offspring may live, loving the LORD your God, obeying his voice and holding fast to him, for he is your life and length of days, that you may dwell in the land that the LORD swore to your fathers, to Abraham, to Isaac, and to Jacob, to give them" (Deuteronomy 30:15-20).

4. Conquest

Joshua, Moses' successor, led the people of God into the Promised Land. In one stunning conquest after another, the Israelites took possession of the entire region. When the battles ended, the land was divided among the twelve tribes of Israel. The people settled down as a nation and finally occupied the land God had given them. Near the end of his life, Joshua charged the people, *"Now therefore fear the LORD and serve him in sincerity and in faithfulness. Put away the gods that your fathers served beyond the River and in Egypt, and serve the LORD. And if it is evil in your eyes to serve the LORD, choose this day whom you will serve, whether the gods your fathers served in the region beyond the River, or the gods of the Amorites in whose land you dwell. But as for me and my house, we will serve the LORD"*

(Joshua 24:14-15). The people served the Lord until after Joshua died.

5. Judges

A distressing pattern developed after the death of Joshua. *In those days there was no king in Israel. Everyone did what was right in his own eyes* (Judges 17:6). For a while the people would be faithful to God. Slowly but surely, however, they would slip into apostasy. Every time that happened, they would fall prey to one sort of trouble or another. Then they would cry out to God, and God would raise up a deliverer for them. This sad cycle was repeated many times. Deborah, Gideon, Jephthah, Samson; these were some of the leaders or "Judges" that God raised up to rescue His people during this period.

It was also during this time that a young widow named Ruth, a foreigner from the land of Moab, married an Israelite named Boaz. She became the great-grandmother of a very important person in the Bible. His name was David. We'll come to him in a moment.

The last of the Judges was Samuel. He was sort of judge, prophet and priest all rolled into one. It was while he governed Israel that the people insisted that they should have a king, just like all the other nations, Samuel prayed about this situation, *And the LORD said to Samuel, "Obey the voice of the people in all that they say to you, for they have not rejected you, but they have rejected me from being king over them. According to all the deeds that they have done, from the day I brought them up out of Egypt even to this day, forsaking me and serving other gods, so they are also doing to you"* (1 Samuel 8:7-8).

6. United Kingdom

So, Samuel anointed a man named Saul as the first king of Israel. Saul, however, disobeyed God and God did not establish Saul's dynasty.

The second king of Israel was chosen and anointed when he was just a shepherd boy. David was the youngest son of a man named Jesse. As long as Saul was alive, David was the king's loyal servant. As a soldier, David won great victories for Saul and spared his life on several occasions. After Saul committed suicide in battle, David finally ascended to the throne. All in all, David was a good king. He was not sinless by any means, and he had his share of tragedy and trouble. His precious son, Absalom, tried to steal David's throne out from under him. The young man died in the rebellion. Still, David was a man after God's own heart. He expanded Israel's borders and brought prosperity to the nation. An inspired poet and musician, David wrote many of the Psalms we find in the Bible.

David had a deep desire to build a temple in Jerusalem, a "house of the Lord" where the people could worship God. God did not permit David to build a house for Him, but God promised to build a house, a dynasty, for David. Promising that one of David's descendants would always be king, the Lord said to David, *"And your house and your kingdom shall be made sure forever before me. Your throne shall be established forever"'* (2 Samuel 7:16).

At the end of David's life, his son Solomon succeeded him as king. Solomon prayed for wisdom and the Lord made him the wisest man in the world. The "wisdom literature" of the Bible – Proverbs, Ecclesiastes, Song of Solomon – have their roots in the reign of Solomon. The king wrote much of that literature himself. Further, Solomon fulfilled his father's dream and built a spectacular temple for the Lord. Alas, later in his life, Solomon began to worship the gods of his many foreign wives. Tragically, even the wisest man in the world fell into folly, but God's promise remained intact.

7. Divided Kingdom

If Solomon became a fool, his son Rehoboam, started out as one. When he took over the kingship from his father, the people came to Rehoboam and asked him to be easier on them than Solomon had been. The brash young man answered them, *'My little finger is thicker than my father's thighs. And now, whereas my father laid on you a heavy yoke, I will add to your yoke. My father disciplined you with whips, but I will discipline you with scorpions'* (1 Kings 12:10-11). When they heard this, the ten tribes of Israel that lived in the northern part of the country rebelled against the king. They set up their own capital in the city of Samaria and worship centers in Bethel and Gilgal. A former official of Solomon's, named Jeroboam, became their first king. The northern tribes kept the name "Israel." The southern kingdom, which continued to be governed from Jerusalem by the descendants of David, took on the name Judah. Though their histories were often intertwined, sometimes as enemies and other times as allies, the two kingdoms were permanently divided.

The northern kingdom was never faithful to the Lord. All the kings and queens of Israel served other gods. God sent His prophets to call the people to repentance. Elijah openly displayed the power of the Lord over the false gods known as the Baals. Elisha worked wonderful miracles in God's name. Hosea said that Israel was like a wife who had turned to prostitution. Her loving husband longed to take her back, but she must forsake her other lovers. In the same way, Israel needed to turn away from serving other gods and return to the Lord. Amos, who migrated north from Judah, also called the people of Israel to repent. What was the purpose of being God's chosen people if they were unfaithful to the Lord? God had chosen them to bring His blessing to the whole world, but they could only do that if they lived in right relationship with Him. God reached out to His people through the prophets. The prophets warned Israel that God would not allow their unfaithfulness to continue, but the people would not listen. Consequently, in the year 722 BCE, the army of the Assyrian Empire captured the city of Samaria and took the people of Israel into exile. That was the end of the northern kingdom.

In the southern kingdom of Judah things were better, but not much. A few of David's descendants were good and godly kings: Asa, Jehoshaphat, Uzziah, Jotham, Hezekiah, and Josiah. Most of Judah's rulers, however, were as rotten as their counterparts to the north. Judah was headed toward the same doom as her bigger sister, Israel.

8. Exile

God sent His prophets to Judah as He had to Israel. Isaiah, Micah, Zephaniah, Nahum, Jeremiah, Ezekiel, these all reached out to the people of Judah and warned them that the same fate that befell the kingdom of Israel was closing in on them. From time to time, under godly kings, the people would repent. They staved off judgement for a few more years. Eventually, however, they would return to their old ways. Finally, in 586 BCE, the Babylonian Empire crushed Jerusalem, razed Solomon's temple and took the people of Judah into captivity.

At this time, however, something strange and beautiful began to happen. The prophets started singing a sweet new song. To the proud people of Jerusalem, the prophets had forewarned doom and gloom, destruction and devastation. To the heart-broken captives of the Exile, however, the prophets began to speak tender words of comfort and hope. The Exile was not to last forever. It was not a final punishment. Instead, it was a wake-up call. It was a clear invitation from God for His unfaithful people to turn back to Him. We find this promise clearly in the prophecies of Isaiah, Jeremiah, and Ezekiel.

The Exile was a very important time in the history of God's people. The descendants of Abraham began to look more closely at what it meant to be God's chosen. In exile, the hearts of the people longed for their God. It was near the end of this period that the prophet Daniel had his ministry.

9. Restoration

By 538 BCE the Persian Empire had conquered Babylon. As God promised through the prophets, King Cyrus of Persia allowed the people of Judah to return to Jerusalem. Under the leadership of people like Nehemiah and Ezra, and with prophets like Haggai and Zechariah, the city of Jerusalem and even the Temple were rebuilt.

The Old Testament doesn't tell us a great deal after that. We have a few more prophecies, like those from Joel, Obadiah and Malachi. What we do see, however, is a pattern throughout Scripture. Time and again God reaches out in love to His people, and time and again these people turn away from Him. So far, from Pre-History to Exile and Restoration, the Bible seems to be a story of unrequited love.

At the same time, we have also heard certain promises of God. Someone will crush the tempter's head. The children of Abraham will be a blessing to the whole world. One of David's descendants will rule over God's people forever. By the end of the Old Testament, however, these prophecies lie largely unfulfilled.

10. Jesus Christ

These different movements converge and culminate in a spectacular way in Jesus Christ. He is the resolution of each of these various themes. He is the One who crushes the tempter's head. He is the descendant of Abraham and Israel through whom all the world is blessed. He is the firstborn, the only begotten Son of God, whose sacrificial death sets God's people free from their slavery – not to Pharaoh but to Satan, sin and death. Like the pillar of fire and of cloud in the wilderness, He is God with us. He is the promised heir of David who rules over God's people forever. Jesus Christ is the climax of the story.

Jesus Himself taught that the Old Testament was part of His story. To a group of His contemporaries who doubted Him, Jesus said, *"You search the Scriptures because you think that in them you have eternal life; and it is they that bear witness about me, yet you refuse to come to me that you may have life"* (John 5:39-40). And in Luke 24:25-27, the risen Jesus rebuked two doubting disciples with these words, *"O foolish ones, and slow of heart to believe all that the prophets have spoken! Was it not necessary that the Christ should suffer these things and enter into his glory?" And beginning with Moses and all the Prophets, he interpreted to them in all the Scriptures the things concerning himself.* Since the New Testament was not written until after the earthly life of Jesus, "the Scriptures" in these passages refer to the Old Testament.

In Jesus Christ, the Old Testament story is continued and fulfilled. In Jesus, God reached out to us in a decisive and ultimate way. Once more God invites us to choose life. Once more God calls us back to Himself. This time, however, it is not with a catastrophic flood or a chosen family. It is not through kings or prophets or an exile. This time, God sends His Son. This time God Himself becomes a human being, a descendant of Adam, Noah, Abraham and David. He becomes flesh and blood and dwells among us, full of grace and truth. In Jesus Christ, God lived among us and loved among us. He told us about the Father's love. He explained to us the Lord's will. He demonstrated to us God's power in the many miracles He performed: healing the sick, raising the dead, walking on water, casting out demons and more.

For a while people were excited about following Him. They received Him gladly at first. Eventually, however, they began to realize exactly who He was, who He is. Then they had to destroy Him. You see, the children of Adam and Eve still have this perverse desire to be gods unto themselves. They want to live life their own way, not God's way. So, the people decided to do away with Jesus. They dragged Him before the governor and demanded His death. *"Crucify Him! Crucify Him!"* they cried (John 19:6).

And then, one more time, the Lord reached out to His people in love. Literally. He stretched out His hands and allowed them to be nailed to a cross. He hung on the cross in agony and pain in order to take upon Himself the punishment our rebellion deserved. For us, God sacrificed His only begotten Son. For us He came to earth as a man, and for us He died a human death. And all who turn to Him and trust His sacrifice receive forgiveness of sins (Acts 10:43).

Yet death could not contain Him. On the third day, He defeated death for us. When the first man and woman sinned, death became the destiny of every living thing. When the sinless Son of God died and rose again, death was vanquished. Thus, He gives the gift of eternal life to all who trust Him.

Christ has now ascended into heaven, to the right hand of the Father. From there He reigns as King of kings and Lord of lords. Now we can see that He is that descendant of David who will reign over God's people forever. He is the child of

Abraham, through whom all the peoples of the world are blessed. Having won salvation for all God's people, He is the One who has crushed the tempter's head. Because of all this, Jesus Christ is the climax of the story and the fulfillment of God's promises.

11. The Church

Before Christ ascended into heaven, He commanded his followers to go into all the world and make disciples. The Book of Acts is the record of how Christ's followers received the power of the Holy Spirit and began that process by being His witnesses in Jerusalem, Judea and Samaria. Empowered by the same Spirit, we are still carrying His message to the ends of the earth. The rest of the New Testament, except for the Book of Revelation, is a collection of profound letters from apostles and other church leaders instructing Christians how to live faithfully.

12. The End

Scattered throughout the Old Testament and the teachings of Jesus and the apostles, and concentrated in the Book of Revelation, we find God's ultimate promise: at the end of human history, Christ will return in glory. He will destroy evil and restore all things into His good and perfect Kingdom. We who know and live the Bible's message echo the Bible's final prayer, *Amen. Come, Lord Jesus* (Revelation 22:20)!

What's Your Story?

There we have a brief summary of the entire Bible. I hope that summary, and this book in general, will make regular, daily reading and study of the Bible easier and more meaningful for you. Of course, there are many rich details to be discovered as you read the Scriptures for yourself. This is just a basic framework. Yet even when you fill in all the details, that is still not the entire story. For the Bible cannot be truly meaningful to us until we realize that it is *our* story. We must each come to a point where we recognize in our spirits that it is to us that God has continually reached out in love. We must admit the ways that we have spurned His advances and that He came in Christ to die for us – for you and me in particular. We must realize that He is *our* promised King. He is *our* richest blessing. He is the One who conquers death and evil *for us.* When we turn to Him as Lord and receive His salvation, we become part of His story.

Chapter Ten

Let's Rock The

World!

Seventy Hours

It takes the average person about seventy hours to read the Bible.[136] Yes, "the whole thing." That means that in 15

---

[136] Jason Carter, "The 70 Most Crucial Hours of 2019" January 6, 2019 https://www.revdrjasoncarter.com/blog/2019/1/6/the-70-most-crucial-hours-of-

minutes a day, most people could read the entire Bible in a year. There are numerous Bible reading plans around which give you 365 daily readings.[137] I think it is an excellent discipline to read the whole Bible in a year. When you do that, pick a translation you like and just plow through it. Some parts may not be as interesting as others, but press on. You may not understand everything the first time you read it. I still don't understand everything. But the first time shouldn't be the last time. You'll read it again, and every time you do, you'll understand more and more. You'll see things you didn't see before and remember things you had forgotten. Of course, you don't have to limit yourself to fifteen minutes a day. That's not how most people read most books. Read for half an hour and you'll finish the Bible in 6 months. Read for an hour a day and you'll finish in 3 months. In any event, every Christian who can read should read the whole Bible several times. As I indicated in the last chapter, the more you read it, the more you'll understand it. The whole thing.

Sometimes, however, instead of reading the Scriptures cover to cover, you'll want to concentrate on one book or portion of Scripture and study it. Read it in several translations. Look at commentaries or listen to online sermons on pertinent passages. Use a few study Bibles and read the notes. I

2019?fbclid=IwAR0cmYDb6g9JJknjielCZjSDsXyZDQLazx4SUbki 2v81bDr_PHd_p43JDrI last visited 3.1.2019.
[137] See Ibid. My favorite Bible reading program has been *Seasons of Reflection*, ©1994, International Bible Society. Unfortunately, that book is out of print, but it can sometimes be found on Amazon.

personally like the *Life Application Bible*[138] and *The Spirit-Filled Life Bible,*[139] but you have a plethora of study Bibles available. Pick a few and try them. I usually do my daily Bible reading on my phone. I've downloaded a couple of translations, and of course, www.Biblegateway.com and www.Biblehub.com are only a few taps away. And they're free. But you may prefer a paper Bible that you can mark up and make notes in. That's fine, too.

So maybe one year you read from Genesis to Revelation. Or you might start with Matthew and read the New Testament before you read the Old Testament. (The New Testament is easier for beginners.) Then the next year you concentrate on the Gospels, or Paul's letters, or Psalms or a prophet or two. Mix it up. Which plan you follow doesn't matter much. What really counts is that you spend time daily in God's Word. Deuteronomy 8:3, which Jesus quoted when He was tempted by the devil to turn stones to bread (Matthew 4:4), talks about how God dealt with His people when they were in the wilderness, after they escaped from Egypt. It says, *And he humbled you and let you hunger and fed you with manna, which you did not know, nor did your fathers know, that he might make you know that man does not live by bread alone, but man lives by every word that comes from the mouth of the* LORD (Deuteronomy 8:3). God's Word is more important to our well-being than daily bread. God's Word is food for our spirits. Most people would rarely consider skipping physical nourishment for a whole day if we didn't have to. Why do we think we can survive without spiritual

---

[138] *Life Application Study Bible* © 1988, 1989, 1990, 1991, 1993, 1995 by Tyndale House Publishers Inc. Wheaton IL.
[139] *The Spirit-Filled Life Bible* © 1991 by Thomas Nelson Inc.

food? Take sustenance. Why starve yourself? Spend quality time in the Scriptures every day.

Personal Reformation

And what would be the benefits of reading the Bible so regularly? Well, look at Psalm 19:7-11:

> *The law of the LORD is perfect,*
>
> *reviving the soul;*
>
> *the testimony of the LORD is sure,*
>
> *making wise the simple;*
>
> *the precepts of the LORD are right,*
>
> *rejoicing the heart;*
>
> *the commandment of the LORD is pure,*
>
> *enlightening the eyes;*
>
> *the fear of the LORD is clean,*
>
> *enduring forever;*
>
> *the rules of the LORD are true,*
>
> *and righteous altogether.*
>
> *More to be desired are they than gold,*
>
> *even much fine gold;*

sweeter also than honey

and drippings of the honeycomb.

Moreover, by them is your servant warned;

in keeping them there is great reward.

Do you ever need personal revival or revitalization? Wisdom? Rejoicing? Enlightenment? Righteousness? These things and more are all promised to those who search for them in the Law of the Lord. This Psalm was composed around 1,000 BCE. At that time the prophets and other Old Testament writings had not yet been penned, much less the New Testament. "The Law" here refers to the first five books of the Bible. When David wrote this Psalm, "the Law" was his whole Bible. What he said about that portion of Scripture, however, is true of the whole God-breathed canon. I urge you to spend regular, daily time reading God's Word and applying it because, along with prayer, that practice will transform your life like nothing else.

Romans 12:2 says, *Do not be conformed to this world, but be transformed by the renewal of your mind, that by testing you may discern what is the will of God, what is good and acceptable and perfect.* The best way to experience godly transformation, according to this verse, is to renew your mind. The best way I know to renew your mind is to read, study, and meditate on the Scriptures. That's my experience, but even more it's what the Bible teaches. Read Psalm 119. This Psalm, which is the longest chapter in the Bible, emphasizes the benefits of deep Scripture reading over and over in 176 verses.

The famous musical virtuoso, Ignacy Jan Paderewski said, "If I miss one day of practice, I notice it. If I miss two days, the critics notice it. If I miss three days, the audience notices it."[140] I find the same to be true with Bible reading. Sometimes I do skip a day, maybe even two. When I do life loses some of its luster, and the people close to me can tell the difference. I always "catch up" on my reading when I fall behind, but it is better when I spend time in the Word every day. Bible reading is a fruitful discipline. It's an essential daily habit for those who want to grow as disciples of Jesus. I urge you to read the Bible every day. You'll sense your life start to change. The change may be gradual, but it will be great. Slowly but surely that practice will bring about a revival, a personal reformation in your life. In other words, it will rock your world.

Why You're Wrong

Rich benefits come from reading the Bible. Conversely, neglect of the Bible has negative consequences. In Matthew 22 a group of self-appointed religious experts, the Sadducees, tried to stump Jesus with a tricky question. Jesus burned them with this blistering reply, *"You are wrong, because you know neither the Scriptures nor the power of God"* (Matthew 22:29). Ouch! The Sadducees thought they knew the Bible, at least the first five books. (The Sadducees didn't recognize the Prophets, the Psalms, or other writings

---

[140] "Ignacy Jan Paderewski Quotes," *AZ Quotes* https://www.azquotes.com/author/28759-Ignacy_Jan_Paderewski Last visited 2.11.19

as Scripture.) But Jesus said they missed the point entirely. That's a sobering reminder to us today. Many people fall into error because, while they may know the Scriptures, they don't know the power of God. We talked about them in Chapter Eight when we explored how Scripture gives us an accurate description of reality. At the other extreme, Michael Brown, in his book, *Playing with Holy Fire,*[141] talks about tragic abuses in the Pentecostal-Charismatic movement. Many of these abuses are committed by people who know the power of God very well, but they toy carelessly with the teachings of Scripture. Jesus bluntly told the Sadducees they were wrong, and the reason was that they knew neither the Scriptures nor the power of God. We need to know both. I'm sure there are places in my life where I'm wrong – opinions, practices, and perspectives. I may not know what all of them are, but I'm sure they're there. The same is probably true of you. That's the bad news. The good news, however, is that I'm willing to be corrected, and I hope you are, too. That's the only way we can grow. Otherwise we become stagnant like the Sadducees. (How sad to be like a Sadducee.)

Fortunately, no, providentially, we don't have to continue to be wrong. We can learn. We can grow. We can be corrected. Remember, *All Scripture is God-breathed and is useful for teaching, rebuking, correcting and training in righteousness, so that the servant of God may be thoroughly equipped for every good work* (2 Timothy 3:16-17 NIV). Regular time spent in the Bible corrects our course. Reading the Bible consistently and trying to apply it to our lives helps us know both the Scriptures and the power of God. Apart

---

[141] Brown, Michael *Playing with Holy Fire* © 2018 by Michael L. Brown, Ph.D.

from that, we're bound to be wrong.

Twice before we've quoted Matt Chandler saying, "It's better to live the Word than to know the Word."[142] He's right. But we can't live the Word if we don't know it. And the best way for you to know the Word is to read it, study it, meditate on it, and apply it to your life.

A Seismic Shift

In 1517 God rocked the western world. There was a seismic shift in society, and it happened largely because people rediscovered the Bible. The Bible was always supposed to be available to people. As we saw in Chapter Four, the New Testament was written in *koine* Greek, the language of the common people. When Latin replaced Greek as the "universal language" of the Roman Empire, the Bible was translated into that language. The Latin translation of the Bible is called the *Vulgate*. The name comes from the Latin word *vulgata,* which means "the speech of the common people and especially of uneducated people."[143] The Bible was intended to be accessible to the masses. During the middle ages, however, society changed for the worse. After the demise of the Roman Empire, Latin was understood only

---

[142] Matt Chandler: Prophecy, tongues, their continuation, and our fears (Convergence, OKC 2017) https://www.youtube.com/watch?v=QFojKyynEI4 Last visited 3.1.2019

[143] https://www.merriam-webster.com/dictionary/vulgate *s.v.* Vulgate. Last visited 1.4.18

by those who were well educated, even among the clergy. Yet the Bible was available only in Latin, and the Church leaders of that dark era forbade that the Scriptures should be translated into the languages of the people. In the 1300s and 1400s, when John Wycliffe and Jan Hus dared to translate the Bible into their national languages (English and Czech), they were exterminated for their efforts. The common people became biblically illiterate and spiritually ignorant. They knew neither the Scriptures nor the power of God. They were totally dependent on the priests for spiritual instruction.

When Martin Luther ignited the Protestant Reformation, one of his foundational tenets was that the Scriptures should be translated into languages the people could understand and read for themselves. Luther's life changed when he began to study the Bible in order to teach it, and he wanted others to be able to read the Scriptures as well. So, Luther himself translated the Bible into German. He famously claimed, "I fought the devil with ink." There is a fantastic legend about Luther hurling an inkwell at Lucifer in his room, but the quote really refers to the brutal blow Luther dealt Satan by making the Bible available to God's people again.[144] Other Reformers soon followed suit and translated the Scriptures into other European languages. The newly invented printing press made it possible to distribute these translations widely, and literacy programs were developed largely to enable people to read the Bible for themselves for the first time in centuries. The demand for Bibles was great, for people were hungry for God's Word.

---

[144] See "500 Years After the Reformation, the Gospel Is Still Worth Fighting For" J.D. Greear. https://jdgreear.com/blog/500-years-reformation-gospel-still-worth-fighting/ Last visited 3.1.2019

Luther's life changed when he began to read the Scriptures closely, and the western world changed when the common people began to immerse themselves in God's Word. Education and health care flourished. Governments and society were transformed. Yes, there were problems, but you and I still feel the tremors and benefit from that earthquake known as the Protestant Reformation. And all that took place largely because people rediscovered the Bible.

Return of the Darkness

Professor Bart Ehrman, a leading sceptic who advocates many of the rumors addressed in this book, sometimes begins his freshman New Testament course at the University of North Carolina, Chapel Hill with these questions: "How many of you in here would agree with the proposition that the Bible is the inspired Word of God?" (Almost everyone raises a hand.) "Now, how many of you have read the Harry Potter series?" (Again, almost everyone raises a hand.) Finally, he asks, "And now, how many of you have read the entire Bible?" (This time scattered hands, here and there, throughout the auditorium.) Then he'll say, "OK, so I'm not telling you that I think the Bible is the inspired Word of God; you're telling me that you think it is. I can see why you might want to read a book by J. K. Rowling. But if God wrote a book – wouldn't you want to see what he had to say?"[145]

---

[145] "Can My Students Believe in the Inerrancy of the Bible?" The Bart Ehrman Blog: The History & Literature of Early Christianity https://ehrmanblog.org/can-my-students-believe-in-the-inerrancy-of-the-bible/ (Last visited 3.1.2019)

Even in the Bible Belt, biblical illiteracy has returned to our culture. Darkness has invaded and pervaded our society once again. I wonder what would happen if I asked Dr. Ehrman's questions of the congregation I serve. I'm not sure how many of them have read *Harry Potter,* though like me, many of them may have seen the movies. More potently, I wonder how many have read the whole Bible. Some have, I know, but I doubt that it would be all. Maybe not even a majority. When the *Harry Potter* series first came out there was heated controversy about whether Christians should read those novels. I'm far more concerned about the scalding scandal that so few believers actually read the Bible. Many Christians claim to value the Bible highly. They believe what they believe the Bible says, but they can't really be sure because they've never read it for themselves. They've never taken seventy hours of their lives to peruse the book they know was inspired by God.

As a result, so many lives are shrouded in moral and spiritual confusion. Our society can barely distinguish right from wrong, and many individuals share that condition. We make up our own moral codes and spiritual schemes, thinking mine is as good as yours, and hoping these empty systems of our own concoction will somehow give us guidance and relief. We don't know what God's good, perfect, and acceptable will is (Romans 12:2). In fact, many think His will is unknowable or irrelevant. Like the Sadducees, so few know either the Scriptures or the power of God.

How did this come about? How did the medieval darkness descend on us again? Maybe it was complacency or laziness. Maybe we've been distracted by the blitz of entertainment options that constantly bombard us, from movies to TV to cat videos on our cell phones. Perhaps we really don't want to know what the Bible says. Like Adam and Eve, we want to be gods unto ourselves. Or, we might think we're too busy for the Bible, or too sophisticated. I wrote this book because I suspect the nasty rumors we've explored have effectively disheartened people from trusting the Bible. Even some believers have been discouraged from devouring the nourishing bread that comes from the mouth of the Lord. We've examined those rumors and found them to be blatantly false or disastrous distortions of the truth.

> ➤ No, the Bible wasn't compiled by conniving bishops who were hungry to build their own power and prestige. Instead it was collected by the people of God, who treasured and saved the writings in which they heard the voice of the Good Shepherd.
> ➤ Yes, the Bible has been copied over and over, but that's to our advantage. The fact that we have more than 5,800 copies of Bible manuscripts means that we can be more confident about the original text of the Bible than we can be of any other piece of ancient literature.
> ➤ Yes, the Bible has been translated again and again, but the various translations are based directly on the Greek, Hebrew and Aramaic texts. The rich variety of translations at our fingertips lets us explore the meaning of the Scripture more fully.
> ➤ No, the Bible isn't just another book. It's the God-breathed Word of the Lord.
> ➤ Yes, the Bible was written in cultures vastly different from our own, but there are sound hermeneutical principles that help us see how the Bible applies to our lives today.

➢ At first glance there seem to be contradictions in the Bible, but in most cases the perceived dissonance gives way to rich harmony when we hear the whole symphony of Scripture. Further, the differences that are most puzzling prod us to deeper spiritual understanding.

➢ The Bible does not assume a primitive, mythological worldview that is inferior to our modern scientific understanding. Rather the Bible expands our worldview by showing us the world as it really is.

➢ And yes, some parts of the Bible are hard to understand, but if we can grasp the great truth that we love because God first loved us (I John 4:19), we have a handle on the whole of biblical truth, and we can build from there.

Let's Rock the World Again!

So, with those nasty rumors out of the way, where do we go from here? In Chapter One, we said that if those rumors are false, the Bible is true. And if the Bible is true, we have God-given guidance for our lives. We have a lamp for our feet and a light for our path. We have clear direction on how to live our lives and what to teach our children. We no longer have to grope in the darkness for something that might seem substantial enough to sustain us. We no longer have to be the slaves of philosophical fashion or societal whim. We have the word of God. The answer to our crucial question, "Is the Bible reliable?" is a resounding "Yes!" So, let's read it. Let's study it. Let's meditate on it. Let's live it.

Remember, we live in an age where resources for the study of Scripture are overwhelmingly easy to obtain. Most of us carry entire libraries in our purses or pockets. Translations,

Bible studies, commentaries, videos, webcasts, blogs, sermons, even books like this one can appear on our cell phone screens when we just tap "go." Audio recordings of the Bible are at our fingertips, so we can listen to the Word as we drive or jog or go about our chores. We really do have the opportunity to be the best-informed generation of believers in history. We could easily be the most biblically literate generation ever, as we said in Chapter One.

We have easy access to the light that will dispel the darkness. It's just a click away. How can we choose to live in the biblical illiteracy that envelops us? How can we continue to stumble in the dark when light is so near? Not since the Reformation and the invention of the printing press has there been the opportunity for such a great spiritual revolution. And the opportunity is exponentially greater today. If we will simply devote ourselves to reading, studying, and meditating on the Bible, and applying what we learn to our lives, we will each experience a personal reformation. When we avail ourselves of every Word that comes from the mouth of God, we will be transformed by the renewing of our minds. But that personal reformation won't remain merely personal. It will spread. Once we get infected by the Bible bug, we become contagious. We could start an epic epidemic of transformation. Then once again, we will rock the world. For all I know, the next Martin Luther may be reading this book. I pray that he or she is. Pray with me for that person. Better yet, *be* that person. We are poised for a new Reformation. The world desperately needs it, and we have the resources to make it happen. Let's rock the world again!

The Girl and the Vulture

A devastating photo appeared in the *New York Times* in March of 1993. It shows an emaciated Sudanese toddler, apparently wearing only a white necklace and bracelet, collapsed on a patch of parched earth.[146] On the ground just behind her a vulture is perched, haunting, awaiting the inevitable. The poignant picture was taken by South African photojournalist Kevin Carter. The next year he won a Pulitzer Prize for the disturbing image. Soon after that, he took his own life. While there were rules, regulations and extenuating circumstances that constrained him in Sudan, he could not bear the guilt and criticism he incurred for taking the photo but not feeding the helpless child. We do not know whether the little girl survived.

Embed that image of the famished girl in your mind, for we have something in common with Kevin Carter. All around us, people are starving for the bread of life. They are just a few feet from the spiritual nourishment they need. The vulture is patiently waiting their demise. Will we help them to the food? Or are we too focused on some other prize? Or perhaps we are too weak and malnourished ourselves. We can't help them. We are barely surviving ourselves because we have tried to live without every Word that comes from the mouth of God.

---

[146] "The Vulture and the Little Girl" Truth Inside of You https://www.truthinsideofyou.org/kevin-carter-the-vulture-and-the-little-girl/ Last visited 3.1.2019 See also "The Right Response with Michael Jr." https://www.youtube.com/watch?v=qV24O1YxTV8&t=1943s Last visited 3.1.2019

One Godly Woman

I shared that story with my wife. She's a godly woman who loves the Lord. When she heard it, she lamented, "Yeah, but I'm not feeding people. I try, but it just isn't my gift." But she was wrong. She is feeding people. I reminded her that some of the teens she taught in Sunday school became ministers and missionaries. Further, at her workplace at least three or four people (that we know about) have come to faith in Jesus Christ, or recommitted their lives to Him, or taken steps closer to faith and become more open to the Gospel. Her influence was probably not the only factor in any of these delightful developments, but she made a huge contribution. And how did she do it? Well, while she has studied and learned a number of wonderful evangelism presentations, she didn't use any of them. She never asked, "Do you know God loves you and has a wonderful plan for your life?"[147] or "If you were to die tonight, do you know for certain that you would go to heaven?"[148] She may have given them a copy of *The (Little) Book of Love*[149] to read, but basically she just

---

[147] "Would You Like to Know God Personally? http://www.4laws.com/laws/englishkgp/default.htm Last visited 3.1.2019

[148] "Evangelism Explosion International" http://evangelismexplosion.org/resources/online-tracts/english/ Last visited 3.1.2019.

[149] Rod Pinder *The Little Book of Love: The Story of God and You* ©2019 Rod Pinder is available at Amazon.com, also at www.PastorRodPinder.com/LittleBook

tries to live her faith and grow in it. She reads the Bible every day and tries to apply what it says. She prays with her co-workers when they ask her to, and they do. She talks about the Lord in a matter-of-fact way, the same way she talks about her family. He's a real person in her life. Sometimes living out her faith means publicly failing in her discipleship, "blowing it" in terms of Christian behavior, then later apologizing. She doesn't show people how to be perfect because she isn't, regardless of how wonderful I think she is. Instead she simply demonstrates how to grow in faith. Some people find that attractive and look up to her example. And her daily practice of prayerfully reading, studying, meditating on, and applying the Bible is at the core of that.

Strength in the Billions

The handful of people my wife has influenced may not sound very impressive. Some people do have remarkable gifts for evangelism, and they influence many more people. But think about the fact that there are 2.3 billion Christians in the world (31% of the world population).[150] What would happen if each of those 2.3 billion Christians influenced just one person over the next several years? There would be 4.6 billion believers! If each of those believers influenced 2 or 3 people, we would run out of population! The planet would change for the better. Can you imagine what would happen to crime? What would happen to family life? What would happen to governments? What would happen to racism and

---

[150]"How Many Christians Are In the World Today?" https://www.thoughtco.com/christianity-statistics-700533 Last visited 3.1.2019

hatred? To substance abuse and human trafficking? What would happen to the people you love? It would be a worldwide revival. It would be a beautiful, godly reformation of the entire globe!

Okay, we may not be able to influence the 2.3 billion believers in the world, but what if you and I and everyone reading this book made a commitment to read God's Word, study God's Word, contemplate God's Word, and seek to live God's Word on a daily basis? What might the Lord do with that? What might God do through informed, committed Christians who know both the Scriptures and the power of God? I have no doubt that God would use our example to bless and influence many. Maybe millions. Maybe billions.

God has shown me a few visions. In essence, they all mean the same thing, but one of them stands out in this context. I saw a vast crowd of people – they looked like the figures on bathroom doors. Most of them were drab gray, but a few of them were shiny gold. The shiny gold people moved around among the drab gray people and touched them, turning some of them shiny gold. They in turn touched other drab, gray people, transforming them, too. Before long the crowd was transformed. A few were still drab gray, but most had become shiny gold. We become shiny gold people, we become radiant when we are transformed by the renewing of our minds. We become shiny gold people when we nourish ourselves on every Word that comes from the mouth of God. Further, when we are learning and living the Scriptures, our goldenness becomes contagious.

I think God is getting ready to rock the world again. I believe He's going to do it through people who feed on His Word and put it into practice. Join the revolution. Be part of this new reformation. Yes, there are some nasty rumors going around about the Bible. We've exposed them as false by examining the facts. But we can do even better. We will eradicate those nasty rumors, we will obliterate them when we daily read God's Word, study God's Word, meditate on God's Word, and put it into practice. It takes the average person seventy hours to read the entire Bible. Read your Bible. Live the Bible. Let's rock the world!

Also by Rod Pinder:

The (Little) Book of Love

The Story of God and You

Coming Soon

The Book of Love

Seven Words to Transform Your World

Preaching in the Power of the Holy Spirit

How God's Word Creates Reality

The Joseph Curve

How God Fulfills Vision

Kill the Old Man (It's an Inside Job")

How to Die to Self and Grow in Christ-Likeness

Tiptoe through the T.U.L.I.P

A Moderate Look at Modern Calvinism

For updates and more information, visit
www.PastorRodPinder.com.

Made in the USA
Columbia, SC
12 January 2020

86402943R00189